Pete Doherty
on the edge

Pete Doherty: on the edge

the true story of a troubled genius

Nathan Yates & Pete Samson

JOHN BLAKE

Published by John Blake Publishing Ltd,
3, Bramber Court, 2 Bramber Road,
London W14 9PB, England

www.blake.co.uk

First published in Hardback in 2005

ISBN 1 84454 176 2

British Library Cataloguing-in-Publication Data:

A catalogue record for this book is available from the British Library.

Design by www.envydesign.co.uk

Printed in Great Britain by Creative Print and Design

1 3 5 7 9 10 8 6 4 2

Papers used by John Blake Publishing are natural, recyclable products
made from wood grown in sustainable forests. The manufacturing processes
conform to the environmental regulations of the country of origin.

Every attempt has been made to contact the relevant copyright-holders,
but some were unobtainable. We would be grateful if the appropriate
people could contact us.

Contents

Acknowledgements — vii

Chapter 1 – The Lust of a Libertine — 1

Chapter 2 – It Could Have Been Anywhere — 7

Chapter 3 – The Pact — 31

Chapter 4 – Albion Days — 49

Chapter 5 – The Libertine — 73

Chapter 6 – The Tender Hooligan — 93

Chapter 7 – Skag and Bone — 111

Chapter 8 – The Pied Piper — 121

Chapter 9 – What Became of the Likely Lads? — 131

Chapter 10 – Can't Stand Me Now — 159

Chapter 11 – Clinical Melancholy — 181

Chapter 12 – She'll Never Forgive You But She Won't Let You Go — 201

Chapter 13 –   What Kate Did   213

Chapter 14 –   A Night at the Circus   229

Chapter 15 –   Chained Melody   245

Chapter 16 –   Babyshambles   259

Chapter 17 –   The Legacy   277

Acknowledgements

The authors would like to thank Pete Doherty and Banny Poostchi, Ben Yates for his invaluable research and commitment, Richard Wallace, Conor Hanna, Gary Jones and Anthony Harwood, Dominic Masters, Colin and Janice Yates, Edith Giffard, Oscar Giffard, Hazel Savage, Liz Cocker, Catherine Lewis, Ian Vogler, our editor Mark Hanks for his patience, Stephen Moyes, Chris Hughes, Greig Box, Jon Clements and others who cannot be named here, but who nevertheless made essential contributions to this book.

CHAPTER 1

The Lust of a Libertine

'I HAVE A VERY BAD RELATIONSHIP WITH
THE FUTURE. WE DON'T GET ON.'
— *Pete Doherty*

The slim, half-naked figure was sitting on the edge of the king-size bed in the honeymoon suite of the Rookery Hotel. Perched on the edge of a white feather duvet, his shoulders were hunched in a pose that betrayed intense concentration. Around him were the opulent Victorian trappings of this four-star, £400-a-night establishment in the central London district of Farringdon: velvet curtains, polished hardwood furniture, a doorway through to a large, airy bathroom containing a Jacuzzi – a Jacuzzi that, later that day, twenty-five-year-old Pete Doherty intended to share with his new beautiful and universally desired girlfriend, Kate Moss.

Pete could have felt himself entitled to soak in luxury after the recent success of his new act Babyshambles. Although his breakaway band had yet to release an album, they were producing songs that filled the void in his fans' hearts after the premature death of The Libertines, with gigs selling out within hours of being advertised. Babyshambles' first single, the thoughtful and poignant 'Killamangiro', had shot straight into the Top Ten in December 2004, proving that the demise of The Libertines and the tragic rift with his former songwriting partner and best friend, Carl Barât, would not spell the end for Pete. Only four days earlier, Pete had played a small gig in The George Tavern in Stepney, where in December his rising fame had led to an interview with Kirsty Wark of BBC2's *Newsnight* programme. Before an ever-widening army of supporters, the gig should have gone down a storm, but, standing up on stage in front of the grubby walls and the venue's retro mirrors, Pete had looked a wreck. His devoted fans had been shocked at his pallid complexion and sunken eyes; his fingers had been stained and blackened, his body painfully thin and withered. Pete had halted the gig after just three songs and disappeared into the night. Beneath the celebrity and the artistic triumph, all was clearly not well.

Indeed, Pete's mind was preoccupied by dark thoughts. Not that he wasn't looking forward to Kate's company; a week later, when reflecting on the events of this day, the planned evening with her would be foremost in his memory. However, at that moment, around three o'clock in the afternoon of 5 February 2005, she had been relegated in his tortured mind. Pete's thoughts were on drugs: how to get off drugs and, most prominently, how to get more drugs. So battered was his arm from heroin abuse that he'd reverted to injecting the substance into other parts of his body. Next to him on the bed was a small plastic bag, a spoon, a hypodermic needle and a lighter. Methodically, Pete picked up the plastic wrap and emptied its contents of beige powder on to the spoon, mixed it and sparked his lighter into a flame. Pete's movements were calm and well rehearsed as he performed an operation that had grown familiar since he'd first taken heroin, five years earlier.

There has never been a rock-star addict quite like Pete Doherty. Although there are similarities, Pete is no Sid Vicious; he is a delicate, complicated character, a softly spoken poet driven to drugs by a profound loneliness, the same sense of irredeemable isolation that also propelled him to fame. But from that seed of sadness grew a whole forest of idealised concepts, a Utopian vision of liberation and fulfilment. To others, it might have seemed that the unhealthily pallid Pete, his arms dotted with puncture marks and flecks of tiny bruises, needed just another fix to satisfy an intense physical craving, but, in Pete's mind, the syringe wasn't just a habit; it was a product of his vision and a tool for realising it.

Of course, heroin did serve as a means of escape for a man who was often depressed; wrapped in its warm haze, Pete was anaesthetised to his pain. Yet it also spelled entry into a magical world where the imagination could reign, a space liberated from the constraints of social convention, money, capitalism, respectable family life, religion, suburbia. Pete believed taking heroin would leave him drifting in the realm of Arcadia, an arena of colour and light where the seemingly life-draining qualities of addiction were transformed, where grimy London was changed utterly, into an ideal England he called Albion.

Along with his rock-star routine performed before crowds of fans, heroin was part of Pete's life project of self-transformation, a symptom of his dedication to hedonism, to becoming a pure libertine. He believed that he was doing something for sheer pleasure, something that signified his abdication from any role within the workings of the society around him. He had started out a rootless child with little sense of who he was or what he wanted. As he grew up, others tried to shape him, squash him into moulds that proved a difficult fit for this complex, fiercely intelligent character. He was meant to be a dutiful, God-fearing son to his father, Major Peter Doherty, Sr. He was supposed to go to university, then to work, and to take up his position as father to his own baby son, Astile.

Instead, Pete gave up his place in the world of work just as easily as he had dropped out of university. He rarely saw his son and had been disowned by his father. He even absented himself from his phenomenally successful group, The Libertines, so often that he was sacked from the band by Barât. His new outfit, Babyshambles, were also thrown into disarray by his repeated failure to show up for gigs. By the time he'd hit his mid-twenties, Pete had already given up much more than most ever acquire in the first place.

The mother of Pete's child, Lisa Moorish, blamed it all on what she called the 'illness' of addiction. In fact, Pete's abdication from the parts others wanted him to play was calculated, intentional and central to his philosophy. He made no secret of his desire to opt out of these roles, telling everyone that he was nobody's man but his own. Instead, he'd promised himself a part that he'd carved out entirely for himself – and not just any part but the main one.

Pete felt that he was doing more than dropping out; in his mind, he was dedicating himself to a philosophy of life that drew on great works of literature. He was so inspired by one of his greatest influences, the Marquis de Sade, that he had even named his first band after one of de Sade's books, *The Lusts of the Libertines*. The eighteenth-century French author after whom sadism was named wrote of sexual perversion, self-destruction and the hypocrisy of society's morals. Satanism, goth culture and even punk rock all later drew on de Sade's writing. As for Pete, he was fascinated above all by the idea of the libertine: an individual unimpeded by moral constraints. He was determined that his music and lifestyle would reflect such a philosophy, whatever the cost.

The results of this uncompromising experiment on himself had been remarkably creative for Pete, as well as destructive. Although at times he risked losing his health, sanity and even his life, Pete had burst on to the music scene from an unlikely beginning. As a teenager, he'd had no contact whatsoever with the world of music; not only was he unacquainted with anyone in the business but he also spent most of his time reading books rather than going to gigs, and he couldn't even play the guitar. Within the space of ten years, however, he came from nowhere to form not just one but two of the most original and stirring bands in British music, and with Carl Barât he formed perhaps the greatest songwriting partnership since The Smiths' Morrissey and Marr. Pete had the capacity to produce songs that sounded like they were either about to explode into something new and overwhelming or were just about to collapse entirely, demonstrating an inherent instability at the heart of Pete's talent to which Carl Barât would attest.

Back in Pete's hotel, down a quiet lane on the edge of the City of London, bankers and businessmen were holding meetings and striking deals. The establishment's antique Victoriana apparently impressed clients, and the little oasis of calm within walking distance of the City's financial institutions proved the perfect setting for important arrangements in which millions of pounds were at stake. The movers and shakers talked in hushed tones over lunch, sipped coffee in the bar and pored over spreadsheets on their laptop computers. With the exception of Pete, it was difficult to find anyone in the place who wasn't wearing a suit. Locked in his hotel suite with a DO NOT DISTURB sign hanging outside his door, he had spent his afternoon scribbling poetry and songs. He, too, had been using a laptop – to ponder over updates to his Babyshambles website and to order hard drugs via email. Empty cans of Stella Artois were strewn across the thick-pile carpet. The room, despite a chilly draught blowing in from the open window, smelled of stale cigarette smoke, while stubbed-out Marlboro butts crowded the ashtray on the bedside table. Pete had inhabited the place for only a few hours and barely noticed that he was well on the way to wrecking it. Paying little thought to his plush surroundings, Pete slid the needle into his vein and emptied the contents of the syringe into his bloodstream. By the time he came down from his high that night, the luxurious hotel suite had vanished. In its place were the plain metal bed and barred window of a police-station cell.

CHAPTER 2

It Could Have Been Anywhere

'THEY WERE DRIVING THROUGH FROM SCOTLAND AND HER
WATERS BROKE, SO THEY HAD TO JUST STOP OFF IN THE
NEAREST CITY. IT COULD'VE BEEN ANYWHERE.'
– Pete Doherty

Pete Doherty, a man balanced on the thinnest of dividing lines between fame and tragedy, fulfilment and self-destruction, was born into a disrupted but ultimately conventional environment on 12 March 1979 in Hexham, Northumberland, a picturesque market town with a lengthy history. Clustered around a bridge over the River Tyne, Hexham lies just to the south of the 1,900-year-old Roman structure Hadrian's Wall, beyond which the bleak, treeless moorlands of the northernmost corner of England stretch away towards the Scottish border. Others born in the same place at the same time as Pete would settle into a community proud of its beautiful surroundings and unique heritage, but even back then Pete was the exception. His pregnant mother was in Hexham purely by chance; the family had been driving from Scotland when her contractions began and Pete's father pulled into the nearest town. Pete left Hexham within weeks, at too young an age to have developed any memories of the place. He was destined never to be part of that community, or any other like it.

Although Pete had relatives in the Northeast, he actually had connections all over Britain. His father, Peter Sr, an army serviceman, was from an Irish family and grew up in west London, while his mother, Jacqueline, an army nurse, was raised in the shadow of Liverpool Football Club's home ground at Anfield. Peter Sr's job meant that he would take his family with him wherever he was posted, and as Pete grew up he found temporary homes at Liverpool, London, Belfast, Coventry, Dorset, Birmingham, Leicester, Ilford, Düsseldorf and Cyprus. His roots were so widely spread that it was hard to explain to himself or others where he was from. The town of his birth came to mean nothing to Pete. In fact, during many of his later interviews, he forgot where he was born, wrongly stating that his birthplace was in the Midlands or the Northwest. This emptiness within would later send Pete on a desperate quest to find himself.

On the face of it, there was little about Pete's family that could be identified as an inspiration for his career as a musician and songwriter. His parents were certainly nothing like the flamboyant libertine Pete would later become. Although they were teenagers in the 1960s, Pete's mother and father had never been involved in the hippie movement. They never took drugs, weren't particularly musical and were anything other than rebellious. Peter Sr opted for the conformity of serving Queen and country, while Jacqueline supported him wherever he went. The couple met while they were both working at army barracks in Aldershot, Hampshire, when twenty-three-year-old Jacqueline Michels was an army nurse and Peter Sr was in the process of working his way up the ranks. The couple, who married in 1976, were practising Catholics and brought their children up as churchgoers.

Although Pete came from what was in some respects a close-knit nuclear family, his father was a distant figure. Sometimes, this distance took the form of a physical separation, while for the rest of the time the division was emotional. Whenever Peter Sr's duties took him into the field of action, he would be away for weeks or even months at a time, but when he was at home Pete found him very strict and unsympathetic to the point of disapproval. Peter Sr, believing he had succeeded in giving his son an easy ride through childhood, was determined to make sure Pete would not be spoiled and that he was given firm instructions to follow. Pete remembers an incident that took place after one of his first evenings away from the family, when he was twelve years old. 'I was coming home from a school disco, a real innocent school disco, drinking lemonade,' remembered Pete, 'and when I got in, he followed me into the kitchen. I was drinking water really fast because I was so thirsty, and he said, "You've been drinking." And I literally didn't even know what he meant. I said, "Yeah, I'm drinking water." And he said, "You've been drinking, haven't you?" I was completely paralysed, completely in awe, and I started crying. He stands me in the middle of the room and tells me to walk in a straight line. And I can't.'

Pete's father believed that his son would break the rules

as soon as he was no longer under observation. He wanted Pete to toe a straight line.

Pete's feelings on that particular occasion of being incapable of living up to his father's expectations – being unable to walk the line, despite being sober – would be a persistent feature of their relationship, while the incident also reflected Peter Sr's particular fear of his son drinking or taking drugs. Another possibility he was worried about was the prospect of his son growing up to be a homosexual, an anxiety that surfaced during another incident, when Pete was eight and his father caught him trying on his mother's make-up, and immediately leaped to the conclusion that the boy had homosexual tendencies. 'He was really worried about it,' Pete remembered. 'He thought the make-up thing meant I was definitely going to be gay.'

Peter Sr had grown up as a working-class Irish immigrant on a council estate in run-down Shepherd's Bush, west London. He'd had a tough childhood in which money was scarce and opportunities few. His parents had split up when he'd been just a boy, his mother, Doris, moving out with his sisters, and the split affected him deeply. He consequently developed a keen sense of responsibility for the family's difficulties, and also a distaste for those circumstances in which he was raised that was so strong he had to escape. In later life, he would distance himself as far as possible from everything to do with the inner-city estate and working-class culture in which he grew up. 'I think the rest of my dad's life has been based on that moment of looking out the window and seeing his mum leave with his sisters,' Pete observed. 'In the end, he just had to get out of London, so he joined the army.'

Peter Sr joined up at the age of nineteen and embarked on a dedicated, impressively rapid scramble up the ranks. From the beginning of his career, he applied himself to the rigorous training routines and strict discipline of military life, aiming to mark himself out from many other recruits who would bail out of the forces by the age of thirty. During the first Gulf War, in 1991, he served with such distinction that he was awarded the MBE in recognition of his bravery in foiling a plot to blow up an oil tanker. As the British Army came under attack following the invasion of Kuwait, Iraqi ruler Saddam Hussein's forces blew up oilfields and related equipment as they were forced into retreat. Peter Sr, diving alongside a tanker off the Kuwaiti coast, discovered it had been primed with high explosives. Despite the threat of it going off at any second, he removed the bomb from the side of the ship and managed to defuse it.

This success, along with similar triumphs in Germany and Northern Ireland, elevated Peter Sr to the rank of major in the Royal Corps of Signals. Although in military circles it's forbidden to mention such matters, he was so highly rated that he was seconded for periods of his career to the elite SAS. His activities in the Special Forces remained secret to the point at which he couldn't discuss them with anyone outside the military, including his family.

The sense of separation that this engendered was augmented further by Peter Sr's origins. As a working-class man of Irish Catholic extraction, he found it difficult to become a fully accepted member of the officer class. The network of snobbery within the communities of officers' families made the Dohertys outsiders at each base at which they were stationed. In this context, Peter Sr's promotion was no mean achievement for a man who had worked his way up from the bottom. He had an unshakeable sense of duty, of being a cog in a much bigger machine. As it turned out, it could be said that it was a case of like father, *unlike* son, although the two men were very alike in one respect: just as Peter Sr was dedicated to his army life, so too Pete Jr would become equally dedicated to opposing all it represented.

Pete Jr's difficult relationship with his father and his contempt for Peter Sr's army idea of patriotism is revealed in the lyrics of the classic track from *The Libertines* album 'Arbeit Macht Frei' (having lived in Germany and possessing a flair for words, Pete Jr could speak the language), which translates as 'Work Brings Freedom', referring to the sign placed with cruel irony over the gates of the Auschwitz concentration camp, where thousands of Jews were worked to death. In the song, Pete describes the hypocrisy of a British soldier, confident in his moral superiority after having defeated the Nazis: the soldier is prejudiced against black people and homosexuals, yet proud of having beaten the Nazis.

Pete's lyrics and poetry would turn out to be often poignantly autobiographical. 'The lyrics are very honest about lots of things that are talked about in interviews,' he would later admit. He would delight in making artistic statements subverting his father's militaristic patriotism; songs like 'The Man Who Would Be King', referring to a Rudyard Kipling story of the same title, would show his admiration for renegade soldier characters, as would the iconic photograph of The Libertines in red Crimean War guards' jackets Pete had stolen.

Following the birth of his first child, Amy Jo, on St

Valentine's Day 1978, Peter Sr was determined to see his children grow up more comfortably than he had done. Jacqueline, his daughters, Amy Jo and Emily, and his son, Pete, grew up in comfortable semi-detached suburban houses on army estates reserved for officers, where they looked forward to the prospect of university places and white-collar jobs. Peter Sr wanted to give his offspring improved lives, to wipe out all traces of the inner-city, council-estate existence from which he had narrowly escaped. This perhaps explains why his son's first impulse was to get out of suburbia as soon as he was old enough and head for the city. 'Deep down, I suppose I always wanted to identify myself with the inner city,' Pete would later relate. 'My dad came from a council estate and he was glad he'd escaped, but that's exactly where I dreamed of going.'

Before that time, however, Pete Jr had to trail dutifully behind his father as Peter Sr's army career took the family from one barracks to another. In the process, Pete Jr was expected to jump through the same hoops as his father. Among these was an insistence on him following his parents' Roman Catholic religion. Bizarrely, Pete, the future icon of sin, had to make his way to Mass and Confession. His introduction to the public performance took the form of singing in church, dressed in full choirboy outfit, all of which he managed to accept without any overt protest. 'I was never particularly troublesome as a kid,' he would remember. 'I was very troubled, inwardly, but I had a very, very, fascistically dictatorial, disciplined childhood. I had a strict, working-class military father. I wasn't into being a troublemaker.'

Major Doherty applied the same disciplined approach to his family as he had to his impressive career, exerting a strong presence over the family unit, and Pete remembered that his father's attitude was one of 'You can do what you want, but, if you don't want to live by the family's rules, don't bother staying here.' At times, Pete wondered how much longer he *would* stay. Despite the fact that they lived under the same roof, weeks would pass without him and his father speaking to each other. The atmosphere was tense at the best of times, and at the worst there would be violent rows. 'I never started any of the fighting,' claimed Pete. 'My dad will revel in stories about scraps and how hard he was, but, if ever there was a slight whiff of trouble about me as a kid, I would get disciplined like you wouldn't believe, and I never even knew what the hell was going on.'

Pete had little intention at this stage of rebelling against his father, developing instead a sense of inadequacy, a feeling of not being able to live up to Peter Sr's standards. He turned inwards, looking for refuge in his imagination, devouring novels and poetry at an incredible pace. He was creating a vivid alternative world of fantasy, developing obsessions with freedom, death and the dark side of life that would later find expression in his lifestyle and music.

But it wasn't all oppression and resentment in the Doherty household. Pete's mother, Jacqueline, was a warm, working-class Liverpudlian Catholic who was very protective of anyone in need of help, showing the same selfless devotion to her children as to the demands of her husband's way of life, and she showered attention on Pete, who she saw as vulnerable. Like Peter Sr, Jacqueline took great pride in bringing up her children in a more middle-class environment than the one she'd enjoyed in her own childhood. Having grown up in a council house in the Liverpool district of Anfield, she was determined to make sure Pete saw himself as different from the Scousers. When the family returned to Liverpool for a period in the mid-1980s, the seven-year-old Pete was sent to a local state primary school – a meal-ticket school that had no uniform – but Jacqueline insisted on sending him out every morning in smart shoes and black trousers. 'I was just this weird kid with a wonky fringe and a QPR shirt with all these scallies,' he remembered later. Not for the first time in his life, Pete felt a sense of total separation from his peers, the sense that he was so different from them that they shared no commonality. They wore jeans or tracksuits, supported Liverpool or Everton and sported short, spiky haircuts. Pete looked nothing like them and couldn't fit in.

Typically, Pete felt drawn to those aspects of Liverpool life that his mother wanted to leave behind, such as kicking a football around Stanley Park and sneaking into the Kop in Anfield stadium on a non-match day to run up and down the terraces. He would later talk with pride about the Anfield of his grandparents, remembering how his grandfather Perry had been the oldest taxi driver in the city. There, as in most of the places where his roaming family rested, he was desperate to overcome his isolation and would acquire a chameleon-like ability to shift his accent and mannerisms as he moved from place to place. At the age of nine, Pete's accent was strong Liverpudlian, but later this would be lost completely. His incredible talent for mimicry would later resurface in his music, with Pete adapting his voice to the requirements of each song, and in interviews he would frequently veer from the perfect Cockney drawl he demonstrated in songs like 'The Boy Looked at Johnny' to the softly spoken strains of the romantic intellectual in songs such as 'For Lovers' and 'Arcady'.

Although the infant Pete tried so hard to make himself popular, to mould himself into someone who would be accepted, his efforts were continually frustrated by his parents. Their desire for Pete to be separate and different was combined with a way of life so nomadic that it inevitably made the boy an outsider, always the new kid at school. In the face of these overpowering forces, the naturally sociable Pete had no choice but to withdraw into himself, becoming a solitary, introverted teenager. This left him even more isolated and dependent upon his family, particularly his mother.

Although the fact sat rather uneasily with his image as a libertine, Pete would later find it difficult to avoid confessing that he was something of a mummy's boy, given that his reliance on Jacqueline persisted into his twenties. As he was being denounced in the press for his drug-taking in December 2004, Jacqueline leaped to his defence by writing a letter to BBC2's *Newsnight* programme, asking the media to lay off her son, a 'sensitive soul' who she worried was 'very vulnerable'. And when Pete was due to turn up for the Brit Awards in February 2005 for a potentially bruising reunion with Carl Barât, she persuaded him to concentrate on tackling his drug problem and bow out of the ceremony, before calling the amazed organisers to tell them that Pete wouldn't be coming, as if he was back at primary school trying to get out of a PE lesson.

Jacqueline's sympathetic treatment of Pete's heroin addiction mystified his father, who could not understand why his son abused drugs.

As well as with his mother, Pete also formed close relationships with the other women in the family, particularly with his paternal grandmother, Doris. While his father was out of the country on operations like the 1991 Gulf War or the Balkan conflict in the early 1990s, Pete lived at Doris's flat in Kilburn, west London, for months at a time. In fact, in his mind, it was the nearest he had to a permanent home, and he loved the greater freedom he could enjoy there, away from his father's control. Later, whenever Pete addressed the difficult question of where he was from, he would cite London and occasionally his mother's home city of Liverpool as his spiritual places of origin.

Until the birth of his younger sister, Emily, Pete was the youngest member of the family and, for much of the time, the only male present. Even after Emily arrived, Pete continued to play the role of the vulnerable doe-eyed baby boy surrounded by protective women. As a child, he idolised his older sister, Amy Jo, keenly following her every move into adolescence and beyond, in anticipation of his own escape. She was the source of illicit tales of the outside world, pubs and gigs. A lively extrovert whose passion for acting drew her to drama school, Amy Jo was something of a rebel herself but was nonetheless very protective of her kid brother, always taking Pete's side during his frequent quarrels with his father. She also encouraged his writing, urging him not to be shy in allowing others to read the poetry he wrote from adolescence onwards.

Pete came to see Amy Jo as a shelter from the criticisms of his father and the hostility of his peers. He also credited Amy Jo (who later became a schoolteacher in Lewisham, southeast London) as the inspiration for some of his most groundbreaking work. During his later fight with addiction, he enthused of his older sister, 'She's great. She respects me and understands me better than anyone. She knows that a lot of the things reported about me are exaggerated. She's very protective of me.'

Pete's relationship with his younger sister, Emily, was less straightforward, however. According to Pete, she didn't show the same level of understanding as Amy Jo. While living at home with their parents, Emily's was close to her father and shared his views on Pete's behaviour. The media storm surrounding her elder brother also got to her. Her friends would rib her about Pete's much-publicised drug addiction. 'Emily always writes to me saying how ashamed she is of me,' Pete lamented. 'She says all her friends wind her up and tell her I'm a junkie. But then, when she wants tickets to Reading, it's all, "Yes, Peter. Love you Peter."'

Pete was deeply lonely, separated from his roots, his peers and even his own father. Denied the chance to explore the world through interaction with playmates, he turned inwards, satiating the hunger of his imagination with vast quantities of reading. He would remember his childhood as one long period of retreat into his interior: 'I had no choice but to disappear into myself, veering between old, flickery episodes of *Rising Damp*, Tony Hancock radio shows, Emily Dickinson, flowers and Queens Park Rangers.' While Pete would later be surrounded by fans and musicians, he always maintained that the source of his creativity remained his deep sense of loneliness. 'I come from a loneliness, I think. Reaching out for another world.'

Pete's voracious reading habit developed at an early age through his wading through many of the heavyweight classics of English literature before he'd even finished primary school. Once immersed in a book, Pete became absorbed in it to the extent that he was lost to his surroundings. It wasn't long before his bookish personality was noticed by those around him; he became self-taught to such a degree that it left several of his teachers feeling intimidated. He also felt a strong connection with certain authors, whose works he would read and re-read dozens of times, and found that he could use the power of his imagination to escape his surroundings. 'I was wandering through my mind,' he remembered. 'I lived inside books and devoured literature.'

Indeed, Pete would frequently appear detached from everyday life, separated from other children not only by parental decree but also by his knowledge and his talent. In a further attempt to keep himself company, he took to writing his own literature, jotting down poems and stories in a notebook during breaks in the playground. Before he'd reached his teens, he'd proclaimed himself a poet.

Pete's mother encouraged her son's project of self-education. Neither Peter Sr nor Jacqueline had been to university, but her relative lack of learning made her all the more proud of her son's intellectual aspirations. Wherever the family were living, she made sure that Pete had access to books and was confident that her super-bright child was destined for great things. Of course, she was eventually proved right, in a sense, although she was seriously mistaken about the direction Pete's talents would take, believing at the time that the boy would one day become a university professor of English.

Jacqueline may be forgiven for her mistake, for Pete during this period showed every sign of heading for academic circles and demonstrated little interest in music. Until he reached his early teens, Pete's cultural input was restricted to poetry and novels. Even when he listened to the radio, he preferred speech-based stations like Radio 4, tuning in to comedy shows such as that of post-war classic comedian Tony Hancock. He didn't have much of a record collection, and couldn't play a musical instrument. His interest in music didn't develop until later in his life, through his interest in words.

Pete's childhood reading list offers a fascinating insight into the workings of his imagination. Almost exclusively, he read the greats of English literature, avoiding thrillers, science fiction and even children's books in favour of material with a greater intellectual content. His gift and a fascination for words fostered a particular interest in poetry, and he became obsessed with a handful of key ideas, one of which was a strong concept of Englishness. The rootless youth who wasn't sure where he came from discovered in literature an English ideal that came to replace any precise location. Much of this mythology was borrowed from the Romantic mystic William Blake, who dramatised England as a blessed realm named Albion (the Latin name for England). In keeping with this classical reference, Blake would sometimes represent the concept of the nation as a god, much in the manner of the Ancient Greeks. In Blake's imagination, the newly industrialised landscape of the late eighteenth century was transformed into a lush, pastoral paradise.

Pete found Blake's idea of Albion's 'green and pleasant land' an attractive one. Blake had aimed to cut through what he saw as the superficial distortions of Englishness – the Satanic mills (ie the growing conurbations of Manchester and London) – to an essential core of national identity. Pete took from these ideas, but his Albion ended up radically different from Blake's vision, based mainly in the city rather than the countryside and focusing on its people rather than its landscape. He began to form his own version of an imagined, mystical essence of Albion, picking up elements for it in literature, film and television. From Dickens, he lapped up the colour and chaos of a comically conceived London and the resourceful urchin the Artful Dodger. From First World War poets such as Siegfried Sassoon, he took the image of the resilient Tommy, the modest lion of a soldier being driven to his death by army top-brass donkeys. In the *Carry On* films starring rough diamond Sid James, he found a cast of eccentric English characters that captured something essential in the liberal, self-satirising national consciousness. The brilliant talent of Tony Hancock who posed as various English figures of fun, the ridiculous rag-and-bone men of *Steptoe and Son*, Leonard Rossiter's grasping landlord in the 1970s sitcom *Rising Damp*, the comic fantasist in the classic 1963 film *Billy Liar* – all were woven into Pete's idea of Albion.

Pete also created an associated concept, a vision of

'Arcadia', which took the form of a dream world free of rules and restrictions, to which he would metaphorically sail on a ship he named the *Albion*. Its isolated inhabitants were said to have lived a simple, pastoral life, and the word Arcadia (originally a region of Ancient Greece) therefore came to mean a rustic paradise. Pete's research into Arcadia unearthed references to the concept in his favourite nineteenth-century English poets, such as the 1909 musical play *The Arcadians*, based on the book by Mark Ambient and Alexander M Thompson. In that play, Arcadia is a land where time stands still, where there are no lies, money doesn't exist and no one has to work. In a similar way, Pete's Arcadia was a mental state, an attitude to life, rather than a place. Sailing to Arcadia in the *Albion* meant bringing England to the state of liberation he imagined, and he spent hours watching repeat after repeat of classic sitcoms and comic movies, feeding his imagined homeland.

Of course, Pete wasn't the only one experiencing a revival of patriotism, as demonstrated by the popularity of Britpop at the time, but Pete didn't come to appreciate the likes of Oasis and Blur until later in life, and his Albion project had much more to it than a 1960s and 1970s retro chic harking back to the golden era of British rock 'n' roll. Pete's patriotic imaginings were far more complicated and individualistic; he was looking for an idea that encompassed all the corners of England in which he had lived during his rootless childhood. 'There's always been a real sense of Englishness and probably nationalism,' he later observed. 'From an early age, I had a fascination with the language and accents.'

During his early teens, Pete felt attracted to another idealised concept: that of the lone artist, such as the nineteenth-century American poet Emily Dickinson. Pete identified with this withdrawn, isolated writer who created beautiful verse from the depths of intense emotional pain. Dickinson, who shrank away from society in her early twenties, had a Puritan religious upbringing whose constraints far exceeded those placed on Pete. Scribbling away in private, keeping the bulk of her 1,700 poems hidden (most weren't discovered until after her death), Dickinson developed a freedom of thought expressed in her development towards free verse, through which she constantly broke conventional rules of grammar and structure.

In his youth, the lonely schoolboy, struggling to find ways of reaching out to his peers, found his difficulties perfectly reflected in her poetry, and Pete would later draw on Dickinson's innovations in his creation of experimental song lyrics and stream-of-consciousness poetry on his Babyshambles website. Just as he tried to communicate through his writing, so Dickinson saw her work as a series of messages that she was sending in an attempt to overcome the cruel indifference of the outside world. Her lines 'This is my letter to the world/That never wrote to me' could have served as a description of Pete's own writing during his school years. The American poet's introspection, like Pete's own, was filled with a morbid fascination with pain and death.

Above all else, Pete cherished the lyrical quality of her poems, comparing the process of reading them to that of listening to much-loved tunes. 'My voracity encompassed

Emily Dickinson,' he remembered. 'It's like your favourite record, The Specials or The La's or The Smiths: you can put the needle on the groove anywhere and you know you're in for a treat.'

Pete went on to find heroes in the English Romantic poets of the late eighteenth and early nineteenth centuries, figures like John Keats, Lord Byron, Percy Shelley and Samuel Taylor Coleridge. He was drawn to Byron's image of a debauched rake who had sex with thousands of women (many of them other men's wives), and who even dropped hints that he'd slept with his half-sister, drank wine from a skull and had a much-publicised affair with the Kate Moss of his day, society beauty Lady Caroline Lamb. Over the next decade, Pete would prove that Byron's example had not been lost on him.

At the age of fifteen, Pete encountered what became perhaps his greatest literary influence when he laid his hands on a copy of the Marquis de Sade's stomach-churning bible of sexual cruelty, *The Lusts of the Libertines*, which powerfully affected him. De Sade's concept of the 'libertine' was the ultimate rebel, one who has complete disregard for the rules of society. In the following subsection of the catalogue of debaucheries, cruelties and pathological perversions de Sade called *The 120 Days of Sodom*, four libertines embark on 447 'complex, criminal and murderous lusts' ranging from incest to mass murder. The extract below gives a flavour of what the teenage Pete was reading:

Gradually perfecting his art on various parts of the body over the years, this famous whip-wielder now thrashes a bitch from head to toe until she's flayed alive; he wears her skin to dinner. This libertine used to squeeze a girl's throat during sodomy, to tighten her anus; now he ties her by a noose. A meal is placed before her, but to reach it she must strangle. Otherwise, she starves to death. This libertine used to adore fondling a whore's tits and buttocks; now he lambasts them with such abominable fury that his victim soon expires in a welter of blood.

De Sade wrote *The Lust of the Libertines* as a series of fantasies and, despite being jailed several times, insisted that he had never carried out most of his criminal imaginings. His aim was to shock, to make a deliberate show of pursuing his own pleasure, whatever the cost. His overblown statement of rebellion and total commitment to hedonism made a huge impression on Pete, who within a couple of years of discovering de Sade would declare that he too was a libertine.

At this time, bent over his books, Pete appeared to be studiously compiling a vast repertoire of learning. In fact, he had embarked on an intellectualised sex-and-drugs fest, piecing together a blueprint for his later life. Given the fact that he revelled in his self-education, it's not surprising that he gained eleven A-star GCSEs and four A-levels, sailing through exams with the appearance of barely trying. By the time he came to apply for a place studying English Literature at the University of London, he had already read far more than most who had completed the three-year course.

Pete took his success at school in his stride; although it pleased his mother, it did not spark in him any real interest, and he had no ambition to amass qualifications just to further a career and make money. What did inspire him was the idea of using his literary abilities to reach out, to write a Dickinson-style letter to the world, and beyond that to become the people's poet that the Romantics imagined. In his mid- to late teens, he set about searching for a way to reach out, to popularise the poetic talents he had developed over his years of writing on his own.

Pete's first attempt to communicate his ideas took the most unlikely of forms: at the age of fifteen, he set about writing a fanzine for Queens Park Rangers football club. Pete was a fanatical supporter, attending all home games and following his team to most of their away fixtures. Here was a community he could join, where he would be surrounded by a crowd of people who all shared the same devotion to the club, while the side's Loftus Road ground, near the BBC Television Centre in White City, was just a couple of miles away from his grandmother Doris's home in Kilburn. A small stadium with a capacity of just 19,100, flanked on one side by a sprawling council estate, it was the butt of jokes from visiting supporters, and during Pete's teens the club drifted towards the lower end of the Premier League, before finally being relegated in 1996.

Pete remembered how his enthusiasm for QPR was linked to an ambition to get back to the roots his parents had denied him. 'I was a fanatical QPR fan, even though it was quite difficult, seeing them play when my dad was stationed abroad. By the time I'd got back to England, I was off with my little scarf everywhere following them. That was my passion. I think, in a way, I wanted to get back to what my mum and dad had been trying to escape from. They wanted to get out of inner cities and I just had this fantasy of inner-city bohemia.'

Pete's memories of this period include many journeys to London on the train from his then home, next to Bramcote Barracks, near the Midlands town of Nuneaton. At that time attending Nicholas Chamberlaine Comprehensive School in Bedworth, he passed the time by reading de Sade. He would sit on the train with a QPR scarf wrapped around his neck, engrossed in a rare eighteenth-century exploration of sexual perversion. It's a fairly certain bet that he was the only fan heading to the game in such circumstances.

Pete's unwavering support for QPR – not exactly a star-studded side guaranteed success, like Manchester United during the same period – reflected a genuine passion for football. As a child, he dreamed of one day taking the field for the team and spent countless hours kicking balls against walls in a bid to enhance his skills. By all accounts, these were far from bad, and he proved useful on the pitch, despite his gangly figure. Sadly, he would never make it on to the Loftus Road turf in a professional capacity, but he did occupy the terraces above with a dedicated regularity, learning everything there was to know about the club and, in the process, developing a nerd-like obsession with QPR trivia.

The QPR fanzine Pete created, *All Quiet On The Western Avenue*, offered a curious combination of chat blended with literary references. Following Pete's accession to fame, the pamphlets – sold at £1 each at Loftus Road by their editor, 'Peter Doherty Jnr' – have since become collectors' items. Written with impeccable command of grammar and spelling, they have Pete's character stamped all over them. The title in itself showed his quest to unite the everyday with the literary, merging the name of Erich Maria Remarque's 1929 First World War novel *All Quiet on the Western Front* with that of the A40 trunk road near QPR's ground.

A typical issue of the fanzine, from February 1995, features on the cover a send-up of then manager Ray Wilkins, whose hair is receding so far that he'll soon end up 'combing his arse'. Inside, a piece titled 'From Behind the Tinted Glass' is a spoof in the style of classic comic author PG Wodehouse in which members of the QPR board address each other in Bertie Wooster terms, such as 'Old Beef' and 'Old Stick'. Further on, QPR defender David Bardsley appears in the guise of a seventeenth-century poet. With most of his literary references sailing over most people's heads, Pete hadn't quite yet realised his ambition to provide poetry for the people.

Meanwhile, Pete had found another potential outlet for his creativity that was to prove much more productive than his fanzine. While browsing the shelves of a Cancer Research charity shop, he discovered what was to be the answer to the thorny problem of reaching people through his art. During the summer of 1994, he wandered into the store near his grandmother's home in Kilburn and spotted an old 7in vinyl record with an unusual retro black and white cover. Curious, he snapped it up for 50p. It turned out to be The Smiths' 1987 single 'I Started Something I Couldn't Finish'. He took it home, played it and was blown away.

The fifteen-year-old Pete listened carefully, playing the

song over and over. 'It changed everything for me,' Pete remembered. 'I could live in that song. It was like a drug trip, even though I wasn't taking any at the time, and I understood at that very moment that I had to start creating. I understood that, in three minutes, you could save the world or find a girl, become anyone, do anything. You could climb mountains or go down sewers. You could drown yourself in your dreams and believe in them. Music made real what I felt deep down in myself without managing to define it, to express it. It was possible. Real.' Listening to The Smiths, Pete realised for the first time that it was possible to combine poetry with music to make something very powerful, something with which he could express himself and yet would appeal to a massive audience. He caught the first glimmer of what he could become.

CHAPTER 3

The Pact

'I WAS TRYING TO WORK OUT A SINGLE REASON WHY
MY LIFE SHOULDN'T EMULATE POETRY.'
— *Pete Doherty*

B y the age of sixteen, Pete had made huge strides in overcoming the obstacles placed in his path during his unusual childhood. He had sought to soothe his profound sense of rootlessness by formulating an idea of a homeland he called Albion. Feeling no link with his succession of temporary homes, he had attempted to reattach himself to his grandparents' origins, forging an idealised inner city as the source of his identity. He had already come across many of the ideas that would mould his future, including the concept of the libertine, the free renegade whose role was to rebel and break the rules. Pete had worked out a way of breaking out of his intellectual shell, making use of his imagination to reach out to people through performance poetry and through music.

It was all beginning to gel together and fall into place, yet Pete still hadn't succeeded in finding anyone who truly shared his ideas. When he wasn't one of an anonymous crowd of QPR fans, he spent most of his time alone, reading voraciously. To outsiders, he appeared bookish, introverted and sullen, nothing like a rebel with his smart clothes, close-cropped hair and polite manner. Inwardly, though, he was troubled, desperately looking for a way out.

Meanwhile, his older sister, Amy Jo, was enjoying her first taste of freedom from the confines of their family. In the autumn of 1996, she left home for Brunel University, in Uxbridge, Middlesex, to study drama. Pete would listen to the stories she'd relate over the telephone of life at university. When she returned home for the Christmas break in her first year, he saw how she had opened up, how her experiences had given her a new sense of freedom. As she enthusiastically recounted her tales of life as a fresher, he saw in her a glimpse of the bohemian liberation he was craving. 'I was this lonely foppish lad living on an army camp, surrounded by barbed-wire fences,' he later recalled. 'She was out there, being free and doing what she wanted. What she was doing was the stuff of fantasy for me.'

Amy Jo talked enthusiastically about a good friend in her drama class named Carl Barât. Living in the same halls of residence, they had spent a lot of time together and grown close. Like Pete, Amy Jo was passionate about the arts, and in Carl she saw the same creative drive. She had also been telling Carl about her clever little brother, 'the poet', and Carl became intrigued. With Pete listening eagerly, she talked about Carl at length, described him as a 'great guitarist' with shoulder-length hair and a washboard stomach. Carl was just the kind of person Pete's parents would warn him against: streetwise and from a large hippie household.

Thinking of the band that had inspired him, Pete built up a picture of Carl in his mind as 'a Johnny Marr type, waiting for me to write words for him'. Before they had even come face to face, he had a gut feeling that Carl was the outlet he had been searching for, someone with whom he could share his dream. Having spent years writing on his own, he imagined a perfect partnership, a rock 'n' roll companionship in the manner of Rolling Stones greats Mick Jagger and Keith Richards.

From then onwards, Pete drove his sister mad with endless questions about Carl on the phone. Weeks before the pair had actually met, Pete had already imagined them teaming up and taking the music world by storm. Eventually, his pestering persuaded Amy Jo to invite him down to Brunel, where he would finally meet Carl. He was so full of excitement at the prospect that he even wrote to Carl in advance, asking if he had any guitar tab for The Smiths. Maybe Carl could teach him a few tricks on the guitar, too.

On the day they met, Pete caught the train to Uxbridge, a small satellite town just inside the M25 London orbital motorway. He arrived at Brunel University to find a grey concrete complex, the university's grounds bisected by the muddy River Pinn, a tributary of the Thames. Amy Jo's halls of residence were no less drab than the army barracks in which he had grown up, leading Pete to believe that either the architect had had a very bad day or the builders had had some spare sacks of concrete they'd needed to get rid of in a hurry. Amy Jo gave wide-eyed Pete a quick tour of the campus, but all he was really interested in was meeting Carl. She took him to her room and told him that she had to go to a lecture, but that she would tell Carl to come round. Pete made himself comfortable, opening the window and looking out over the dreary vista.

A few minutes later, Carl turned up at the room, ready for babysitting duty. While it's true that he wanted to meet the talented sixteen-year-old of whom Amy Jo had spoken so excitedly, he didn't particularly relish the prospect of being stuck in a room alone with him for hours. After all, how much could he really have in common with a schoolboy?

The meeting got off to a poor start when Carl opened the door a crack and was hit by a powerful smell of urine. He later confessed to having thought, I'm not having that. She never told me she had an incontinent brother. He held his breath and poked his head around the door. Pete was far taller than he'd imagined, standing in a 'nasty, plastic, squeaky-when-you-move' black jacket, looking out of the window with his back to the door. It didn't look promising. Carl decided to sneak off quietly and leave him there.

Twenty minutes later, Carl felt guilty. He'd promised to look after Amy Jo's brother, and the least he could do was make sure he was there when she returned, so he came back and introduced himself. Much to Carl's relief, the smell turned out to be coming from the polluted river.

Carl came face to face with Pete the teenager for the first time and was immediately struck by his dark-brown, almost black eyes, as round as saucers and full of innocence. Pete was painfully polite and old-fashioned, his voice quiet almost to the point of being inaudible.

To Pete, on the other hand, Carl looked just as he'd imagined: slim and stylish, with long, dark hair and a kind of Oscar Wilde elegance that immediately attracted him. Carl looked the part, and when he spoke Pete could detect the same eloquence and poetry of his own speech, along with a trace of punkish attitude. Within minutes, they became engaged in what would become a defining element in their complex relationship: intense competition.

'From the first minute, we were asking each other these competitive questions, trying to make out we knew more than the other,' Carl remembered. 'We got the dictionary out, seeing who knew the most words. We spent that first day arguing for hours.'

With Pete's high expectations of Carl, the reality was inevitably different, although it was no less passionate. With the two young men constantly provoking each other, the conversation would veer wildly from intelligent banter to angry shouting matches. Pete later admitted that their relationship was tense from the very beginning, admitting, 'We didn't really get on, but I was fascinated by ideas he had about himself and the country. I'd never met anyone like him.'

Then Pete got his hands on Carl's dust-covered guitar. Carl admitted that he'd not played for months. He felt like he'd taken his musical career as far as it would go and was sick of playing the same old songs, tired of people asking, 'Carl, can you play "Wonderwall"?' Pete dusted it off and started to play a song he'd written named 'The Long Song'. Of course, Pete's musical career was still in its infancy, and he couldn't play to any decent standard, managing only to belt out a few clumsy chords. Nevertheless, he kept playing, ignoring the fret buzz and the bum notes.

Carl wasn't impressed by Pete's skill, but he did admire

his persistence. Years later, he remembered, 'He was really shit, but he wouldn't give up and I knew he was going to get better.' Even at this early stage, it was obvious that the guitar was the perfect vehicle for Pete; he could see himself as a Bob Dylan-style figure, a minstrel singing his carefully crafted lyrics to the folksy melody of an acoustic guitar. Despite his lack of technical skill, he was already showing signs of his talent as a performer, and his shyness evaporated as soon as he started playing.

Pete eventually finished his song and passed the guitar to Carl, eager to see what Carl was capable of. The older student played Pete's song back to him, adding a little flair of his own. The result impressed Pete, who saw his own clumsy efforts transformed into a slick performance, with Carl's lithe fingers dancing on the fretboard. Pete remembered later how he was 'open-mouthed' at Carl's ability, and Carl responded with a flourish.

Carl certainly had a kind of charisma when he picked up a guitar. He'd been playing gigs in pubs since he was sixteen, including a stint with a band of friends who had called themselves The Riot, and it showed. But, even though he had played to an audience many times, he wasn't used to the level of enthusiasm Pete displayed at his performance. Normally, people asked him to bang out the same old Oasis songs but Pete showed a much deeper interest. Something about Pete brought the best out of him.

Desperate to be taken seriously, Pete introduced Carl to his concept of Arcadia, describing it as 'something that a lot of people had laughed at'. Carl, however, responded differently. 'We had the ultimate togetherness, me and Carl,' Pete later recalled. 'I didn't think anything would

36

ever come between us. I believed in him, and he was the one person who never laughed when I told him about Arcadia. He could genuinely see that I believed in it.'

Carl was fascinated by Pete's ideas and tastes, and, in fact, he shared many of them, including a passion for British acting greats like Peter Sellers. 'With Carl, it was glaringly obvious that we'd found each other,' Pete observed later. They were both dreamers, although Carl had become very disillusioned, displaying a cynicism matched by Pete's apparent naïveté. As Carl sat there, skinning up and casually playing riffs, Pete babbled enthusiastically about Tony Hancock and The Smiths, *Rising Damp* and Chas 'n' Dave. For Pete, it all somehow fitted together – music, literature, television and poetry – and Carl could see that this was something the boy really believed in. To someone who'd become resigned to the way things were, it was a breath of fresh air. Carl had never heard anything like it.

The summer after he took his A-levels, Pete decided he needed a break from life in the barracks living according to his father's rules, so he packed a suitcase full of books, scraps of his own writing and a few clothes and caught the train to London. As Pete sat on the train, reading, he imagined the journey as being the fulfilment of a fantasy, a fable of escape. Even though he had been to London many times before, this time was different. For a start, he was relieved at having finished school, having always hated institutions, and now he had the double bonus of being able to leave both the barracks and school behind at once. 'Wherever we lived, I just knew I had to get to London as quickly as possible,' he later remembered, 'and that's what I did. I was like a greyhound out of a trap as soon as I left home.'

Pete crashed at his grandmother Doris's cramped council flat in Ainsworth Close, Kilburn, which was like a second home to Pete – not that he really felt that he had a first home. He'd stayed there many times with his family while his father was abroad on duty, coming down to watch his beloved QPR play and sell his fanzine at Loftus Road.

Sleeping on his grandmother's sofa might not have been comfortable, but Pete found something magnificent in the hardship, exaggerating it and likening himself to his down-at-heel artistic heroes. Instead of being a lad staying at his grandmother's, he was slumming it in the city, living like the mid-twentieth-century writer George Orwell, author of *Down and Out in Paris and London*. Kilburn itself wasn't quite the inner-city bohemia he'd fantasised about, but now at least Pete was left to his own devices, and the flat was within a short bus ride of Camden, the creative melting-pot of culture he'd glimpsed during his many stays in the city. Now, living with his grandmother gave him the support he needed at the same time as a new freedom, and Pete felt like he was embarking on the first stage of a pilgrimage. Now he had a base from which he could reach out to other poets, musicians and free thinkers.

Of course, there were also more prosaic matters to think about, such as money. Having never had a proper job before, Pete was unused to the demands of self-sufficiency, but he romanticised menial work and poverty, imagining himself 'lying in the gutter but looking up at the stars', in the words of another of his heroes, Victorian playwright and wit Oscar Wilde. Pete saw his life experiences as creative tools, and he believed that dabbling in destitution would give his writing an authenticity and breadth he had been lacking, sheltered in a middle-class home.

Pete's obsession with all things romantic and unconventional drove his every move. He found his first job after leaving school not in a shop, a factory or an office, but in Willesden Green Cemetery, a mile away from his grandmother's home – not perhaps the average school-leaver's first choice, but Pete had by then developed a morbid fascination with death, likening himself to the poet John Keats, who died at just twenty-five years old from tuberculosis and whose verse is filled with meditations on death. Pete regarded himself as being 'half in love with easeful death', to quote the literary genius, and overlaid his time spent in the graveyard with the ideas he'd borrowed from Keats and other artistic figures, such as the often morbid Emily Dickinson.

The reality of his job at the cemetery was more mundane. A grave-digging machine opened up a six-foot-deep hole in the ground and, once the coffin had been placed inside and the funeral service was over, Pete's job was to shovel earth inside to fill it in. The same task was repeated over and over again, a procession of groups of tearful relatives passing by one after another.

During his time at the cemetery, Pete developed a grim sense of humour. One of his colleagues was a man in his sixties Pete referred to as 'Old Joe', who educated Pete on the financial benefits of attending funerals, describing how it was possible to pick up large tips from grieving families. Pete found Old Joe's cynical attitude uncomfortable. 'We ended up looking forward to funerals, so it all got a bit twisted, really.' Worldly Joe took Pete under his wing, teaching him how to skin up and smoke properly.

Eventually, the cold reality of burying dead bodies took its toll on Pete's state of mind. The cemetery was a lonely place, and Pete had been plagued by a profound loneliness for most of his life. He became fixated on the darker side of human nature. Inspired by reading the Marquis de Sade, his mind turned to thoughts of perversion, death and self-destruction. His idea of freedom, too, began to take a darker turn, and he began to fantasise about the idea of self-harm, a preoccupation that would lead to a habit of cutting himself with razor blades. In an effort to live out his ideas, Pete drove himself into a state of depression, later describing how during his time at the cemetery he had been 'in a bad way' and wanted to be 'a million miles away'.

By the end of the summer, Pete felt down on his luck. When he wasn't shovelling earth, he was practising the guitar and his singing, although he still couldn't read music. Partly thanks to Carl's influence, he had been branching out musically, listening to an eclectic mixture of The Beatles (Carl had recommended *The White Album*), The Velvet Underground, The Doors, the blues and jazz of Billie Holiday and Ella Fitzgerald, and even Newcastle folk group Lindisfarne. He already knew from The Smiths that pop could encompass poetry, but, as his interests developed to take in The Sex Pistols and The Buzzcocks, he incorporated a particularly English rebelliousness: the nihilistic, anarchic, anti-establishment sentiment of punk. Although Pete liked The La's and The Stone Roses, he wasn't interested in the charts and would instead listen to music from any decade, fashionable or not. Just as he would read classic literature, he'd listen to classic albums from the 1970s and 1980s and earlier.

During this time, Pete scoured the pages of weekly music paper the *NME*. By now, he was anxious to get his own band together. Carl had to be in it, of course, Pete by now being convinced that the pair of them could craft the kind of songs that he said 'England was starved of'. Unfortunately, Carl was elusive. They would meet and stay up all night, swapping ideas and singing until dawn, but then they would go for weeks without seeing each other.

Pete was disappointed with Carl, with whom he felt he had a special bond that Carl didn't fully appreciate. While Pete was a positive influence on Carl when they met, Carl was far less encouraging in return. 'Carl was like a lot of people I met around that time who wanted to put me down and keep me in my place,' Pete remembered. 'I wanted to prove to him that he was wrong.' Pete was hoping that Carl would help him break into the music scene, but instead Pete remained a quiet outsider. It seemed like his dream was slipping away.

That August, Pete got his A-Level results and learned that he'd gained a place to read English Literature at the University of London. In some ways, it seemed a natural progression for Pete, a gifted teenager who had spent most of his life immersed in books, but in the event he found that he couldn't stick at education any longer. He half-heartedly attended some of his lectures and seminars, but before he'd completed a term there he realised that a prescribed programme of study wasn't for him. He loved literature, but there was something about his degree course's formal, institutionalised approach that repelled him, and he found the tutor–student relationship stifling. It wasn't his idea of what writing should be about.

Much to his mother's horror, Pete told her that he was dropping out of university. This came as a blow to Jacqueline, who had been grooming her children for university and middle-class jobs all their lives. Pete, of course, didn't see it that way; he felt that he'd already jumped through enough hoops. Doing well at school was easy for him, and so would university have been, but it was the path his parents had put him on, not the path he had chosen for himself. He felt that, by staying on at school to gain his A-levels, he'd already done enough to please them, protesting, 'Amy Jo and I, we're the first generation of my family to stay on at school and do any exams at all.'

For Pete, the best thing about his university experiment was the student loan he received, which relieved the financial pressure he was under, leaving him all the more determined to spend time on his poetry, songwriting and, of course, learning to play the guitar. He wasn't just dropping out; he was forming a clear idea of where he was aiming and how he was going to apply his talents. He was ambitious, but not in a way his parents could recognise.

At this time, Pete saw his life as a reflection of his ideas, almost a work of art in itself. He would later delight in confusing the media with varying inconsistent accounts of his younger years, dressed up in colourful language. In one interview, Pete later claimed that he'd never made it to university because he 'fell in love with a girl called Evelina who wore a plastic crown'. The couple had been due to get married in Sweden, Pete attested, but said that he 'never went to the airport'.

Indeed, in an effort to live out poetic extremes, Pete almost wilfully deprived himself of real, practical relationships, preferring instead to dream of what might have been. His tendency to become carried away with relationships and the idea of an extreme, sometimes unrealistic love would later resurface in spectacular fashion with his relationship with Kate Moss. One former girlfriend, Tabitha Denholm from DJ duo Queens of Noize, described how Pete used to 'climb in through my window and serenade me on the end of my bed'.

Driven by his desire to break into the music scene, Pete found work behind the bar of thronging Filthy McNasty's Whiskey Café, near King's Cross. A haven for music lover and a haunt for writers, artists and hardened drinkers, Filthy's was renowned for its regular poetry readings and live music, attracting hordes of bards, musicians and hangers-on, all crammed together on the bare wooden floors. Pogues singer Shane MacGowan was a regular, routinely drinking himself into oblivion, while writers Irvine Welsh and Will Self had also made appearances at the so-called 'Vox 'n' Roll' words-and-music nights. The walls of the establishment, bearing a variety of rock 'n' roll posters, had been stained a muddy orange-yellow by years of cigarette smoke, the leather sofas were worn and the ambience was dingy and dark.

Pete couldn't have asked for a better job. It wasn't an easy job, tending the hectic bar amidst the noise and smoke, but Filthy's was the ideal place to meet the young bohemian set and certainly more stimulating than a graveyard. Everyone there either wanted to be, thought they were or, indeed, were something. The Vox 'n' Roll idea had been devised to put musicians and writers together in order to capitalise on the links between literature and music, and in such an environment Pete found exactly the combination he'd been looking for. The promotion of audience participation and the proximity of performer and audience had a profound effect, later forming a crucial part of Pete's philosophy for The Libertines and Babyshambles of breaking down barriers, inviting the crowd to flood the stage and even to enter his home. It gave Pete the chance to break out of his shell and have a go himself, performing his poetry and even trying his hand with his guitar.

Perhaps most importantly, Pete was now getting to see Carl regularly at the Filthy McNasty's scene, and they were developing a close if stormy friendship. Pete soon discovered that Carl was much more volatile than he had at first appeared. 'I realised he could be completely out of control. Sometimes on a night out he couldn't even keep still.'

Carl, it turned out, was loud and difficult to pin down, prone to impulsively leaving a conversation to chat up women, get another drink or more drugs, or disappear completely, which to Pete made him all the more fascinating. Carl started taking the introverted Pete out on wild all-night parties at his friends' houses, introducing him to the crowd of musicians and would-be rock stars he'd come to know. It was a new world to Pete. A year older and more socially confident, Carl was very popular, especially with women, and Pete found that sticking by him made it easier for him to meet girls; rather than having to go it alone, Pete could rely on his banter with Carl to attract their attention. Sometimes, however, it looked more like Pete just wanted Carl to himself.

Drugs were commonplace in Pete's new cultural *milieu*. By now, he was regularly smoking cannabis and beginning to experiment with other drugs, seeing them as a source of adventure, of yet more experiences to fuel his creativity. He was drawn to drugs not simply because he was looking for a good time or trying to fit in; like almost every choice he made in his adult life, his decision to indulge formed part of his obsession with ideas about creativity and art. Pete's reading of writers such as opium addicts Samuel Taylor Coleridge and Thomas de Quincey left him with a sense that drugs, creativity and self-destruction were intimately linked.

Around him at Filthy's, he found plenty of poets and musicians with similar ideas, many of whom were taking drugs – cannabis, speed, acid, cocaine, even heroin and crack cocaine. They became part of everyday life for Pete. Not ashamed of his habits, he told his mother he smoked cannabis. She was horrified, warning him ominously (and, it turned out, prophetically), 'Every heroin addict started with cannabis.'

With his new hectic lifestyle, Pete wasn't earning enough from his intermittent bar work, particularly as he was spending more and more money on drugs and alcohol, so took another job, as a labourer on a building site. With his slight frame, Pete stood out among the bricklayers and hod carriers, but he saw his new job as harking back to his working-class roots. And, to his surprise, he found that his fellow builders were just as fond of drugs as the musicians and artists he'd met. 'All the labourers were taking speed, acid and poppers,' he remembered. 'I started dealing to them to make a bit of money on the side and took speed myself.'

By this time, Pete and Carl had become inseparable. Their paths were now intertwined: both were searching for something and both possessed a talent they were yet to fully exploit. Like Pete, Carl had now dropped out of university, disillusioned and dissatisfied with the direction it was taking him, and they moved in together into a dingy flat at the Holloway Road end of Camden Road. The place was so small that they had to sleep together on a single bed, but it was a start. Now they had all the time they needed to play music and share ideas. For Pete, this was a crucial step towards getting together the band he had dreamed of.

As it turned out, Pete wasn't the only one preoccupied by the darker side of life; Carl, too, was haunted by the idea of his own destruction, being visited by a recurring vision of himself alone and broken in a bedsit, watching daytime television and eating beans on toast. This image of his supposed future later inspired the song 'Death on the Stairs', which describes the misery of ending up washed-up and ruined. Carl felt that he was trapped in a drab, controlled life, later confessing, 'I felt like a person who locks it all up and goes through the motions.'

Pete knew exactly what his friend was going through, having had similar thoughts, and this shared sadness bound them together. Ironically, Carl's fear of insignificance provoked him to pursue nihilistic ideas, which he shared with Pete. In a fit of angst, Carl tried to persuade Pete to enter into a suicide pact whereby they would kill themselves together, either by jumping off a high building or by shooting themselves. He had it all planned out in disturbing detail.

Later, Pete would recall how Carl had tried to talk him into entering the suicide pact while they were sitting by a canal in London's East End. Looking into the dark water, it had seemed to Carl that there was only one way out: straight to the bottom. Pete, however, was convinced that there was an alternative to the dismal conformity of everyday existence that had driven Carl to despair – the way to Arcadia, a life without boundaries and constraints – and persuaded Carl that they could live out the dream.

As Carl later put it, instead of plummeting to their deaths from the top of a skyscraper, 'We threw ourselves into eternity. And it worked.' For Pete and Carl, an ordinary existence was a fate worse than death, and the only way out was to pursue their ideas to their conclusion. Filled with a new self-belief, they made a new pact, less nihilistic but just as determined as the one Carl had intended. 'We decided it's either the top of the world or the bottom of that canal,' Pete recalled. 'We were going to sail the good ship *Albion* to Arcadia.'

CHAPTER 4

Albion Days

'IT WAS BIT LIKE FINDING A MANHOLE COVER AND
LIFTING IT UP AND THEN GOING UNDER.'
— *Carl Barât*

'ALL THAT WAS FANTASY IN INK BECAME TRUE:
THE SEARCH FOR ARCADIA AND THE UNDERWORLD,
LOVE AND CRIME AND MELODY.'
— *Pete Doherty*

In London, with his new best friend by his side, Pete intended to embrace a life that was as exciting and chaotic as he could make it. The close bond he had developed with Carl gave him the perfect platform from which to pursue this aim, and he set about it with gusto. In wholehearted pursuit of his Arcadian dream, Pete would defy all conventional codes of conduct and morality. He and Carl, and everyone around them who jumped aboard the 'good ship *Albion*', set out to live the lives of libertines before The Libertines had even come to be. It was a philosophy of life that Pete was determined to pursue as far as he possibly could.

Pete and Carl's flat on Holloway Road was cheap to rent, as well as being near the heart of London and the Camden music scene, but it was also thoroughly squalid. It had no door and one of the dirty windows was broken. The pair had borrowed their single mattress from a student house just up the road, and it was full of lice. And, to top it all, they'd moved in with a bizarre stranger. 'We had nowhere to stay and we met this anorexic woman who said we could stay,' Carl remembered. The woman, who called herself Sasha, was in her late twenties and was very thin, apart from her large, artificial breasts. 'She had the body of a fourteen-year-old boy with these two huge plastic knockers,' Pete later recalled.

Rather than recoiling from Sasha in horror, as his parents would have done, Pete befriended her and included her in his musical plans. Sasha would come into the room he shared with Carl and watch them play, sometimes joining in to tap out a rhythm. Sitting squashed together on a lice-ridden bed with nothing but two guitars and a pile of clothes, Pete and Carl were already showing signs of the vocal interplay that would later be a defining element of The Libertines' style. They didn't yet have a band – no lead singer, no bassist, no drummer – just each other and some idea of what they stood for.

It was in their ramshackle flat that Pete and Carl bumped into their neighbour, 'Scarborough' Steve Bedlow, who staggered in loudly one night with two French girls on his arms. Pete and Carl had just come in from a night out and tried it on with the girls, who weren't interested and disappeared off home.

The following morning, Pete and Carl peered out of their dirty broken window and saw Steve hanging out his flared jeans on the washing line in the garden. They popped out with their guitars and were soon talking with him about music. Steve was a loud, charismatic Yorkshireman who liked his beer and parties. He had a few songs of his own, and Pete and Carl were sufficiently impressed to invite him to join them in forming a band. Steve wasn't so sure at first – he'd been in several bands before, and he was used to having a bit more equipment to play with than a couple of guitars and a bed to sit on – but he was swept up with Pete's enthusiasm and agreed. Pete and Carl appointed him lead singer.

With Sasha roped in to do some drumming for them, Carl, Pete and Steve had something resembling a rock group. They called themselves 'The Strand' and started recording demos, using whatever equipment they could lay their hands on. Steve would come around every morning at about eleven o'clock for a beer and they'd try to put songs together. Steve handed a tape to Adam Evans at Camden-based label Food Records, who'd signed Blur back in 1990, but Adam was unmoved by the poor recording, so they tried a more direct approach, barging their way into the building, guitars under their arms, and playing their songs live. The record company's bosses were startled but not impressed, the stunt earning them nothing but a rapid escort to the door.

By coincidence, living directly beneath the happy family of Pete, Carl and Sasha was *NME* photographer Roger Sargent, who had shot covers for Oasis when the Mancunian Britpop heroes had been in their prime. Sargent would later become close friends with Pete and Carl, and would take some defining images of The Libertines in his capacity as their official photographer, but back then he knew them simply as neighbours from hell, as he was constantly disturbed by the loud banging, shouting and singing coming from upstairs.

Sasha knew that Roger's flatmate was a music journalist and, desperate to please the young men who'd adopted her as mascot-cum-drummer, she knocked on the door to the photographer's flat one day and handed them a demo tape.

However, she didn't make the best impression on Roger or his flatmate, who was also in the music business, as they were used to seeing a string of men entering and leaving Sasha's building on a daily basis, sometimes even ringing their doorbell by mistake. 'Sasha was twenty-nine but she looked like she was nearly fifty,' Pete explained. 'She was very thin and into smack. Roger wasn't impressed with us. I think he threw the demo tape straight in the bin.'

The demos might not have been going down too well, but these were nevertheless exciting times for Pete. Things were starting to fall into place. For a start, he'd never heard anyone else perform the songs he had written. Composing poetry and lyrics had always been a very solitary process for him, but now he could share his creativity with Carl and Steve, and he was thrilled by the results. 'Seeing someone play a song I'd written just blew me away,' he later recalled. 'It was the first time I'd got to do that, and in a way I could tell then that it was something I'd always wanted, almost without realising it.'

Immersed in their self-created world, Pete and Carl invented their own language of idiosyncratic slang, based around their alter-ego pet names for each other (Pete was Pigman while Carl was Carlos or Biggles). Their private tongue was full of references to literature, film and classic TV programmes, and it was so unusual and archaic that Steve was often mystified by the surreal dialogue between the two. The pair's shared eccentricities would later come across perfectly in interviews and would form an integral part of The Libertines' image. During one typical interview in 2003, Pete described this exciting, uncertain period: 'Money didn't really figure that much, as long as we had enough for a packet of bennies, a couple of drinkies and to take a bird to the pictures.' The terms 'bennies and drinkies' for cigarettes and alcohol sounded more like something 1950s comedian Tony Hancock would use after being force-fed a diet of classic English literature than the street slang of twenty-first-century London.

Pete and Carl soon came to realise that their nascent band needed a proper name that reflected their ideas and philosophy. Pete suggested The Albion, reflecting his vision of Englishness, but soon realised that the name meant very little to people who were strangers to his philosophy. Rather than communicating what the band were about, Pete realised that it was 'a shit name for a group'.

Eventually, Pete found inspiration in the works of the Marquis de Sade. Ever since he'd read *The Lusts of the Libertines* a couple of years earlier, Pete had been fascinated with the concept of book's eponymous subject, an individual unimpeded by moral constraints. Carl and Steve agreed that the name 'The Libertines' summed them up perfectly as a band searching for freedom and truth, with a lifestyle to reflect it. Even though the name had its origin in the taboo literary works of an eighteenth-century Frenchman, its obvious connection with liberty meant that everyone would grasp at least some of its significance. Indeed, such was the name's power that Pete and Carl would later bicker endlessly about who had come up with it.

Pete soon realised that the band's line-up wasn't good enough as it stood. They needed a bassist, for one thing, while having Sasha in the group was proving to be the source of all kinds of problems, as she was smitten with Carl. The situation soon took a turn for the worse when he woke up one morning to find her straddling him. 'We didn't do very much, and when Carlos Barât finally got his kit off, the contents of his trousers didn't seem worth the unzipping,' said Sasha, remembering the unsatisfactory experience. Pete found the sexual surprise hilarious, but Carl was less amused. Her flakiness, too, soon rankled with him. 'I used to wake up with her at the end of my bed in tears with all her hair ruffled up and hollow cheeks,' he recalled.

The atmosphere in the flat became increasingly tense, with Pete constantly ribbing Carl about his new 'girlfriend', repeatedly pointing out that Sasha was in love with him. Subjected to his endless jibes, she grew to hate Pete, and her behaviour became increasingly unstable. And he started to suspect that she actually wanted to kill him.

One day, Pete's fears were confirmed when Sasha became convinced that Pete had stolen money from her, grabbed a pair of scissors from the flat and marched down to the Prince Charles cinema in Soho, where he'd landed another part-time job. Pete took one look at her and ran away screaming. Sasha gave chase, cornered him and lunged at him with the scissors, almost stabbing him in the stomach. 'I ran after Pete,' admitted Sasha. 'One: I wanted to talk to him about a banking mix-up. Two: I wanted to know why he was shrieking like a banshee. Three: it's instinct to chase something that runs away.' Luckily, Pete held her off. They both called the police and two squad cars turned up, sirens blaring.

After that episode, Pete decided to get out of the flat as quickly as possible. After all, what was to stop Sasha sneaking in at night through the empty doorway and stabbing him in his sleep? Carl, too, felt that he wasn't safe from her. 'One morning she burst through the door and emptied a tin of cat food on my head,' he remembered. 'She didn't even have a cat.'

As they were moving out, Sasha uttered a final desperate cry for attention. 'She left a note on the door saying, "Goodbye, cruel world," and I found her trying to gas herself in an electric oven,' Carl remembered. He and Pete hastened their exit and never returned.

The duo soon found themselves a new flat a safe distance up the road in Camden where they were joined by Steve, whose time in Delaney Mansions was also up after his disgruntled landlord had taken exception to him squandering his housing-benefit money on beer rather than rent. The new arrangements, with all three members of the band living under the same roof, gave extra impetus to The Libertines project. The band found themselves a new drummer, a man called Zack, and set about writing songs. The process was somewhat hit and miss, but perseverance paid off. Carl remembered, 'I played Pete my batch of half-baked potatoes, and he played me his. A few of them gelled together and made a few of our earliest songs.'

Pete and Carl found that they were more creative as a partnership than they had been solo; their ideas and influences bounced off each other, evolving into something new and different. Eventually, they got together enough material to perform a gig. In true Libertines style, the venue was to be their new basement flat. They invited anybody and everybody they could find in Camden – friends, friends of friends, willing strangers – and kitted out the basement with a drum kit and amplifiers, lit a few candles to add a touch of bohemia and made sure that there were plenty of crates of beer around. Pete was especially keyed up at the prospect of playing his first ever live gig with a band.

On the night of the gig, the turnout was good, although it was never going to be a challenge to fill the cramped basement. The quartet started off by playing mellow, laid-back tunes – still raw, but without the loud, brash sound for which the band would later become famous. This handful of early songs included versions of 'Pay the Lady', 'Breck Road Lover' and 'Dilly Boy'. Pete and Carl delivered an electric performance on the makeshift stage, and the crowd went wild. Unfortunately, so did the people in the flat above, but for different reasons.

Suddenly, the lights cut out. Everything went silent. After a quick check, it was discovered that there was no money left in the electricity meter – an embarrassing technical hitch, but not an insurmountable obstacle. After a quick whip-round, an Austrian girl provided the 50p they needed, and on went the show. Pete didn't show her much gratitude for saving the gig – later on that night he thought it would be funny to dress up as Hitler and corner her in the bathroom. Carl remembered, 'She came out in tears and slapped him round the face.'

The gig, however, was a great success and, as the guests left, Pete and Carl were still buzzing with excitement, recognising that night as the beginning of something big. Carl was just as dedicated as Pete to pursuing the Arcadian dream, later remembering, 'It was like we were on board the ship and just throwing the ropes, and it cast off.'

Pete believed utterly in his band and what they stood for. With his crew on board the *Albion*, he felt that he had the force behind him to realise his aim of reaching out to the world. 'Walls need to be knocked down,' he observed. 'You can't blow them down. And you do that as a group – a group believing in the same thing.' From that night on, Pete, Carl and the rest of the band were hooked on the atmosphere of intimate, passionate gigs.

Just as Pete was determined to invite the audience into The Libertines' world, and even their home, the band were wide open to new members, and a bewildering array of musicians came and went during this period. Later, Pete would remember, 'Every man and his dog from Poplar has been in the Libertines. We've had a few members come and go. It's been a pretty sordid affair, really.'

When Zack left to join a band called Cactus Camel, he was replaced by a bass player called Justin, who was from Essex and had a Mod haircut. Justin quickly developed a reputation for telling tall stories, once telling them he'd written a song and then proceeding to sing Arthur Lee's 'Signed DC'. He didn't last long. Then a bassist called Gary played with the band briefly before leaving, claiming that he was off to Afghanistan to join the Taliban in their fight against British and American troops. 'We only had about three practice sessions with him,' Pete remembered. 'He seemed like a really nice guy as well.'

With members arriving and dropping out with alarming rapidity, Pete and Carl were desperate to find someone else who would complete the core of the band. Luckily, Steve had plenty of musician friends and told them that he knew someone who might fill the gap – a young bassist named John Hassall. Pete and Carl had their reservations about John because he came from a wealthy family and had been to public school, a background that didn't really fit with the anti-establishment, rebellious image they wanted to foster. Their opinion of him brightened, however, when Steve told them that he had a lot of music equipment stored at his mother's house – including amplifiers and a beautiful Rickenbacker bass – along with a basement that would be ideal for rehearsals.

Steve took Pete and Carl along to meet John at Camden's Dublin Castle pub, which was a perfect place for Pete and his Libertines to hang out. A Mecca for Madness fans and a key venue for countless up-and-coming bands, the Dublin Castle had a grand musical heritage. The bar itself was traditional and unpretentious, with terracotta wallpaper, benches upholstered in faded coverings and small red lamps dotted around beneath plastic plants.

When they met John, the place was crowded, as usual. John was sitting with his friend, future Razorlight singer Johnny Borrell, and wearing a train driver's hat. The first thing Pete and Carl both thought was: He's too good-looking. Indeed, at a couple of years younger than Pete, John had the chiselled features of a male model or a member of a boy band.

Pete and Carl were concerned by the fact that John had been to public school, but they were willing to reserve judgement until they'd heard him play. In contrast to Pete and Carl's slumming-it, street-urchin appeal, John did nothing to hide his classic good looks and inherited wealth, which seemed to fly in the face of everything the band were about. In an effort to find some common ground, they had a chat about musical influences, and John admitted that he was obsessed with The Beatles, confessing that he'd bought every one of their albums, in chronological order. It turned out that

John wasn't so impressed with what Pete, Carl and Steve were trying to achieve; to him, it all sounded a bit over the top, but he told them they could come round to his place for a jam, if they liked.

After their first meeting, Pete and Carl weren't sure about John, but Steve insisted that he was a great player, so Pete persevered and turned up for further discussions. 'Pete turned up on my doorstep with a book of poetry under his arm, stroking my cat,' John recalled. The following day, Pete showed up again, this time with Carl, and the three of them held a jam session.

John, it turned out, was terrific. Despite his rather more staid musical background, he immediately picked up on Pete and Carl's style and had the ability to create basslines on the spot for songs he'd never heard before. He provided the tight rhythm that the unruly band needed, especially in the absence of a committed drummer, while having him in the band would provide them with a place to rehearse. There was a minor sticking point in that John wouldn't commit, claiming that he was in another band, but Pete could live with that. He knew that John could be useful, even if he only played with them part-time.

Although Pete was convinced that John's musical ability and professionalism could benefit the band, he was beginning to have serious doubts about Steve, who seemed increasingly to be out of control, frequently gatecrashing parties by climbing in windows. He'd moved into a squat above a disused pub in the Angel called The Empress of Russia with what Pete described as 'assorted psychedelic types'. Steve was every inch the libertine, but he took the lifestyle so far that it began to affect his performance. Every time they had a gig at a bar, for instance, he would get drunk before the first set. At one bar, during a gig where the whole band played while sitting on barstools, Steve fell off his, drunk, halfway through the set.

As Carl remembered, 'One funny thing that kept happening was that we'd be at a venue and people would be like, "When are you on?" And we'd reply, "About five minutes." And they'd say, "Oh. Well, isn't that your singer?" Then we'd look down and find Steve lying on the floor, dribbling, and we'd have to kick him to get him up. Then he'd get really angry on stage and kick the shit out of all our equipment and start fighting with the bouncers.'

The problems with Steve surfaced again when the band played at The Empress of Russia. Pete enjoyed the idea of playing in what he described as 'splendid rotten rooms of the derelict mammoth building', and to him the pub was the perfect venue. With a growing following of friends and groupies, the gig was set to be a success. John's friend, Johnny Borrell, made a spectacular appearance. Pete noticed him as soon as he walked in, spotting 'a tangle-haired young Greek, one day to become Johnny from Razorlight, appearing in a pair of night-vision goggles and feather boa and bowler hat'.

Unfortunately, with wayward Steve in tow, the band just didn't gel. It was one thing to be a libertine, but it was quite another to be so drunk that you couldn't perform. Carl began to see Steve as a liability and tried to convince Pete that they should drop him from the band, not least because he attracted the wrong sort of crowd. As Pete later explained, 'When we were called The Libertines with Scarborough Steve singing, we got banned everywhere because we attracted a little band of fucked-up kids everywhere we went who knew they could sell gear at our gigs.'

Pete was less critical than Carl of Steve's lifestyle and personality, but he also began to wonder if the vocalist was really contributing. Pete wrote most of the songs and felt that he could sing them better than Steve could, while Steve was increasingly distancing himself from the group, often not involving himself in the band's operations.

The tension came to a head one time when Steve was away at the Glastonbury Festival and Pete, Carl and John decided to go to Odessa Studios in Hackney to record a demo without him. Their previous efforts at making demo tapes had been appallingly poor, but Odessa had the equipment with which they hoped to produce something of far higher quality. Unfortunately, they were still suffering from the perennial problem of having no drummer, but a seasoned professional by the name of Gwyn Mathias behind the mixing desk had the answer. He made a few phone calls and before long they were joined by 'Mr Razzcocks', a Cockney drummer in his mid-fifties who always wore a baseball cap. The new foursome recorded The Libertines' first demo, 'Pay the Lady', without Steve. When he found out about the demo, Steve took the hint and disappeared for a while.

The band's situation now appeared to be much simpler. Mr Razzcocks (real name: Paul Duffour) might have been a little on the mature side, and with questionable fashion sense, but he was a great drummer and he wanted to play with The Libertines again. John, too, was increasingly keen. And then came perhaps the oddest addition of all: a well-to-do young cellist named Vicky from Notting Hill. Together, the five of them would play anywhere that would have them.

Sometimes gigs ended up costing them money, but it was all about trying to get noticed, whatever it took.

Pete's eagerness to reach out to an audience knew no bounds. When Mr Razzcocks said that he had a contact in an old people's home and might be able to arrange a gig there, Pete jumped at the chance. Playing covers of old classics to pensioners wasn't his ideal scene, of course, but he ended up enjoying every minute. 'We did all the old musical numbers,' he later recalled, 'and it was really amazing. They loved it.' However, he also remembered that the excitement proved a little too much for some of them: 'A woman died during the show. These were old, old people, and we played a few of our own songs, and that's when she copped it. And some woman kept shouting out, "I saw you at the Palladium in 1949. You haven't aged at all."'

For Pete, gigs in old people's homes were all part of the dream, and he revelled in them, transforming his experience of such events into a kind of romantic poetic odyssey. Carl and John's idea of success, however, was fame and stadium gigs. Carl's frustration at not hitting the big time was a source of strain on his relationship with Pete. While for Pete there was a certain attraction to the idea of being an undiscovered, frustrated artist inhabiting the fringes of society, Carl had more straightforward ambitions: he wanted to be a star. Their friendship, always passionate and unpredictable, gave way to petty rows. Pete had an uncanny ability to wind up Carl by picking on Carl's obsession with hygiene and manners, exploiting this foible to full effect.

'We had some real fights,' Carl later admitted. 'When we lived in a squat in Camden Road once, Pete was winding me up because we were frustrated, angry and bored with running down to record labels and saying, "Honestly, we're gonna make you so much money; please listen to this," and getting snubbed by their A&R men. Around that time, we just had this massive fight. He was acting like an arsehole – although he probably thought I was being one, too – and he was drinking some water from a bottle, because he knows I've always hated slobbishness, as it seems so barbaric and unnecessary. Anyway, after he wound me up, I was so angry at him that I just booted this bottle right out of his face.'

However, such was the creative spark between Pete and Carl that even the deterioration in their relationship proved to be an artistic inspiration. Indeed, as Pete acknowledged, the friction prompted them to write the song 'Death on the Stairs'. This trend would later be repeated, the poignantly autobiographical 'Can't Stand Me Now' and 'What Became of the Likely Lads?' charting the breakdown of Pete and Carl's friendship during the making of The Libertines' second album. Even when they were barely speaking to each other, Pete and Carl usually managed to have a successful working relationship. 'We had some kind of inner storm in common that drove us together,' Carl remembered, 'even though a lot of the time we didn't actually want to be together.'

Pete, as always, remained utterly positive about the dream he was pursuing. 'Despite everything, you knew there was goodness there,' he noted. 'Something to believe in. Something that was good, pure and untainted by anything.'

The Libertines finally got their first proper gig as a full band – cellist and all – at The Hope & Anchor on Upper Street, Islington, on 11 September 1999. Dressed in suits and sporting cropped haircuts, they looked like The Beatles and

sounded like a 1950s skiffle band. It was clear that they still
had a long way to go, but such an unconventional line-up
couldn't fail to attract some attention. As it happened,
Johnny Borrell had turned up that night with *NME* writer
and future Razorlight manager Roger Morton, who liked
what he heard and took to following The Libertines closely.
Indeed, he reviewed another of their gigs – at The Bull &
Gate in Kentish Town on September 18 – in the *NME*, where
he described them as 'fresh, wry, flowery and savage', hailing
them as 'the most alluring thing since opium lollipops'.
Morton got in touch with Pete and Carl and told them that
that he was interested in managing the band.

For Pete, that was it. He'd made it. Ever since leaving home
and dropping out of university, his parents had told him that
he was wasting his time. He felt that his father, particularly,
had done nothing but look down on him as a dropout, a
failure neglecting his potential. He didn't see his parents very
often, but the few encounters they'd had over recent years
hadn't gone too well. His father poured scorn over his new
life in London, dismissing his down-at-heel urban digs and
everything that went with them. 'I remember Dad dropped
Mum off once at one of my digs,' Pete remembered. 'He
stuck his head around the door and said, "It's a shithole, isn't
it?" That was all he said. Then he went.'

Despite his rebelliousness, deep down Pete wanted his
father to be proud of him, and now he felt he deserved some
support. He was, after all, in a proper band. It might not have
meant much to his parents, but, to Pete, being mentioned in
the *NME* meant that he'd come of age. And, as if that wasn't
enough, Roger Morton was their manager. Unfortunately,
Peter Doherty, Sr, had little interest in his son's

accomplishments in such an area. Pete felt like he'd been written off, and nothing he later did changed that.

Just as his band appeared to be taking off, Pete enjoyed further successes with his poetry, becoming involved with regular Sunday-afternoon poetry sessions alongside the surreal spectacle of someone with the moniker 'Worm Lady' at the Foundry, a bohemian hangout on Old Street. Pete couldn't compete with Worm Lady on the grounds of weirdness; the gravelly rhymes of her works such as 'Fish Fucker' and 'Tooth Fucker' echoed around the venue and were lapped up by an attentive audience. Nevertheless, Pete was growing in confidence as a performer and even started putting on his own 'Arcadian Cabaret Nights' at the Foundry and at Finnegans Wake, Islington. Indeed, he spent many a night in north London, performing poetry and preaching his idea of the Arcadian dream, telling the story of a ship called the *Albion* that would sail to a mythical English paradise. 'The purpose of life,' he would proclaim, 'is to be happy and reach Arcadia.'

Occasionally, the music and the poetry would merge into one and Carl, John, Mr Razzcocks and sometimes even Steve would perform in gigs at the Foundry, sporting their then-trademark suits and Mod haircuts. While Carl and John were looking for bigger venues, Pete persuaded them to play regular acoustic gigs at Filthy McNasty's, where Pete was well known and always welcome.

For Pete, this was the perfect combination: the life of a libertine and the opportunity to create and perform. He wanted fame, but he wasn't desperate to be recognised by anyone walking down the street. His idea of success was limited to the world that he believed understood and appreciated him, the world of poets and songwriters. He believed he'd found his rightful place in inner-city bohemia, that he was exploring a Dickensian underworld of rogues and romance, music and poetry. As he later enthused, 'All that was fantasy in ink became true: the search for Arcadia and the underworld, love and crime and melody.'

Pete and Carl might not have always seen eye to eye, but through the shared prospect of achieving fame and recognition with their new manager, their relationship improved. When times were good, Pete saw Carl as an ideal companion on his journey to Arcadia. 'We'd run around town together, in our own little dream, with our own view of the world,' he remembered. 'We'd be in football stadiums in the dark, creeping about, jumping over fences down by the river, just having adventures. Initially, the plan with the band was to get on stage, enjoy ourselves and be enjoyed, while the songwriting was just a dream we had.'

The songwriting might have been a dream, but, like many of Pete's dreams, it would become a reality. With recognition from the *NME* and fame on the Filthy McNasty's stage, Pete embarked on a period of intense creativity, piecing together versions of what would become some of the classics of The Libertines' first album, *Up the Bracket*. The ease with which lyrics and music were flowing left Pete feeling like he was capable of achieving anything. 'We were following melodies down the street,' he observed. 'We thought we had the songs that were going to save the world and get the girl and cut the ribbon.'

Carl was equally amazed by Pete's creative surge. 'It was just natural, the way it happened. We were blessed, and lucky.'

Pete and Carl developed a complicated songwriting relationship, their seemingly contradictory character traits uniting over a common love for music. In some ways, the pair resembled Lennon and McCartney, each taking complementary roles, with Pete exhibiting McCartney's dauntless optimism and Barât displaying Lennon's weary pessimism. However, as Pete explained, their roles were rather more fluid than that. 'Take "I Get Along", which I wrote with Carl,' he said. 'He came up with the phrase "I get along, I get along…", and that's quite poppy and optimistic. Then I wrote the verses and the "Fuck 'em" bit. I was saying, "I was really fucked up. You saw me there. I don't know what to do." And then Carl goes, "I get along…" – but it works the other way as well. I suppose the joy of it, for the songwriter and the listener, is the unpredictability of it. There isn't really a formula.'

However, even when Pete and Carl were firing on all cylinders, writing songs often proved to be a source of tension in itself. They would collaborate so closely that they would often forget who had written which line of a song, which would result in fierce arguments. Pete was extremely proud of his talent with words, and his desire to be in control of the process irritated Carl, who sometimes felt that Pete was pushing so hard that their collaboration was suffering. Pete admitted, 'Sometimes it would happen, and then sometimes we'd sit down with guitars and something would be missing. I'd say, "Come on, let's get on writing a tune," and Carl would say, "Don't say that. Don't force it. How can you say that? It's got to happen naturally." It normally started a row.'

For Pete, of course, rows were an inevitable part of the

process. It was as if his creativity thrived off chaos of all kinds. If his songwriting partnership with Carl was turbulent, then his life was a storm. He was committed to an 'anything goes' attitude that would lead to a whole host of bizarre experiences. As an example of this behaviour, he would later describe some time he spent in a disused factory on Albion Road in Stoke Newington, taking acid and all manner of drugs with a character who called himself 'Delvin the Wizard'. The factory was in fact a good place to rehearse for free, and Delvin allowed the band to perform there. 'We used to put on all these gigs there,' Pete recalled. It was like the psychedelic underground.' It was there that Pete also encountered 'Sandra the Wood Nymph'. 'She used to play with us quite a bit,' said Pete. 'She was a French dancer who used to crawl out of a plastic egg with fire around her.'

Pete's libertarian lifestyle encompassed all things colourful and chaotic, and he had reached a point where almost nothing was forbidden and he would try anything at least once. This no-holds-barred attitude applied to his sexual encounters along with his other lifestyle experiments. Although for most of his life Pete had been pursuing girls for one-to-one relationships, however fleeting, he was now branching out into group sex and homosexuality. Sometimes he would persuade women into threesomes and even full orgies, having sex with men and women in the same night. The women would include steady girlfriends such as Katie Lewis – nicknamed 'Bapples' because of her large breasts – who remembered that Pete was into 'all kinds of kinky stuff. He got me into threesomes with him and Carl when we were completely off our faces on drugs. He was having sex with men and women. It broke my heart the day I walked in on

Pete in the shower, delicately soaping a naked man. It was all part of him being just wild. Pete has got a lot of love to give, but I'd warn any girl who goes out with him – like Kate Moss – that the love might not all be in her direction.'

As one woman who slept with both Pete and Carl during this period observed, 'They weren't what you'd think of as a gay couple, and they both preferred women, but they were up for anything – orgies, the lot. Women and men wanted to have sex with Pete, and he was out to have a good time. He was up for anything with anybody he fancied.'

Indeed, Pete was so liberal in his approach to sex that he even decided to become a male prostitute to make some extra money. To this end, he and Carl signed up with an agency as a male escort, which involved him dressing up in kinky costumes and provided the opportunity of having sex with men in hotel rooms in return for money. Carl remembered, 'We thought it was about taking women out to the theatre or escorting them to dinner, but it was about shagging old men in hotel rooms.'

Pete found he couldn't stick the job for long. 'It only lasted for about five minutes,' he admitted. 'I got all dolled up, but I couldn't deal with it. I used to push the drinks trolley over and make a run for it.' However, he continued his rent-boy enterprise by touting for business in gay pubs such as the Quebec at Marble Arch and the King's Head in Chelsea, where he would hang around the bar until he met a client, most of whom would be older gay men who often took him back to their homes. Pete told them that he was offering a masturbation service only, and although he was cautious he nevertheless sometimes ended up in difficult situations.

On one occasion, Pete ended up in Chelsea in the house

of an elderly gay man who asked him to perform favours he'd made clear weren't on the menu. He locked the man in his bedroom and ran for it.

Pete would charge £20 for each handjob, which was a sizeable sum for him at the time, representing almost half his weekly income from state benefits. At the time, he felt that he was providing a useful service and didn't think that working as a male prostitute was dishonourable. 'There was no shame, because I kind of knew that they were just lonely pissed-up old queens,' he protested later. 'And twenty quid was a lot of money!'

Pete's bisexuality was nothing new in rock-music circles. Flirtation with sexuality and gender roles was so commonplace in the music business that one of Pete's predecessors as a self-destructive genius of British music, Richey Edwards of The Manic Street Preachers, once declared, 'All rock 'n' roll is homosexual.'

With Pete, however, there was a difference. While figures like Bowie exaggerated and even fabricated their gay affairs in order to shock, Pete genuinely *did* experience homosexuality, throwing himself into areas that others merely pretended to have visited. Afterwards, he neither tried to turn them into public-relations stunts nor attempted to deny them.

The shared homosexual adventures were an important and oft-overlooked aspect of Pete and Carl's relationship. The fact that they had these experiences while existing in this bohemian world of squats, prostitutes and pub gigs meant that the way in which they related to each other was changed permanently, affecting their interaction even much later, after they had become famous. As a result of their sexual secrets, they became closer, their relationship taking on an intensity that was reflected in the way each seemed able to predict what the other was going to say, in their conversations together in their own private language, and in the way their dialogue took on the quality of spontaneous free association. However, it was also reflected when things weren't going so well. Indeed, the rows Pete and Carl engaged in were furious and highly emotional, rank with jealousy of each other and each other's friends, Pete becoming resentful of Carl's friends in the Primrose Hill set and Carl obsessed by Pete's affinity with his other close friend, Peter Wolfe (who would later become known as 'Wolfman'). And both, of course, were jealous of each other's successes.

Pete's sexual experiments were in direct opposition to the attitudes he'd grown up with as a child. His father, Peter Sr, had held a very negative attitude to homosexuality, and the possibility of Pete turning out to be gay had been one of his greatest fears, and of course finding the eight-year-old Pete using his mother's make-up once did little to alleviate this. When Pete later admitted to working as a rent boy, one imagines that Peter Sr must have been beside himself with disgust.

As an adult, Pete seemed to take delight in becoming everything his father appeared to despise and was determined to rid himself of the shackles imposed by society that made sex with a woman permissible for him but sex with a man forbidden. His ideas in this area were heavily influenced by the Marquis de Sade, whose works include passages about anal sex, among many other acts. Elsewhere in his writings, de Sade expresses an open-minded attitude to homosexual encounters, on one occasion insisting on being sodomised by his manservant, for example.

Just as he followed de Sade's views on homosexuality, Pete also experimented with sado-masochistic sex. This isn't to say that he was involved in anything as extreme as the tortures outlined in de Sade's prose, but he did take things to the edge. On one occasion, Katie Bapples was shocked to find that Pete had sliced her chest open with a razor blade, while another of his girlfriends, Tabitha Denholm, reported that she had enjoyed 'torture sessions' with him.

Pete was living the life of one of his rake heroes, exploring his sexuality and imagination in as many directions as possible, and it was the innocence with which he approached this deliberately dissolute life that was perhaps its shocking aspect. Far from appearing worldly and knowing, he retained the dreamy eyes of the poet and the ability to talk as if he were quoting verse. 'I believe that at the core of everything I do there is an innocence,' he explained. 'I don't care how soppy that sounds. There is a belief in dancing and unity through music, and fuck everything else. Everything else just upsets my nan.'

Pete would practice the art of seduction with a gentle, charming manner that betrayed little of a commitment to vice. The enterprise was, he said, under the control of Pitzia, the goddess of Arcadia. Later, he would come to see this period before he and Carl were famous, when the pair were at large on the streets of London, as perhaps the nearest he had ever come to achieving his dream. 'The girls, the drugs and the drink – that's all that we were doing before we got signed,' he noted. 'This is all something above and beyond mere pleasure-seeking principles... The Arcadian Dream. That's where I'm heading: Arcadia. Don't spare the horses.'

CHAPTER 5

The Libertine

LIB·ER·TINE (LBR-TN) N 1. ONE WHO ACTS WITHOUT MORAL
RESTRAINT; A DISSOLUTE PERSON. 2. ONE WHO DEFIES
ESTABLISHED RELIGIOUS PRECEPTS; A FREE THINKER.
ADJ MORALLY UNRESTRAINED; DISSOLUTE.

By the time he'd turned twenty-one, Pete could claim that he'd come of age as a libertine. He'd already experimented with almost all manners of hedonistic behaviour, tasted most drugs and most varieties of sex, and managed to avoid any full-time work or study. He was certainly living a rock 'n' roll lifestyle; all it lacked was the rock 'n' roll. So far, The Libertines had little more to them than an inspiring name and a few well-written songs. The group was among dozens of other small-time players in the bubble of activity surrounding Filthy McNasty's, the Dublin Castle and other bohemian venues, such as the Foundry. Beyond Pete and Carl, the band didn't even have an established line-up of artists and existed on borrowed labour and instruments. Part-time manager Roger Morton had got them only one gig in an entire year – at the retro Blow-Up at the Metro Club on

Oxford Street – and his laid back style had led Pete to wonder if he'd abandoned them.

Change, however, was just around the corner in the diminutive shape of music lawyer Banny Poostchi, who had heard about Pete and Carl through her friend, Alex Clarke, at Filthy McNasty's. Pete and Carl, now apparently managerless, met her at Filthy McNasty's in May 2000. Neither was confident that this would be the breakthrough they had been looking for, but at least they were in the right place for a drinking session.

Pete's first reaction to meeting Banny was one of surprise. She wasn't what he had expected, and he didn't quite know what to make of her. 'She was wearing a fur coat and she talked like a BBC newsreader – very bright, very confident,' he later admitted, adding that he was immediately impressed with Banny's razor-sharp intelligence and shrewd business sense. An Oxford University graduate in her early thirties, Banny had been a lawyer for Oasis and was working for Warner–Chappell Music Publishing and the Mirror Group. With these weighty credentials in music and the media, Pete and Carl had to take her seriously, although Pete felt that such a focused, determined character couldn't be part of their world. Her musical tastes were different and she shunned the hedonism in which they engaged, never touched drugs or drank to excess.

Despite the obvious differences, however, the three of them struck up a friendship. She enjoyed Pete and Carl's high-spirited lust for life, while they saw in her a drive to succeed that could carry them anywhere. As Pete put it, 'She was a lady of vast ambition, like Margaret Thatcher.'

After further meetings, Pete and Carl became convinced

that her favourite in their circle was Steve. The northerner was very much on the fringes of the band, but Pete believed that Banny liked Steve's looks and wanted him as the frontman. As soon as she agreed to take on the band, tension developed between her and Pete, who hated being controlled and being told that Banny knew best. One early row erupted over a photo shoot that Banny had secured through her media connections and at which Pete had rubbished the photographer, accusing him of being half-blind (although the pictures he took actually turned out to be pretty good).

The contest between the unruly, often out-of-his-mind, 6ft 2in Pete and the tiny, soft-spoken Banny seemed from a distance an unequal one. In fact, the new manager was capable of imposing her will ferociously and would fix Pete with a steely stare through her glasses and order him to smarten up his act. For a time, at least, Pete would kick against the will of his new manager, but he would buckle under after a fight. It was a tense situation that couldn't last forever.

Banny paid for the band to record a demo that consisted of one song, 'Love on the Dole', a light, jangly guitar-riff-laden take that was a long way from the harder, brasher sound the band would later develop. Pete had once again stamped his literary hallmark on the music, as the title came from a 1933 novel of the same name by Walter Greenwood that laid bare the working-class poverty in Northern England in the 1930s. Like George Orwell and many of his other literary heroes, Pete identified strongly with the working class, and this was demonstrated in the lyrics of the song, with Pete mockingly inviting the listener to 'drink a toast to the ruling classes'. He felt that he could use music to reach out to people of all walks of life and unify them. Later, he said that music was 'the last refuge of the working class, along with football'.

The demo might have been a success, but Banny's early efforts to mould The Libertines into shape were wrecked by the group's continuing instability. Carl was determined that the wayward Scarborough Steve should be excluded from the band while John was losing hope of the outfit ever making it to the big time. The final straw came for him when he found that Pete had once again booked the band for a Filthy McNasty's gig, on the same night that he'd already arranged one at indie venue the Monarch in Camden. The dispute left John fuming; he told Pete to forget his band and walked out, taking Mr Razzcocks with him.

At this stage of their career, none of The Libertines believed that they had a serious chance of achieving fame. They were so convinced they would always be on the fringes of the music scene that they would split at the slightest provocation. Pete, who had begun taking heroin earlier that year, was engrossed in his new hobby and had little respect for the project of making a commercial success out of his music. For the time being, he was happy just playing his songs and performing his poetry among the cliquey Filthy McNasty's crowd.

Carl was as frustrated as John was with what he saw as Pete's reactionary, uncompromising attitude. Frequently drunk and drugged in a cramped rented space in a building that was falling apart, Pete and Carl ended up having furious rows on a daily basis. By the end of the summer, the situation had become so bad that Carl had moved out to follow a fling with a female fan, taking up residence in the Camden home of his fellow would-be rock star Johnny Borrell.

Pete followed his example and moved to a cottage in Tottenham, which he shared with Steve. He got by through small-time drug deals, selling weed and speed around the music scene, although he would do almost anything to make enough money for drugs and alcohol, even posing as a minicab driver in a battered old estate car.

After going their separate ways from the Camden flat, Pete and Carl barely spoke to each other and gave up rehearsing altogether. They simply weren't ready to commit to a coherent enterprise, let alone one that would make money. By December 2000, Banny was faced with a band that had been whittled down to two frontmen who rarely spoke to each other, with no drummer and no bass player. She realised the situation was beyond her and jumped ship.

That false start could have spelled the end for The Libertines, leaving its members to tread the well-worn path into obscurity. Pete continued to perform, holding jamming sessions with Steve and anyone else who expressed an interest, but he remained largely separated from Carl for almost a year, while John floated in and out of the picture. At that time, he lived on the dole in Tottenham and Whitechapel and even spent some of the time homeless, crashing at friends' houses. However, despite the rift between him and Carl, he never gave up his faith in music, rehearsing with the previously exiled Steve on an almost daily basis.

For Carl, these were depressing times. With the band all but broken up, it was only the seemingly slim chance of getting things back on track that kept him going. 'I ended up without any money or a house,' he remembered. 'I didn't even have any drink, so I couldn't hit the bottle. I was really sofa-surfing, and sleeping rough as well, but I always had this thing with Pete, so I was never completely alone.'

John would later see the months the band spent apart as a period of development, a chance to grab some necessary breathing space. 'Pete and Carl were on their own for a period, and I think that was a good thing,' he noted. 'I may have physically left, but I didn't really leave at all. It was the right time to have a break.'

With Carl unwilling to rehearse and the band effectively put on hold, Pete returned to his first love: words. He threw himself back into poetry, regularly performing his work at arty venues like the Foundry and Finnegans Wake. He felt at home with poets and those who followed them, feeling that only they could recognise his talents. Success in such a circle wasn't about making money and being a star; it was about reaching his artistic potential. Eager to gain an audience, Pete became a regular contributor to underground poetry-based publications. He loved to have an intellectual audience, something that he felt was harder to come by in the music business. The modest recognition he achieved on the poetry circuit was well within his control and was a far cry from the uncontainable media frenzy that would later surround him.

That August 2000, a group of thirty-five Russian poets and artists came over for a week to the Foundry as part of what they called a 'cultural exchange', supported by the British Council in Moscow. To Pete's delight, a counterpart four-day trip for Foundry regulars to Moscow was scheduled for the end of September. The trip was open to anyone who responded with a title and description of a job they would do on the tour. Offers to contribute towards the cost of the trip also helped. Every pound contributed was matched by a pound from the British Council Paupers' Relief Fund. From this mixture of self-funding and government generosity, a group of fifty Foundry regulars embarked on what would be a wild and wonderful trip to Russia. Pete was one of them.

The city of Moscow was still an unusual place for an Englishman to visit, despite the final parting of the Iron Curtain more than a decade earlier. The prospect of visiting the Kremlin and walking around Red Square would have been intriguing for anyone when such activities had been the exclusive preserve of MI6 agents until relatively recently.

For Pete, the experience was more than thrilling; it was life-changing. The exchange trip took him to the DOM, a new bar, gallery and performance venue in central Moscow that ran programmes of poetry, art, theatre and music – and of course served plenty of vodka. His performance poetry was hugely successful with the Russian audience there, who were eager to soak up everything to do with the West. The experience had the flavour of going on tour with a band – a sensation he would later want to repeat again and again.

The trip was intellectualised excess and debauchery from the very start. On their first day, the group stormed Russia's Channel 1 TV station with plastic guns and clown masks, their antics beamed into the homes of a million Russians watching primetime breakfast TV. The next few days were pure chaos, involving Russian noise machines, a flea circus, a 'twelve-hour opera oubliette' and, perhaps most bizarrely, engaging in a spot of maggot-racing on an 18in-long track called the Larvadrome at the DOM. This championship attracted an eager and eccentric crowd of drunken poets placing a flurry of bets on the contenders of each heat: six three-day-old maggots, set side-by-side in stalls.

Organising such an event wasn't an easy job, as Foundry regular Stephen Haines explained: 'The spectators were getting too excited. They were crowding in, and it was getting very difficult to get the maggots in the stalls. Contrary to what people might think, maggots are very receptive. They pick up on such a feverish atmosphere, and it disturbs them. I think we lost at least three good racing maggots, apart from the one Kenny ate!'

Pete and his fellow poets were accused of foul play when the favourite, 'Mr Wiggler', went down early during the final stage of the championships. Excitable Russian maggot racers claimed the party from the Foundry had tampered with the fastest maggot by secretly feeding it bacon so it was too full to crawl quickly.

During his stay in Moscow, Pete and his companions ran riot on the streets of the city, consuming vast quantities of alcohol and partying hard every night. They embarked on what they called a 'mathematical' trail through the city, visiting the sights in an order based on the names of British nuclear warheads. Their final act was the sowing of poppy seeds in Red Square. To Pete, the whole affair was gloriously wacky.

With Pete in Russia was Tam Dean Burn, an actor who had appeared in the film of Irvine Welsh's *Acid House* and would later star in Scottish soap *River City*. Tam would often compere when Pete was giving readings at the Foundry and would later share the bill with Pete at the Burns an' a' That Festival at the Gaiety Theatre in Ayr in May 2005. He has fond memories of that Russia trip, remembering, 'I turned up without a clue where I was going, and the guy at the airport met me with a bottle of vodka. It all got a bit blurred after that. The trip has gone down in legend. Who says you can't mix poetry and a rock 'n' roll lifestyle?'

The Russia trip proved such an important success for Pete that he came to see it as a golden moment in his life, remaining forever nostalgic about the country. He developed an image of Russia as a promised land, building on his experiences in Moscow to imagine a place that would suit him even further, a city that shared his name: St Petersburg. Pete felt that Russia was the country that most resembled his dream land of Arcadia, and he was anxious to recreate the feeling back in England. His time there left him with a taste for performance, touring and vodka, and on his return to London he was more eager than ever to make a success of The Libertines. However, Carl remained a distant figure, caught up in his own world of parties, drugs and women.

Pete and Carl might not have been getting on at that point, but if restricted to music their relationship was at least sometimes bearable. Indeed, their common love for music eventually led to a crucial change in the summer of 2001, when Pete's then girlfriend, Francesca, introduced him to the music of New York rockers The Strokes, who were then taking the British music scene by storm. On the strength of just five songs, released over two singles, the US band were being hailed as the saviours of rock before their first album had even been released. (On its release that October 2001, *Is This It* received rave reviews.) Pete and Carl bought tickets and went up to Liverpool together to watch them play at Lomax's, at L2.

L2 was renowned for staging landmark gigs for up-and-coming bands just before they made it to the big time. At the club's previous smaller site, a young Liam Gallagher had left a message in the toilets for visiting Manchester United fans. The new venue was still cheap and cheerful but much larger, and that night it provided the scene for an effervescent atmosphere at The Strokes' concert. Fresh from an outstanding performance at the Reading Festival a few days earlier, the band put on a terrific show, and hearing them play changed everything for Pete and Carl. Confronted by a band with such a raw, frenetic style, clearly influenced by 1970s punk groups such as The Velvet Underground and Television, the estranged pair were inspired to resolve their differences and get back to the business of making music. It should have been *them* up there on stage, after all, living that life and performing their music.

At the same time, Banny was equally stirred by The Strokes. She was instantly reminded of the energy she had identified in the fledgling Libertines. Inspired by the emerging rock revival, Banny got back in touch with Pete and Carl, telling them that now was their time, that if they pulled themselves together she would get them signed. She had decided that the band were going to sign for a major record label and she had set her sights on Rough Trade, the label that had just launched The Strokes' career.

Founded by Geoff Travis in 1977, Rough Trade

specialised in European post-punk and alternative rock of the late 1970s and early 1980s, having in the past signed the likes of punk and post-punk groups The Fall, The Slits, The Virgin Prunes, Young Marble Giants, Essential Logic, Scritti Politti and Stiff Little Fingers, the more poppy Aztec Camera and even, most famously, Pete's heroes The Smiths. Branching out in the 1980s as far as the country music of Lucinda Williams, the label had retained its strength in alternative music. To Banny, Rough Trade was the perfect home for The Libertines, but Pete and Carl didn't truly believe they would get signed. At that stage, they were more worried about mustering enough cash for day-to-day costs.

'Before we got signed to Rough Trade, times were pretty desperate,' remembered Pete. 'We were both homeless and Carl owed the County Court £230. That doesn't seem like that much now, but back then it was like, "Where the fuck are we gonna get that from?" We signed a special agreement with Banny, who said, "I'll pay your £230 if you sign this contract." We didn't think about it; we just did it, because she said she was gonna get us signed to Rough Trade eventually.'

This time, Banny was armed with a very clear vision of what the band should be. She felt that their often gentle, whimsical acoustic style had to be taken by the scruff of the neck and given a much heavier, electric edge. Instead of experimenting with whatever form of music they felt like, she believed that The Libertines should have a distinctive sound, one which had more in common with the snarling punk of The Sex Pistols and the exuberant rock of Oasis. Indeed, Banny had been closely involved in the 1990s Britpop scene in her legal work for Oasis, and she wanted to recreate some of the energy of this rock revival. Banny was in pretty good step with the way the music world was moving when she related her intention for Pete and Carl to be the English Strokes (a comparison the two men would come to detest) and bought them a guitar and a bass.

Banny knew the band couldn't make it without a solid, permanent line-up, and one of her first acts in her new reign was to recruit Gary Powell as drummer in October 2001. Gary wasn't quite the odd one out that Mr Razzcocks had been, but he certainly injected a different flavour into the band. A quiet, serious character, he was born in New Jersey but his family had moved to Birmingham in the 1980s, leaving him with a bizarre half-American, half-Brummie accent. He had been introduced to drumming in the US, where he'd played in a marching band, a drum-and-bugle chorus and in the Pennsylvania Army Cadets' band. He ended up doing some session work down in London after joining an agency, playing with various bands, until Banny approached him in October 2001. His musical background, however, was soul and jazz, his style precise and professional – the perfect foil for the wilfully sloppy Pete and Carl.

Carl remained adamant that Scarborough Steve should not be part of The Libertines' line-up, and to Banny's dismay the vocalist eventually left the group, for what would be the final time, to pursue a modelling career with the Select agency in New York. He would later find the musical role he was looking for as lead singer in another band, The IVs. Despite his banishment, Pete's relationship with Steve remained close, and years later he would often be seen playing with Pete and his breakaway band, Babyshambles. For now, though, Pete and Carl needed to strengthen their line-up. John was still not interested in returning, but his friend Johnny Borrell agreed to help out on bass.

Pete had ambivalent feelings towards the manufacture of the new, commercially viable Libertines. It was a process that didn't come naturally to him, forcing him to strike compromises on the type of music he produced and the people with whom he worked, but he accepted the new situation out of desperation. While he had never shared Carl and John's lust for fame, he had grown hungry for recognition beyond the incestuous confines of the McNasty's scene and was uncharacteristically willing to knuckle down to the will of the manager. 'We were skint and angry,' he remembered of that time. 'There were American bands coming over here and cleaning up, and we were furious and desperate, really, but we had strong ideas and a lot of passion.'

Pete was ready for a fight and spent the rest of 2001 in a whirlwind of frenetic rehearsals. Together with Carl, he put together a new body of songs, some of which the now-absent Steve had worked on, such as 'Horror Show', 'Up the Bracket' and 'Time for Heroes'. The hardships and insecurities of a year on the dole, failing to get on and failing to make music together, gave their music a new edge, a hardness it had lacked before. It was, in fact, just what they'd needed. As John would later comment, '[Pete and Carl] were both basically homeless and had very little money, and that pent-up frustration went into the music. We were all angry young men, in a way.'

Banny was so determined to sign with Rough Trade that she brushed off an approach by James Mullord, from the small independent label High Society Records, taking him to one side in a pub and telling him frankly, 'They aren't signing to you.' The flat rejection jarred with Pete, who got on well with James and wasn't inclined to dismiss him just because his label wasn't big enough. For the time being, though, he decided to do whatever Banny wanted, vowing to follow the Gallagher brothers' advice and roll with it, just as Oasis had done in their early days.

After dozens of phone calls, Banny managed to persuade James Endeacott, a talent scout at Rough Trade, to put the band in a studio to demo some songs. Pete was elated by the news, but his enthusiasm was rapidly punctured when Carl told him that Borrell had left the group after only one rehearsal, opting instead to go on tour with Alabama 3 without bothering to mention he'd quit. His departure left The Libertines without a bassist on the eve of their biggest break to date. It was too late to find a replacement, so Pete and Carl decided that they'd take turns to do the job themselves.

Pete, Carl and Gary met Endeacott for the first time at rehearsal rooms in Old Street in October 2001. Pete later described the occasion: 'This funny-looking fella in a baseball cap with frizzy hair popped his head around the door and said, "Do you mind if I sit in?" We said, "Yeah, make yourself at home."'

The group played a showcase of four songs: 'Time for Heroes', 'Up the Bracket', 'Boys in the Band' and 'Horror Show'. Endeacott was impressed and asked them for an encore, but he didn't commit.

A few weeks later, Banny called the Rough Trade talent scout to invite him to a Libertines performance at the Rhythm Factory in Whitechapel on 17 November. Endeacott was already booked to see Irish folk singer

Cara Dillon at the Spitz Club that night, but he was curious to see more of The Libertines and decided to turn up at the gig after midnight. As he walked in, he was struck by the spectacle of Libertines fans in action. 'It was like walking into another world. The place was full of freaks and bohemians,' he observed. He realised that the band had already carved out a dedicated fan base like no other, who would follow The Libertines' every move – and buy their music.

Gary's own memories of that gig are somewhat different. A perfectionist by nature, he despaired when things started to go wrong. 'I didn't have a drum kit at that point in time, so we borrowed this horrible gold kit. All the toms were put together with bits of string, and there was a big metal clamp with cymbals hanging from ropes. It was the worst kit ever. As soon as I started playing, I broke one of the heads and couldn't play any more. Carl and Pete started breaking strings and didn't have any replacements. We did two or three songs and then I had to go into the audience to ask people if they had any guitar strings on them.'

Despite the setbacks the band had faced there, the Rhythm Factory gig convinced Endeacott that he had to sign them. Gary, for one, couldn't believe it when Endeacott invited the trio to do a demo at Nomis Studios in west London, before an audience of himself, Geoff Travis and Jeanette Lee. At Nomis, they hammered out four songs before Jeanette interrupted to say, 'We're going to sign you.'

'It was ecstasy,' Pete remembered of that moment. 'It was what we wanted. It was the happiest moment of my life, easily.'

Still carrying the guitars Banny had bought them, the

trio made their way across the Thames to the Players' bar on Charing Cross Road, where they proceeded to get totally, blissfully drunk.

Pete was full of excitement for days afterwards, telling everyone he'd ever met that he was about to make it big, and word spread across the London music scene that The Libertines were at last going to be signed. John Hassall, hearing that his old friends were heading for a record deal, called Carl and offered to rejoin the band, but Pete and Carl were still bitter about the way he had walked out on them with Mr Razzcocks the previous year and had played with them only sporadically since then. After a difficult decision, the making of which moved Pete to tears, they opted to accept John back, on one condition: that this time he would play for them until his fingers bled. And so the final Libertines quartet was born.

Friday, 21 December 2001 saw Pete, Carl, Gary and John heading off to accept the best yuletide gift any of them had ever received: a record deal with Rough Trade, scheduled to be signed on the afternoon of the last working day before the holidays (although, typically, The Libertines still managed to risk it all by turning up late). Striking this deal had been Pete's dream for so long that he couldn't believe the label was really going to go through with it, having convinced himself that it would pull out at the last minute, that the whole thing would suddenly fall through. All the band were in a in state of nervousness, so much so that they got off at the wrong Tube station and struggled to find their way to the label's offices on Golborne Road, west London. Endeacott waited for them for so long that he began to fear they wouldn't turn up, but the foursome eventually made it to the label's offices to find the contract awaiting their signatures. Next to it was a piece of cake and a bottle of champagne. Later on Pete celebrated further with a big fat line of high-grade cocaine.

Pete's drug habits had previously been limited to cheaper material. While scamming the dole and scraping a living, he had ingested plenty of dope of all kinds – speed, ecstasy and, more recently, heroin – but the kind of £60-a-gram rock-star fodder that he was now able to afford has previously been beyond his means. The signing represented the promise money that, of course, would ensure a plentiful supply of purer, better drugs. On the day of the signing Pete 'sparked up like a Christmas tree'.

With the cocaine surging through his system, Pete was jumping for joy, leaping around, hugging Banny and picking her up off the floor. It was a moment of supreme personal triumph. 'Just being in a position to record a song – that was pure fantasy,' he later remembered. 'Even having our own guitars seemed almost impossible.'

However, the day the contract was signed was marked by an event that Pete the poet instilled with symbolic meaning. Still intoxicated by drugs and the band's sudden rise to recognition, he experienced a surreal omen of evil. 'After the signing, everyone went to see British Sea Power, I think, at the Water Rats, but we lost each other. I ended up going back down to Filthy's with some people, but at around three in the morning Carl and I both happened to be at the same place – Percy Circus – at the same time. So, we'd both come from different directions and bumped into each other, and then we saw this tramp on a bench. We hadn't said anything to him, but he just came up to us and he went, "It's the worst thing that could happen to you." It really freaked me out.'

Carl, however, saw things differently. 'I was laughing about it,' he recalled.

Bad omen or not, these were high times. Within days, Pete and the rest of the band went shopping for guitars. They each received huge bundles of cash for Christmas and immediately spent £10,000 on instruments and other equipment. Pete wanted a space in which they could rehearse twenty-four hours a day, and, as he and Carl were effectively homeless, they demanded a flat of their own. All of their requests were granted: the band were fixed up with round-the-clock access to Ruse rehearsal rooms in Old Street and were given the keys to 112a Teesdale Street, Bethnal Green, the flat that would become known as the notorious Albion Rooms.

The sudden influx of money came as a shock to Pete, who had become used to scraping a living through claiming the dole, doing part-time jobs and selling drugs. Suddenly, instead of having to worry about the price of a pint of beer, he had enough cash to buy a round for everyone in the pub – and that was exactly the kind of extravagant gesture that he would make, often with thousands of pounds' worth of rolls of banknotes stuffed in his pockets. Shortly after the deal was signed, Pete and Carl emerged from a bagel shop in Brick Lane to be confronted with a homeless Geordie woman begging for some change. Carl pulled a brown envelope out of his pocket containing a wad of notes worth £1,500 and thrust it into her hands. Later that day, Pete gave another £800 to a man who asked him for money on the Charing Cross Road.

Pete and Carl felt like finally they'd made it through the

storm of the past couple of years, after having disappeared down a metaphorical manhole on the day they'd first moved in together on Holloway Road. 'We came out of the manhole the day we signed to Rough Trade,' said Pete, relieved at their good fortune – as was Carl, who felt like they had emerged from a 'nuclear winter'. However, despite his elation, Pete would later come to regard this exhilarating period with mixed feelings, believing the seeds of The Libertines' sorrows were sown when they signed to Rough Trade, describing it as 'the best and the worst day of my life'.

CHAPTER 6

The Tender Hooligan

'THE HAPPIEST EXPERIENCE WE HAVE EVER HAD IS BEING
TOGETHER AS THE BOYS IN THE BAND, REACHING THE
LISTENERS' HEARTS AND WAKING UP CUPID, TOO.'
– Pete Doherty

While the Libertines had finally signed a record deal –
and with Rough Trade, of all labels – they had yet
to play a gig in their current (and final) incarnation. They
took that step at west London's Cherry Jam on 21
February 2002. While Pete was nervous about whether the
new line-up would gel, at least the venue was of a familiar
type – a small, dark basement with low ceilings and a
capacity of only 150.

The show was much hyped, and tickets were sold out
well in advance. To Pete's annoyance, they were now being
touted as the 'British Strokes', and as a result there was a
great buzz of anticipation among music lovers and critics.
The *NME* was poised, ready to introduce thousands of
curious readers to this exciting new rock band.

Wearing leather jackets and with dishevelled hair, Pete
and Carl burst on to the stage with an energy inspired by

nerves combined with large quantities of cocaine. They thrashed out their songs with a force that bordered on the uncontrollable, playing twice as fast as the rhythm section. Pete and Carl swapped places at the microphone, falling into each other. Soon enough, things degenerated. Only two songs in, Pete and Carl began to push each other around and tear at each other's shirt.

The entire set hovered on the brink of violence and ruin, but the band played on regardless, churning out what would become the classic punk-influenced tracks for which they would become known – songs like 'Up the Bracket', 'I Get Along' and the future single 'What a Waster', many of which would end up on the first album. The gig laid down a precedent for future performances, mirroring on stage the intensity and fragility of Pete and Carl's relationship.

Despite the messy show, however, with Gary and John struggling valiantly to hold it together, the audience loved the spectacle. It would be the start of a long and fruitful relationship with the *NME*. The music paper's James Oldham gave the band a glowing review, opining that they had 'the lyrical dexterity of The Smiths, the taut energy of The Jam and the raw melodies of The Strokes'. Oldham had watched the gig with Pete and Carl's ex-neighbour, photographer Roger Sargent, who was blown away with their performance and captured some of the most vibrant images of his career. After the gig, Sargent harassed Rough Trade into making him the official band photographer. Now even the band's own photographer also worked for the *NME*.

Only two days later, The Libertines achieved the massive coup of playing with the band that had both inspired them and helped to create the conditions that led to them getting signed, supporting The Strokes at Leeds University and the Birmingham Academy. They'd hardly played together in their current form, were supporting one of the biggest bands of the year and were playing before far larger audiences than ever before, but they didn't disappoint. There was no sign of the fact that their career as a unit had only just begun. Gary was a force behind the drums, giving the band a new tightness and fluency.

Pete relished the experience, but he found the large, anonymous crowd less responsive than the smaller cliques he'd grown used to at intimate pub gigs and poetry performances. This was his first real taste of the big stage, and he wasn't sure he liked it. 'Playing to 4,000 people in Birmingham was the most astonishing thing,' he said at the time, 'but people didn't seem like they wanted to dance to songs they didn't know, which I can't ever understand, so I thought that maybe they didn't dig it. Ideally, I'd really want people to come away thinking, Wasn't that really good fun, just jumping up and down for half an hour? I want movement in the crowd. I think that, up until now, people that would want to dance have been put off because they've been looking around at the audience and seeing nothing but a load of industry scum.'

Again, the *NME* gave Pete's band a helping hand by arranging a short UK tour in March on which The Libertines would be supporting The Vines, another highly popular new US band, thus ensuring that they attracted even more media attention. This was the first time The Vines had played in the UK, and their tour was much anticipated, while it also provided the perfect opportunity for Pete and The Libertines to develop a solid fan base.

The first venue of the tour, the Free Butt in Brighton, was

packed with journalists. Unfortunately, Pete and Carl displayed what can only be described as a self-destructive streak, deciding to perform a twenty-minute 'jazz odyssey' to the puzzled crowd. Improvising might have worked in the more forgiving arenas of bohemian north London pubs, but in front of a massive, expectant crowd they risked making fools of themselves.

Pete realised, with some sense of alarm, that he was truly on his way to stardom. He loved the feeling of being on stage, playing to a crowd, but had a growing fear that fame was a beast that he would not be able to control once it was fully unleashed. He realised that he was reaching the point at which people would recognise him away from the stage, that the effects of his success would soon intrude into his everyday life. Pete knew the transition would be difficult for him, as he couldn't help but care what people thought about him, what they wrote and what they said. He remembered, 'I started getting paranoid, wondering if people were looking at me and recognising me everywhere I went.'

The band, meanwhile, were developing a cult following. On 23 May, having already performed earlier in the evening with British Sea Power at a crowded, eager Cherry Jam, the band bundled their equipment on to the tour bus and drove to their second venue of the night, the packed 333 Club, to perform an explosive show that many critics regarded as their best so far.

That spring, The Libertines were faced with a difficult choice: what would be their debut single? There were several possibilities; songs like 'Up the Bracket' and 'I Get Along' pushed all the right buttons, but Rough Trade was looking for something raw and in-your-face, a statement of intent.

In the end, the band chose 'What a Waster', a song that,

amazingly, had started out as a ballad but had been given a complete overhaul to fit with the band's new, harder style. The song's lyrics were deliberately provocative, all blasted out in Cockney accents against a raw, raucous, super-energetic soundtrack that echoed the classics of punk rock. Indeed, Pete took great delight in pouring forth a stream of taboo language, knowing full well that he was writing a song that could never be played on daytime radio, but he loved the song's directness, describing it as 'probably the most self-explanatory song in the history of pop'.

The single was released on 3 June 2002 to coincide with the Queen's Golden Jubilee and became an overnight hit, climbing into the Top Forty, despite being banned from the airwaves. The double A-side on Rough Trade, featuring the live favourites 'What a Waster' and 'I Get Along', was produced by former Suede guitarist Bernard Butler. Pete was impressed by Butler's credentials; an obsessive *NME* reader and a musical sponge who had soaked up music heritage since his first encounter with The Smiths, Pete knew everything there was to know about Suede. Carl, on the other hand, didn't even know that Bernard was Suede's former guitarist, much to Pete's amusement. 'That's what I like about Carl: he knows nothing about bands,' Pete observed fondly. 'He doesn't know Bernard Butler or even Suede. It was his little brother who told him about Suede.'

On the face of it, everything pointed towards a successful working relationship between Bernard and Pete, who had a lot of respect for Suede. Pioneers of Britpop and with a style incorporating elements of everything from glam rock to The Smiths, the band had drawn on many of the same musical influences as Pete had, with Bernard admiring Johnny Marr just as Pete admired Morrissey. On a personal level, however, there were immediate problems. Pete found Bernard a difficult man to get along with, as he had always shunned the libertarian rock 'n' roll lifestyle that Pete swore by and disapproved of hard drugs and what he saw as irresponsible, destructive behaviour. Before he quit Suede at the height of their fame in 1994, he had always been the quiet one, reluctant to indulge in the excesses enjoyed by his three bandmates.

Pete felt uncomfortable with Butler in the producer's chair. Rough Trade had originally chosen him because it intended The Libertines to be a big London band, just as Suede had been, but Pete felt that this intimidating figure was too controlling, demanding hard, nine-to-five graft in the recording studio.

Ironically, Butler had left his own band after complaining of troubles with their producer, Ed Buller. As Bernard later admitted, 'When I left Suede, I didn't do it because I fell out with people. I did it because I didn't want the producer we had [Ed Buller] to mix an album. It was a case of call my bluff – it was him or me. It was a stupid mistake. I was stupid enough to go for it. It shouldn't have gone that far.'

While Pete might have had problems with Butler, there was no question that the product of their affiliation was terrific, and 'What a Waster' turned out to be a great single. Expecting – perhaps even provoking – the usual disapproval, Pete played it to his father and was shocked by Peter Sr's reaction. 'He started eating my cigarettes,' Pete remembered. 'I'd never seen him like that before. He was eating cigarettes and telling me to fuck off. He started dancing around the room and saying it reminded him of the Goldhawk Road in 1969.'

Pete's bosses at Rough Trade liked the single so much that they took out a full-page advert in the *NME* that simply featured the lyrics, while among the song's other fans was Radio 1's Mark Radcliffe, who managed to create a version sufficiently edited to be broadcast as his show's single of the week.

The CD single also featured 'I Get Along', a defiant statement of musical individualism, and 'Mayday', a track described by Pete as a cross between the theme tunes of classic sitcoms *The Likely Lads* and *Steptoe and Son*. Taken as a whole, the disc was full of character and spelled out much of what The Libertines were about: the rebellious hedonism, the belief in music, the cultural backdrop of English comedy. All the same, Pete felt that he'd compromised himself in making it, and at times he found he couldn't bear to listen to 'What a Waster', feeling that it reflected Rough Trade's preoccupation with a punk revival as much as it expressed his own musical identity. 'We were supposed to be part of this fucking punk-rock revival, but that wasn't us,' he later protested. 'It was a load of bollocks some twat in a record company had started. It was nothing to do with what we were about.'

On the whole, though, Pete believed his band's debut single was a 'fucking brilliant' achievement, although for him the lyrics later proved to be disturbingly prophetic, the song's meaning becoming warped almost beyond recognition in the media storm surrounding Pete's drug habit.

It was while posing for the publicity shots for the debut single that Pete hit on the idea of the band wearing the bright-red Crimean War guards' uniforms he'd got from an army-memorabilia store on Brick Lane market, in

London's East End. Pete loved to imagine himself as the renegade soldier, like the World War One Tommy in Siegfried Sassoon's poem 'Suicide in the Trenches' or the reprobates in one of his favourite movies, *The Man Who Would Be King*. Wearing his guard's jacket casually draped over his T-shirt, he looked every inch the deserter on the run, an image of rebellion that held particular resonance for Pete, whose father was an army major. In one shot taken by Roger Sargent, Pete is seen standing proud in his red tunic while Gary, Carl and John are off to his right. Brass buttons undone, moptops dishevelled, unsmiling expressions of defiance fixed on their faces, they appear bloodied, battle-worn and ready to mutiny. The stunning picture became the band's most iconic image.

Pete had every reason to be delighted with the way the publicity machine was working in his favour, and found himself blessed with another stroke of luck when he and Carl appeared on the cover of the 8 June issue of the *NME*, the week of the Queen's Golden Jubilee. The paper was looking for a British band to fit in with the patriotic times, and the Englishness of The Libertines, combined with the fact that they had recently released their debut single, made them the ideal choice. The two founder Libertines were pictured draped in the Union flag, while Pete rammed home the patriotic message still further by wearing a 1982 England World Cup squad football shirt.

The accompanying interview was given in the Dive Bar, Soho, appropriately while the annual London ritual of the May Day riots was being staged outside. The piece consisted of a riveting ramble through the pair's colourful past, with Pete and Carl talking about how they had lived in brothels.

The cover shot signalled the first spark of the *NME*'s exploding interest in the band. From then on, the paper would run news and reviews on the band in such profusion that it sometimes took on the aspect of a Libertines fan sheet. Many in the rock world have attributed this intensive coverage to the prejudices of the *NME*'s journalists, although, in fact, the decision to follow the group closely was a commercial one; the *NME* found that The Libertines generated a huge response from its readers.

At the time, Pete was typically candid and controversial about the role of the *NME* in gaining the band notoriety, observing that 'Rough Trade owns the *NME* anyway, so anything we get from that angle is always gonna be a compliment. Basically, keep the *NME* supplied with drugs and they'll write nice things about you.'

With the single out and many column inches of publicity in the bag, Pete and the band were eager to go out on the road. On the day of the Queen's Jubilee celebrations, the band took the opportunity to get some punk-style publicity by playing an alternative gig across the road from Buckingham Palace, where the spectacle of an unholy alliance between ageing rock stars and establishment figures was being aired across the nation.

Pete found that the standard of gigs The Libertines could expect to play had suddenly rocketed beyond recognition when, on 27 July, the band donned their trademark guards' jackets to support the legendary Sex Pistols at Crystal Palace. Pete was characteristically undaunted by the prospect of sharing the gig with John Lydon, aka Johnny Rotten. Hearing Lydon backstage going off on a rant, he taped the punk legend on his portable Sony and played the results down the microphone when he went on stage. The mischievous stunt didn't go down too well with The Sex Pistols' fans, however, one of whom threw a can of what had originally been Heineken in Pete's face. Pete picked the missile up and drained the remaining contents of unidentified liquid into his mouth, then rounded off the performance by flinging his guard's tunic into the rowdy masses.

The summer of 2002 also saw the recording of The Libertines' debut album. Too busy pursuing a solo project, Bernard Butler wasn't available to produce, so Rough Trade decided to bring in Mick Jones, former guitarist of The Clash and half of the famous songwriting partnership with the late Joe Strummer. Then in his mid-forties, Mick had been at the very centre of the punk movement during the late 1970s, The Clash's classic album *London Calling* setting a benchmark for any group since trying to capture the raw energy of freedom and rebellion.

Mick, it turned out, was something of a libertine himself, having been in and out of jail during The Clash's heyday for a series of minor crimes. His friend Jeanette Lee at Rough Trade gave him a load of demo tapes to listen to, and he liked what he heard so much that he turned up to meet the band at the Depot in Camden, where they were rehearsing. Although he wasn't there when Mick arrived, Pete soon made a spectacular appearance.

'The first time I met Pete, he rode into the middle of the studio on a scooter, with a bag of carry-outs hanging from the handlebars,' laughed Mick. 'I remember thinking, What an entrance! He's a unique individual. He has an enormous amount of talent; his ability as a songwriter and a performer cannot be measured. Not just him, but all of the band.'

Unlike Bernard, Mick didn't look down on Pete's

behaviour. He was on Pete's level, and Pete could see that straight away. The punk veteran showed such respect for the band that he was even wearing a Rough Trade 'What a Waster' badge. Incredibly, though, given his generally nerdy familiarity with British bands, past and present, Pete didn't know who the man with the badge was. To a largely disbelieving public, Pete would later assert that The Libertines hadn't been directly influenced by The Clash, since they'd never really heard their music. But, once he realised the gaping hole in his knowledge, he didn't delay in quizzing Mick repeatedly and listening to all the music he could persuade Mick to lend or play to him.

Pete and Mick hit it off straight away, their relationship displaying none of the awkwardness that Pete had felt with Bernard. He felt that Mick understood him, as Mick too believed in the idea of breaking down barriers between the musician and the listener, adhering to the principle that music should be open to all. Ultimately, Mick's more understanding attitude proved more effective in keeping Pete under control; whereas Pete had fought against the strict regime imposed by Bernard, with Mick in charge he was instead inspired to devote his energies to recording an album.

Mick, too, was dedicated to his work. It wasn't just a job to him; he loved the process of making music and, with him buzzing enthusiastically around the equipment, the band was spurred on to produce some great music. 'He danced to our songs – the Mick Jones shuffle,' Pete remembered, grinning. 'We knew that, if he danced, they were good.' Indeed, Mick's warmth and zeal were a breath of fresh air, and Pete was full of admiration for him, praising his 'natural feel for music, and for people too'.

Pete came to realise that there was more than one way to

produce music. After working with Butler on 'What a Waster', he had become disheartened with the process of producing music commercially and had begun to doubt that he could force himself to go through the creation of a whole album. When Mick came on the scene, however, Pete found new optimism. 'Mick is very direct,' he enthused at the time. 'He comes from another decade, a less absurd one, while Bernard Butler came from a more recent decade. It seems there are two ways to do things: to either follow something along the same direction or follow another path. If we get led along two different paths, though, we get lost.'

Under Mick's relaxed but nonetheless influential guidance, Pete's creativity flourished. He'd expected that the band would turn out only a second single before Bernard Butler returned, but the recording sessions were going so well that Mick expanded the studio time to a week and managed to record twenty-nine songs, twelve of which would appear on The Libertines' debut album *Up the Bracket*. Pete found that he could work well with Mick's methods, which gave him the freedom he needed to craft his songs. As Pete later explained, 'Being in a studio should be free – not financially, but spiritually and physically. You should be free to experiment with ideas. There is no regime. OK, you might be recording a single, in which case you get that done, but it's gotta be like a fella with a paintbrush, not like some anal graphic designer who's all rigid.'

That same summer, the band found themselves abroad for the first time, playing at a sequence of festivals in Sweden, Germany and Japan, where, at the Summersonic Festival in

August, Pete discovered new heights of rock 'n' roll excess. On the first night, 17 August, Pete and Carl embarked on a crawl through the pole-dancing bars of Osaka until eleven in the morning, and then the next night, in Tokyo, they ransacked bars in the early hours, before returning to the Hilton Hotel with booty consisting of bottles of gin and an umbrella. They then burst into James Endeacott's room and trashed it as he lay in his bed, spraying spirits all over the floor and blowing up the fruit bowl with firecrackers.

Pete revelled in the unpredictability of live acts, enjoying being on stage even when things went badly wrong. At the Reading Festival on 24 August, The Libertines achieved a disaster of spectacular proportions when Carl's amplifier blew up on the first song. As the band limped through the rest of the set, they met with indifference from the Main Stage crowd. Carl took the débâcle on the chin, particularly as his mother and father had come along to the gig, but Pete impishly responded by switching to a performance of 'Ha Ha Wall', a song in which Carl didn't have a role, just to rub it in. Carl was furious, and the performance degenerated into a slanging match and a scuffle between him and Pete as they disappeared backstage.

The next day, The Libertines were performing again, this time at Leeds. Pete and Carl arrived at the venue with raging hangovers after drinking until eight o'clock in the morning and again produced a shoddy display, this time without the excuse of a technical hitch. Carl felt that Pete was continually trying to upstage him, trying to turn him into a figure of fun, while Pete argued that Carl was being precious about his image. Again, there was a row, this one ending with the befuddled Pete swinging wild punches in the vague direction of his bandmate. Carl was ready to hit back with a vengeance, but Gary brought a halt to the contest by grabbing him by his long tresses. By the end of the night, Pete's on-off girlfriend, Tabitha Denholm, wound up with a black eye and Carl's shoes were filled with urine.

The Libertines on the road around Britain that autumn proved a volatile force that could explode at any moment. In Manchester in October, the band's support act, Left Hand, were given a beating by some nightclub bouncers, an experience that somehow inspired them to pour curry powder into another pair of Carl's shoes. The next day, Scarborough Steve, who had turned up for the ride, woke up with swastikas and the words 'I AM A QUEER' written across his face. Unfortunately, he'd walked around Manchester city centre before he'd noticed the prank.

Every night of that tour, set up to promote the forthcoming *Up the Bracket* debut album, Pete ended up drugged and drunk out of his mind. He felt trapped on the tour bus, frequently retreating to his cubbyhole hideaway at the back of the vehicle to smoke yet more smack and crack. He was seeing at least two women regularly at this stage – Lisa Moorish of support act Kill City and Tabitha Denholm, future member of The Queens of Noize – although there were also many other less regular companions. On one occasion in Scotland, Pete smuggled four girls on to the tour bus, hid them in his tiny dressing room, locked the door and promptly forgot about them for six hours. The prisoners escaped only when one of them, Hannah Bays, managed to get hold of group photographer Roger Sargent on her mobile phone.

Venues like Coventry, Bristol, Cardiff and Exeter passed in a blur, with Pete's excesses in each place being colourful enough to warrant a weekly Libertines bad-behaviour bulletin in the *NME*. The band's ex-policeman tour manager was eventually sacked after Pete had a particularly furious row with him in Southampton on 18 September at Joiners. He later told the *NME* that he'd never before witnessed such scenes of drug-fuelled debauchery after twenty-two years of working with rock stars.

As winter approached, the mayhem didn't stop. In November, the band turned up at a legalised brothel with a Rolling Stones theme in Switzerland where Pete distinguished himself by being sick all over a prostitute's breasts and being chased down the street. In Munich, he slept with a girl who offered him a ride on a tandem, only to escape from her flat stark naked, riding the same vehicle in pursuit of another conquest. (When he caught up with the second girl, he found that Carl was already kissing her in a corner of a bar.)

Back in England, the *Up the Bracket* album was released in October 2002 to an enthusiastic reception. As with the debut single, Pete had had a hard time recording it, later admitting that he was 'in a mess' and ascribing his difficulties to 'too many girls, too many drugs'. Aside from the maelstrom of his home life, he was finding the creative process of recording intensive and exhausting, demanding hour after hour of solid effort at RAK Studios in St John's Wood. But at least the creative pangs had been soothed by Butler's replacement with Jones.

For all the trials that the album caused him, Pete was pleased with the result, recognising that he'd stamped his personality all over it, expressing himself on several levels in the title alone. ('Up the bracket' was a catchphrase of Pete's favourite *Carry On* comic, Sid James, and means a punch in the face.) The retro Englishness of the allusion sprang from Pete's childhood obsession with TV classics and expressed his intention for the album to give the listener a metaphorical punch in the chops. It was also, however, a reference to snorting cocaine.

Pete promised the album would deliver a stimulating wallop, and it did, giving fans everything they'd hoped for and more. The Libertines' tale of life in England, London in particular, was exciting, funny, scary, sleazy and always rough round the edges. The better it got, the closer it sounded to falling apart. From the arrogant entrance of 'Vertigo', Carl's effortless swooning tone had already won the listener over. It was a journey the fans wanted to be a part of.

One of the album's best offerings was 'Time for Heroes', which best described The Libertines' state of mind at this time, being a love story about riots, class war and young lungs coughing up blood. The subject matter wasn't obviously romantic, but the band nevertheless managed to turn it into lyrical mythology. They could have made being battered to death by Englishmen in baseball caps look decadent. As always, Pete found a way to add layers of meaning to his lyrics, even making a reference to Bill Bones, a character from Robert Louis Stevenson's classic novel *Treasure Island*.

'Death on the Stairs', meanwhile, showcased their songwriting ability, notably Pete and Carl's effortless exchange of lyrics, while 'Boys in the Band' was a celebration of how the band had made it, describing an energetic romp through the world of drugs, women and knees-ups that was now available to them. It was a theme that would disappear in later Libertines material, making way for tones of regret and sometimes sorrow, but for now they were loving their music and their lives as brand-new rock stars. The song also showed Gary's often-neglected influence, its complex, tight rhythm changes hinting at his background in jazz.

Elsewhere, the album's title track was another tale of love and hate, sex and fights. More than any other song on the album, it was a quintessential anthem of the modern East End of London.

Alongside the riotous celebrations on *Up the Bracket* are some eloquent and sentimental meditations; 'Tell the King', for instance, is tender and reflective, containing the line 'You know how I feel out of place till I'm levered off my face', while 'Radio America' is an ambling plea for love. In 'The Good Old Days', meanwhile, Pete raises the spirit of Celtic warrior queen Boadicea, before dispensing with the idea of good old days with the line, '*These* are the good old days.' The song also contains a brilliant line that hinted darkly at Carl and Pete's future, which states that to lose one's belief in love and music is the beginning of the end.

'Horror Show', meanwhile, touches on heroin abuse, although without the detail that would follow in later material, taking a tone that's entertaining and funny without trying too hard.

Taken as a whole, the album is as English as the Sid James quotation it was named after, yet it outsold The Strokes' debut in Japan. It's a brilliant album produced by a brilliant band, the most exciting debut since Oasis's *Definitely Maybe*. The detail and emotion that Pete and Carl invested into a story by juggling lines between them for a three-minute song hadn't been heard before, and the entire album formed a thrilling combination of punk arrogance and a sincere, lyrical romanticism. In the words of Morrissey, it was the contradictory sound of 'sweet and tender hooligans'.

The fans, of course, loved it, and were left hungry for more, waiting eagerly to find out what The Libertines would do next.

CHAPTER 7

Skag and Bone

'WE COULD STAY AT HOME, MAN/CALL THE
SKAG AND BONE MAN.'
– Pete Doherty and Carl Barât

While Pete's music career was moving ahead in leaps
and bounds, he was also making rapid progression
deeper into hard drugs. His addiction to heroin, which he
followed up with a dependency on crack cocaine, developed
during the same period in which The Libertines really took
off – an uncomfortable fact for those who would later
blame his drug-taking for the break-up of the band.

Before spring 2000, Pete was at large on the London
music scene, along with many other would-be rock stars
much like himself. He played gigs in smoke-filled pubs,
drank gallons of lager and took copious quantities of weed
and speed. Ten pints of Stella Artois and a dab or two of
amphetamines to him constituted a good night out, and
among his crowd such behaviour was pretty much run of
the mill. Pete saw himself, and was seen by others, as a
young man about town, having a good time. Two and a half

years later, on 19 October 2002, the new-born rock star would be pouring his heart out in the *NME*, telling the world how he had become addicted to smack and hadn't a clue what to do about it.

The difference between Pete and thousands of other young Londoners was his attitude to the substances he took. Even before he smoked his first cannabis joint, back when he was sixteen, Pete had made drugs a part of his intellectual landscape. Reading the Romantic poets, he was quick to pick up on their obsession with the use of drugs to fire the imagination, to free the individual from what William Blake called the 'mind-forged manacles' – the chains of society internalised by each of its members. Pete had wanted to be a free spirit back then and was already plotting his escape from the confines of his childhood; reading Coleridge and Blake inspired him to regard the project as one that would benefit from chemical assistance.

When his mother, Jacqueline, found out that he was a regular cannabis smoker at the age of eighteen, she immediately feared for his future, warning him that it would lead him down the destructive road to heroin. This, however, was a prospect that did little to scare her son, who had already thought a great deal about using the opium derivative. Pete classified it as the ultimate agent of escape, a narcotic passport to new heights of creativity, after poring over Thomas de Quincey's *Confessions of an English Opium Eater* again and again during his late teens. This nineteenth-century autobiographical account of addiction spells out the Romantic obsession with drugs in its fullest form, emphasising the effects of opium on the imagination, ascribing to the drug the power to generate the most vivid spectacles. In the context of poetry, this power was inspirational and creative, although de Quincey took pains to point out that its consequences were sometimes far from pleasurable; the book presents harrowing scenes in which the author is driven to terrifying hallucinations after taking opium. In one passage, for example, the sea mutates into a vision of thousands of faces twisted in agony: 'Upon the rocking waters of the ocean the human face began to appear: the sea appeared paved with innumerable faces, upturned to the heavens: faces imploring, wrathful, despairing, surged upwards by the thousands, by myriads, by generations, by centuries: my agitation was infinite, my mind tossed and surged with the ocean.'

This passage, worse than a scene from a horror film, is nevertheless a source of fascination for anyone who holds the imagination in such esteem as Pete did. The young poet believed in suffering for his art, and it seemed that opium could produce both suffering *and* art. He lapped up the passages that de Quincey wrote of his enjoyment of opium, describing its 'divine luxuries'. The quote 'Opium! dread agent of unimaginable pleasure and pain!' stuck in his head like a promise.

In a typically candid moment, Pete later described how his first taste of heroin led directly from these ideas about opium: 'My dealer was always smoking roll-ups and I asked, "Is that opium?" I had a romantic vision of taking opium. I didn't think of it as smack. He was loath to sell it to me and told me, "You'll regret it. I don't want to be the one who got you hooked." But it was my decision, no one else's. You can't spend your life blaming others for your actions."

In fact, Pete had been considering this step for years before he eventually took the plunge at the age of twenty-one. While other addicts could cite personal crises or peer pressure as the original pressures behind their habits, Pete made the decision on his own during a period when he wasn't experiencing any particularly acute troubles. At the time, he had recently moved into a flat in Whitechapel after Banny's first attempt to kick The Libertines into a commercially viable state had failed. True, he was estranged from Carl, having spoken to him seldom since they had gone their separate ways from the shared flat in the Holloway Road in Camden that spring, but he was still hanging around with Scarborough Steve, going out to pubs and clubs, signing on the dole and doing bits of jobs to keep himself going. He was still playing his music and keeping The Libertines dream alive.

In the event, he came to heroin as a man who was doing something he'd always dreamed of. Just as he felt his life had imitated his art in many other respects, so Pete took up this most notoriously self-degrading habit as if it was just another stepping stone to his promised land of Arcadia – not because he wanted to hide from something, but because he expected it to add to his experience of life.

The first time Pete smoked heroin, the sensations he experienced seemed to live up to his expectations. 'The first time I had heroin, I was twenty-one, walking round the streets of Whitechapel on a Sunday, smoking brown my dealer gave me and thinking I was cool,' he later recalled. 'I've no idea how much I took that first time or how much it cost. He gave it to me for free. As it got into my bloodstream, I noticed it exaggerated parts of me that were already there: solitude and loneliness. Then I started getting all these creative thoughts.'

Although Pete was quite capable of producing music before he'd first tried heroin, he found that de Quincey was right about its effects on the imagination, believing that it helped him to create. The Libertines' debut album *Up the Bracket* was so good, Pete felt, because he'd been on heroin during the recording sessions. In the early stages of his heroin use, Pete was actually quite pleased with the results of his indulgence, although even at this point a certain ambiguity crept into his attitude. It became clear that, while his inspiration had been enhanced by heroin, he still didn't want to glorify it. 'Drugs have never been the driving wheel,' he noted. 'They're just part of creating music. I just want to play, so I take heroin to enhance my creativity. A lot of my lyrics are heroin-related, but they're never a celebration of it.'

Pete's descent into heroin was unusual in that it had intellectual origins, but the rarefied seeds of his habit only helped it to develop into a full-blown addiction. The process took around six months; by the time The Libertines signed to Rough Trade in December 2001, Pete had already been smoking heroin for several months, with increasing regularity. 'I kept taking it,' he admitted. 'I didn't get hooked straight away; it was a gradual thing. It was six months to a year later before I started taking it every day.'

Pete's appetite for the new drug was given fresh impetus in the autumn of 2000, when a small-time Asian dealer of his acquaintance provided him with some high-grade china-white heroin, a sack of which he'd smuggled back from India by stuffing it up his rectum. Pete found the effects of the china white 'amazing', taking as much of it as he could manage.

Along with the heroin came a new group of friends who began to hang around Pete's East End flat. They were what Carl called 'the brown people' – ie those who shared an interest in smack – and included characters such as the bank robber Will Brown and a man named Peter Wolfe, universally known as 'Wolfman'. This gaunt figure, invariably dressed in black from top to toe, became a huge influence on Pete. Wolfman was an ex-plumber in his mid-thirties who was the veteran of three suicide attempts, a mental breakdown so severe he'd ended up in an asylum, and many unsuccessful bids to break into the music business. Born in Maidstone, Kent, of Irish extraction, he'd been married to a Polish countess and had shared a flat with Pogues wild man Shane MacGowan. He'd also had a near-death experience when his heart had stopped beating after his third suicide attempt, on the north London landmark Primrose Hill on Easter Monday 2000.

Pete met Wolfman two years after he almost passed into another world, and he was immediately drawn to this character, scarred by fifteen years on the fringes of showbusiness. Pete spoke of his new friend in reverential tones, showing respect for his songwriting talent where others had dismissed him as a smack-addicted nearly man, while also appreciating his softly spoken, often macabre sense of humour. The affection, it turned out, was mutual; as Wolfman described it, 'Pete turned up at my flat and started hanging around, saying he was in a band. He's a great fucking person – sometimes really awful, but sometimes very kind. Maybe he was the first person to look at me through eyes that didn't say, "This guy's a cunt."'

Wolfman has been blamed by some Libertines fans with

leading Pete into heroin addiction, whereas, in fact, as he rightly pointed out, Pete made his own decisions. The fact that neither Pete nor Wolfman could dispute, however, was that Pete's choice was to take as much heroin as possible. As Wolfman put it in an entry in Pete's diary, 'He's fit, he's toned, he's ready to get super-stoned.'

Days and nights of epic binges followed. Sometimes they would be literally gory affairs. On one occasion, Pete remembered the pair becoming so out of their minds on heroin that they began howling together like wolves, then carving their names into each other's chest with a razor blade. When they'd woken the following afternoon, the floor of Pete's flat had been covered in blood. The scene could have been taken out of Pete's favourite de Sade writings, reflecting a preoccupation with self-harm – another point he had in common with his new friend.

During the early Wolfman era, which began in the spring of 2002, Pete was taking heroin by rolling it up in a joint with some cannabis – a creation he called a 'booner' – or by chasing the dragon – ie heating it on foil and inhaling the smoke. He was trying to convince himself and others that it was possible not to become an addict if you didn't inject the drug. This was a myth that Pete would relate to all and sundry, although he would later admit that he'd been secretly aware that he was slipping into dependency.

Of course, intravenous use was the next step on the road, as the more heroin he smoked, the less of an impact it made on him. The desire to repeat the extreme sensations of his first hits (and Pete wasn't one to deny himself something he wanted) led to him injecting straight into his bloodstream.

117

Pete crossed the line into intravenous heroin use during an abortive recording session in New York in May 2003. He'd managed to make plenty of drug-using friends in the Big Apple, despite never having visited the place before, on this occasion meeting a fellow Englishman who was also a heroin addict and inviting him back to his hotel room. Carl walked in on the scene to find Pete's new friend filling two syringes. 'This guy, who was obviously preparing to introduce Peter into the world of jacking up heroin, turned to me and said, "Pleased to meet you. I don't think there's enough for you,"' Carl remembered. Furious that Pete had sunk so far into his addiction, he'd picked up the needles and smashed them against the wall. 'Peter seemed kind of pleased I'd done it,' he observed.

Pete's progression on to crack cocaine was less premeditated than his acquisition of a heroin habit. His commitment to total hedonism made him open to the idea of taking any kind of drug, but he had never fantasised about crack, specifically. The crystallised cocaine was a relatively recent creation and hadn't been the subject of much poetry, outside rap. The mythology surrounding it spoke of gang warfare in the inner cities of America, R&B music, bling jewellery and designer-label sportswear. It was all alien territory for the man who wrote of his distaste for Englishmen wearing baseball caps.

However, by this stage, Pete had become less interested in the image and more interested in the drugs. He had been introduced to cocaine in powder form when he'd signed to Rough Trade in December 2001, having been too poor before that time to spend money on the music industry's staple stimulant. 'We could never afford coke,' he lamented.

'That was too expensive. It was always heroin.' Having tried the drug of the rich and famous, however, he found that he enjoyed the experience. He wanted more, and with his newfound wealth he bought it by the ounce.

In February 2002, Pete turned up at King's Cross train station looking for cocaine. He got what he wanted from a dealer on the street, who threw in a small rock of crack for good measure. Pete wasn't sure how to use the block of yellow-white crystal, but he didn't think for a minute about throwing it away. 'I didn't know what to do with it,' he confessed. 'I just put it in my little tin.'

With the help of his well-informed friends, it didn't take Pete long to work out how to smoke his first rock, whereupon he found its effects were even more intense than those produced by heroin, though very different. Soon he was talking about crack as if it was the love of his life. He felt that it was a beautiful drug, referring to it as 'lovely crack'. In a strange parallel to some of the words a distressed Carl would say about him, Pete confessed, 'It's like you're in love with someone. You never really stop loving that person. It's like a family member who's a bit troublesome, but you love them anyway because you know they're all right, even if the rest of the world can see the truth – ie they're not all right. They're in your blood.' His affection for crack became such that he lovingly scrawled pictures of his pipes in the diaries he called 'the Books of Albion', referring to the devices – made out of taped-together Evian bottles – by the affectionate nickname 'Pipey McGraw'.

Pete found that heroin and crack worked almost as opposing forces in his mind. He would smoke pipe after pipe of crack, using the super-strong stimulant to give himself a series of short, intense highs. Over a few hours, the effects would build up so that Pete's state of mind between highs was strung taut, leaving him unable to concentrate or sleep properly. Then he would use heroin to come down from this mental hyperactivity, slipping into a calmer, less excitable state. During this period, one of his girlfriends, Lucy Evans, noted that Pete lost three stone in weight as his dual addiction took a grip on him.

Many of Pete's friends – Lucy included – found his crack and smack habits so difficult to deal with that they ended up cutting him out of their lives. As he moved further into drug abuse, he found disapproval wherever he went, even from those who, like Carl, who were no stranger to Class A drugs themselves. Pete, however, had gone beyond what was acceptable, even in the libertarian world of music, but he would brook no criticism of his behaviour or attempts to control it; the hostility of others served only to drive him further into the arms of the only people who now appeared to understand him: his new smack- and crack-taking friends.

After The Libertines' first album was released in October 2002, Pete's drug-taking began to reach crippling proportions. Perhaps unsurprisingly, the song on *Up the Bracket* that gave him the least difficulties was 'Skag and Bone Man'. Pete wrote the track in the space of a summer afternoon and got the recording done the same evening, and its lyrics, which suggest the appeal of staying at home and calling up a drug dealer, capture his obsession with hard drugs, both brown and white.

CHAPTER 8

The Pied Piper

'A FEW FANS WERE ONLY FOURTEEN YEARS OLD.
IN SOME CASES, I HAD TO PHONE THEIR MUMS TO LET THEM
KNOW. SOME OF THE KIDS WERE EMBARRASSED WHEN
I FIRST PHONED. SOME MUMS CAME ROUND AND SAT
WITH THEM WHILE I PLAYED.'
– *Pete Doherty*

For Pete, getting signed to Rough Trade Records was the most stunning success thus far in his project of turning fantasy into reality. He didn't see it as the end game, however, but as another rung on the ladder, a means of gaining access to more of what he wanted. Now the fame and fortune he had dreamed of were within his grasp, he was determined to live that dream in his inimitable manner. He'd never cared about the conventional trappings of wealth; flash sports cars and flats in Notting Hill or Chelsea meant nothing to him. Indeed, he hated the materialism he associated with the suburban, lower-middle-class values of his parents. The alternative, bohemian existence he had been leading in the pubs and squats of the East End was the way of life he had chosen, and he would use his money not to escape from what others saw as squalor but to fuel more of the same, on a massively expanded scale.

The scene for this lifestyle experiment was the Albion Rooms, bequeathed to them by Rough Trade as part of the deal they signed with the label. The flat was located in the backstreets of Bethnal Green, an east London district that held all of the features of Pete's beloved inner city in abundance; drugs, prostitution, crime and grime – the capital's Dickensian underworld was laid out on Pete and Carl's doorstep. In reality, the top half of a Victorian brick terrace turned out not to be theirs in any conventional sense, but that didn't concern Pete, who didn't believe in the idea of owning a home, in shutting himself away in a private box where everything belonged to him. He wanted to demolish the bourgeois concept of home ownership, replacing it with a bohemian place of shelter where people he liked could crash in pauses between indulgence in sex and drugs. It was all about breaking down the barriers Pete saw in the society around him. He wanted to be at one with the public, particularly those who were his fans, and regarded anyone who liked his music as part of one big, happy family.

What Pete and Carl created was in effect an updated version of a hippie commune, a place where members of their circle had the freedom to come and go as they pleased, sleep, have sex, take drugs or order a pizza. Dozens of people had keys to the flat, and there would be a stream of arrivals and departures all through the day and night. Everyone Pete and Carl had met during their adventures on the streets of London was invited to the non-stop party. As Pete explained, 'All the people whose floors I'd kipped on, everyone who I'd scrounged a spliff off, were invited to live at the Albion Rooms, in a giant Arcadian reverie.'

Pete, of course, didn't believe in hoarding anything,

particularly money, and, as soon as the first cash from Rough Trade was deposited in his bank account, he withdrew the lot and carried it back to the Albion Rooms in a brown paper bag, which he then emptied on to the floor. The heap of crisp £50 notes was an exhilarating sight for Pete and Carl, and they immediately ordered a king-size consignment of drugs. Later, they began to pelt each other with screwed-up bundles of banknotes. Later still, and by this time comprehensively drugged up, they decided to iron the notes and stash them in neat piles in the fridge.

A few days after the cash had arrived and Pete and Carl had moved into 112a Teesdale Street, the band's photographer, Roger Sargent, turned up for the press shoot for their debut single, 'What a Waster'. Letting himself into the Albion Rooms with one of the many keys in circulation, he was greeted by the debris of a celebration that had lasted all week. Money was littered everywhere, along with drug paraphernalia, wraps and powder smears all over the tables. The flat looked like a scene from the 1998 glam-rock film *Velvet Goldmine*. There were piles of books of poetry, classical literature, even a biography of Russian mystic Rasputin; mounds of videotapes of French films; and dozens of CDs and old LPs by jazz guitarist Django Reinhardt and French singer Françoise Hardy. Pete and Carl, of course, were still out after a night on the town, eventually arriving home for their own photo shoot three hours late.

The decadent mess that Sargent witnessed on that occasion developed over the following months into full-blown chaos. The pair had chosen their respective bedrooms, but in the event people crashed wherever they wanted. Thick velvet curtains hung from the windows, casting the place in a permanent gloom, and on the lounge wall was a giant fish-eye mirror. A cast-iron spiral staircase led up to Pete's room, which contained a bed made out of four mattresses piled on top of each other. The place was never cleaned; in the living room were scattered cans of lager, Rizla packets and cigarette butts, while in the kitchen empty packets of takeout were thrown in a mound over what had been the bin. There was little evidence of food preparation; the cupboards were empty, the fridge contained only four packs of Stella and wads of cash. In the bathroom, the sink was clogged with matted pubic hairs and the toilet was caked in limescale and smears of excrement. The flush mechanism was broken, too, and so Pete, Carl and their guests emptied bottles of Evian mineral water into the bowl instead. The place stank of stale tobacco and rotting leftovers.

Soon after settling in, Pete and Carl developed the Albion Rooms into a musical commune. At the time, The Libertines were recording an album and playing live gigs in front of thousands of people at venues like the Reading Festival, but Pete loved the intimate atmosphere he'd found at Filthy McNasty's and other small venues and wanted to break down the formalities of performance in the same way that he'd destroyed the barriers most people place around their homes. He didn't believe in the division between the artist and the fans, the division that placed the performer on a distant, remote stage. Carl agreed, asserting, 'It's such a load of old bollocks, that wall, that unnecessary divide, which is why we like intimate gigs. We want everyone to be involved.'

At mainstream venues, Pete and Carl's commitment to breaking down barriers between audience and performers would culminate in stage invasions where crowd and band became one seething mass. Pete loved it. 'Can you get a buzz better than that?' he breathed. 'It's communion. It's like being washed away in the ocean, carried aloft on a wave.' After a set, he and Carl would infuriate venue security guards and tour managers by inviting the fans backstage into their dressing room, as if all of them were their friends.

Pete extended the communion by pioneering guerrilla gigs, impromptu performances put on at short notice in places where there was no stage, such as the Albion Rooms, where many of these events took place. Pete, who by this time had bought himself a laptop computer, would send out invitations to the fans via the band's website at www.libertines.org. Dozens would turn up outside his front door in Bethnal Green, paying sometimes £5, sometimes £10, sometimes nothing at all to mount the narrow flight of stairs to the flat above. Inside, they would press up against the kitchen cabinets or squash together on the couch and the steps of the spiral staircase to watch Pete and Carl jolt around their microphone stands.

The sound was often melodious but never popular with the neighbours. Next door, a middle-aged German woman was driven to distraction by the noise of the gigs, which typically carried on well into the early hours of the morning. Pete nicknamed her 'Vizzels' because her complaints would usually begin with reference to her pet budgie, who was so disturbed by the music that he 'vizzelled' in distress. On one occasion, the burly bird fancier became so infuriated with the racket that she arrived at the front door brandishing a hammer and a chair leg. Whenever she screamed, Pete and Carl would deliberately play louder. She and other neighbours called the police countless times.

The fans, on the other hand, were thrilled to find themselves in such close proximity to their heroes, being treated to a performance in Pete and Carl's own flat. As Pete's future tour manager Matt Bates put it, the relationship between the stars and their audience was unparalleled: 'Peter doesn't mind playing to one person or 10,000. The little shows are where he really comes into his own. He will do a gig, get his guitar from the tour bus and sit in the street and do a second gig for his fans. There isn't another rock star in the world who would do that.'

While other names in music hid behind armies of bouncers and secluded themselves in gated mansions and chauffeur-driven cars, Pete and Carl mingled freely with the people for whom they were performing. Pete saw himself as a troubadour-type minstrel figure and would allow the fans into every aspect of his life, sharing his home, his thoughts, his diaries, his music. As he described it, 'I let them write on the walls, put on records, flick through books, make cups of tea.'

Pete also adopted a paternal attitude to the younger members of his fan base. 'A few were only fourteen years old. In some cases, I had to phone their mums to let them know. Some of the kids were embarrassed when I first phoned. Some mums came round and sat with them while I played.'

Sometimes, when Pete and Carl fancied a change from performing in their own flat, they would track down a fan with a spare room and hold a gig there. Following The Libertines could land you with a live performance in your own living room.

Pete's aim of total accessibility was an intentional rebellion against the constraints of the music business. He felt a genuine distaste for the idea of making money from his music, preferring the immediacy of live performance in return for a few pounds to an orchestrated commercial enterprise that involved little contact between artist and audience. He wanted the kind of contact with fans that had become rarer with the development of television and better audio equipment. He much preferred live music to the sanitised, recorded version delivered through an impersonal CD. By happy coincidence, his preferences dovetailed neatly with new technology that was taking music beyond the era of mass-produced recordings. The internet provided him with the ideal forum on which to publish his own music or poetry uncompromised by the wishes of a record company. What's more, he could do so inexpensively, according him the chance to include plenty of discussion of the philosophy behind his work. This project was the purpose of his spin-off group, Babyshambles.

While other stars jealously protected their precious private lives, Pete exploded the idea of privacy by posting his most intimate thoughts on the internet. The Libertines ended up with seven fan websites, where the irrepressibly populist Pete could often be found engaging with his public, musing on his existence and pouring out unexpected message-board confessionals. The Libertines' fan club, The Albion, meanwhile, provided members with a quarterly magazine entitled *The Albion Chronicle*, and on his babyshambles.com site Pete loaded instalments of his diary, *The Books of Albion*, which included no-holds-barred admissions about his drug habits and love life, with each weekly entry describing online another episode of The Libertines saga. One passage, for example, told of a girl from the north of England packing her bags and leaving her boyfriend in order to move in with Pete at the Albion Rooms, while another described how Pete once went missing from his hotel room after a gig in Birmingham, only to reappear with his guitar in a battered case. The website later revealed that he'd taken a cab from Birmingham to London in order to fetch the instrument.

One of the many fans who visited the band's homepage broached the subject of Pete's love life, remarking, 'You just can't buy entertainment like this!' Indeed, Pete's day-to-day existence was more eventful than a soap opera, and through the window in cyberspace people could follow his antics as though they were his closest friends. As Pete himself realised, he was living out not just his own fantasies but other people's, too. It was a new form of stardom for the internet age.

Pete's open-door policy for his home and his life created a loyal fan base like no other. His burgeoning cult status turned him into a Pied Piper figure, a musician followed everywhere by a queue of devoted admirers, to whom he would talk about his ideas of Arcadia, play music and demonstrate how to give themselves a Libertines tattoo. He would be continually surrounded by women in their late teens and early twenties who would follow his every word. Many of his fans were extremely well informed about Pete, The Libertines and their ideas, having read about Albion and Arcadia on the internet, while a large proportion were educated, often still at university. At last, Pete had found a like-minded crowd who were intelligent and who shared his outlook on life. The mythology he had created in order to forge his own identity was now being adopted by them; the wandering, rootless individual had become a talismanic figure for other young people who had been lost children. It was a symbiotic relationship between Pete and his closest followers. Their presence fulfilled his need to reach out to people who understood him, while in turn they used him as a model for their own identities.

Pete knew that his project meant laying himself bare to his public, but he revelled in every minute of it. 'Being naked is what rock 'n' roll's all about, and opening the door and being honest with people,' he pointed out. 'If you can put on a great show and get people dancing, that's as important as anything.'

Pete showed how far he would go in taking care of his fans' needs during one gig, the legendary event in Wolfman's Chelsea flat in Gunter Grove, Fulham, on 28 May 2003, when more than 100 people crammed themselves into the tiny apartment. Pete told the fans that they should all write something on the wall using brown paint, which was provided in tubs, along with bottles of beer. As the venue warmed up, one teenage girl told Pete she had to go home to her parents' soon, asking him if he would mind playing her a song before she left. He took an acoustic guitar into the garden and played a whole set just for her.

It was inevitable that this intense rapport between Pete and his fans would sometimes develop into sexual encounters. Once the gigs were over, some of the fans would be invited to stay, and the aftermath of guerrilla gigs in the Albion Rooms was usually a highly charged affair. Pete would be snorting cocaine off the table, smoking his crack pipe and holding forth in front of a gang of devoted groupies, most of whom wanted to have sex with him or Carl or, possibly, both. Girls were readily available and Pete took to groupie sex with a passion, sleeping with dozens of women. Sometimes he would have sex with several girls in the same night, while on other occasions he had two, three and even four in his bed at once. Many of these hardcore fans shared Pete's liking for cocaine, crack and even heroin. There were orgies of sex and drugs that lasted all night.

For Pete, this was a terrific success rate. After being quite shy with women during his teens, he was now beginning to catch up with the more sexually experienced Carl. The pair even wrote an affectionate tribute to the groupie phenomenon with the track 'Boys in the Band', which featured on the *Up the Bracket* album. Although the duo had been famous for less than a year at the song's conception, plenty of experience went into the lyrics which spoke of the adulation of fans, specifically women prepared to 'get them out' for the band.

For the boys in this band, some of the fans would do virtually anything, exhibiting the kind of dedication that other groups in such a cynical era could no longer expect. Pete felt that he'd achieved this through giving the fans his affection; he believed that he'd given them love and that they gave it back in response. The experience left him ecstatic. 'The happiest experience we have ever had,' he enthused, 'is being together as the boys in the band, reaching the listeners' hearts and waking up Cupid too.'

CHAPTER 9

What Became of the Likely Lads?

'AS OF RIGHT NOW, OUR LIVES ARE MUCH LIKE BEFORE, EXCEPT THAT NOW WE LIVE THEM IN FRONT OF OTHER PEOPLE. BUT WE DON'T YET KNOW WHAT KIND OF EFFECT ALL OF THIS WILL HAVE ON US. MAYBE, IT WILL CONSUME US, AND IT WILL BE THE BEGINNING OF THE END.'
– *Pete Doherty*

Pete welcomed in New Year 2003 at the Albion Rooms on a high. True, he'd been smoking crack all night, but his euphoria wasn't just the product of chemical inspiration. The Libertines were at that point riding a wave of apparently unstoppable success. The *Up the Bracket* album had sold 100,000 copies since its release the previous October, while the group's guerrilla gigs had developed a cult-like following with an ever-increasing circle of fans. The band had supported The Strokes, headlined a string of their own sell-out gigs and made festival appearances at Reading and Leeds. Pete was living the life he'd always fantasised about, producing music for an adoring public, having sex with dozens of beautiful girls and taking lots of drugs. It all sounded so great, but lying in a mess of crack pipes, books, poetry, videotapes, CDs and old records, Pete was exhausted. His lifestyle was exacting a terrible toll.

By his own admission, in fact, Pete was taking too many drugs and seeing too many girls, and the combination was messing with his sensitive artist's mind. On top of that, there was strain on his relationship with Banny and Rough Trade, who wanted him to go on tour and produce singles and albums, whether he felt in the mood for it or not. It was a business for them, not the kind of spontaneous expression that Pete believed in. He felt as if he was on a 'conveyor belt', part of an assembly line in a factory producing rock 'n' roll. It was a view that might have appeared less than fair to Banny and the label, both of whom demonstrated amply that they cared about him and his music, but Pete felt that they were forcing him to make compromises, and, of course, the nature of the production process meant that this was bound to be true.

Pete's growing addiction to crack and smack, combined with his complicated love life, meant that he was even less likely than usual to toe the record label's line. He'd put up with Banny's scheme when it had seemed that his future had depended on it, but now that he'd broken into stardom he started to question whether such a degree of control over himself and his music was really necessary. After all, he wasn't particularly interested in the money that the production machine created, needing cash only to pursue his lifestyle. Expensive as that was (he was now spending around £1,000 a day on drugs), Pete felt that he didn't really need to continue pushing himself so hard to do what other people wanted.

Pete refused to be ordered around by Rough Trade. He

delighted in misbehaving and did everything he could to persuade Carl and the others to join him. On 4 January, for instance, just days before The Libertines were set to fly out to the Eurosonic Festival in Holland, Pete and Carl absconded to France in a van with Stéphane Moreau, head of French punk label Dialektik Records. Without bothering to mention it to Banny or Rough Trade, the two Libertines had agreed to do a recording session with Dialektik in the provincial city of Nantes.

They had met twenty-nine-year-old Moreau while on tour in France on 2 December 2002 at a gig at Le Chabada in Angers, in the Loire Valley. He had offered them a recording session without ever believing they would accept. To his surprise, however, they had agreed.

The plan was that Moreau would pick them up at the Albion Rooms and take them across the Channel. When Moreau turned up, however, he realised that Pete had made no effort to organise the trip. Gary was on holiday in Cyprus, John Hassall had other commitments, Rough Trade hadn't even been told, but Pete and Carl were ready. They brought along Alan Wass, guitarist for Libertines support band Left Hand, to play drums.

Pete and Carl hardly slept for the next four days, keeping themselves awake with large quantities of cocaine. As always, Pete's creativity was given a boost by the spontaneity of the occasion; during a ferry trip of just a few hours, they wrote several songs. On the evening of 5 January, they arrived in Nantes, where they got straight down to business in the Garage Hermétique, an improvised studio.

Back in London at Rough Trade, the record bosses were incredulous that the pair were prepared to wander off and breach their deal in such an offhand manner. Banny put in dozens of calls to Pete and Carl on their mobiles. The pair had been scheduled to turn up for an interview with the *Guardian* on 6 January and a gig in Holland three days later, for God's sake. Pete and Carl, of course, didn't care; they threw the mobile into the bin and kept on playing. 'Rough Trade were scared,' remembered Moreau later. 'They knew they couldn't control The Libertines, so they let them do it – with only one request [for me]: "Bring them back alive for the gig in Holland."'

Once the recording had been completed and the mixing done – a process that took only half a day – the Dialektik van drove to Groningen, Holland, where James Endeacott and Banny were waiting for the runaways. The lawyer and the Rough Trade man were fretting over what was at stake, which wasn't only money but also Rough Trade's reputation. Moreau remembered, 'They gave Pete and Carl a tremendous dressing-down. Banny was kissing them; the others were shouting at them. Peter and Carl were like little boys. They knew that they had done a damned stupid thing, but they liked it.'

Banny and Endeacott led Moreau into a room of the local Hôtel Mercure in order to conduct some intense negotiations. Eventually, Dialektik managed to acquire the right to release two of the songs recorded on the illicit session, while two other titles, 'Narcissist' and the ballad 'Through the Looking Glass', would later be released on The Libertines' self-titled second album.

Although the trip to France was typical of The Libertines' behaviour, some interpreted it as a reflection of Pete's burgeoning egotism. Those who worked with him increasingly saw him as arrogant and unrealistic, believing that his ego had inflated to monstrous proportions under the influence of fame and mind-bending chemicals. Carl, meanwhile, although accompanying him willingly on their rebellious jaunt to France, believed that The Libertines should carry on what they were doing, that Banny was right in wanting them to go on tour and pump out more records, and Gary and John believed the same. A gulf was developing between Pete's attitude to the music and Carl's and, because the two issues were related, it was also a division between their attitudes to drugs.

The emerging rift was reflected in the fact that Pete and Carl were beginning to move in different circles. Although still supposedly living together in the Albion Rooms, Carl was spending less and less time there and 112a Teesdale Street had become overrun by Pete's other friends. Instead, Carl had grown close to Danny Goffey from Britpop sensation Supergrass, and was developing a circle that encompassed actress Sadie Frost and other members of what Pete scornfully dubbed 'the Primrose Hill set'. To Pete, these people were insupportable in their self-seeking ambition; he felt that they had nothing in common with his commitment to real music, which he wanted to play for live audiences in East End squats. (Ironically, this attitude was compromised when he later began an affair with Sadie's best friend, Kate Moss.)

Despite his scorn, Pete was in reality more ambivalent towards this more mainstream celebrity set; he was once found in tears on Goffey's doorstep during a party, apparently upset at his failure to be accepted by Carl's new friends. Many who knew him believed that Pete's

135

attitude was just another symptom of the continual playground jealousy that existed between the two Libertines frontmen, with Pete being upset that Carl fitted in better with seasoned celebrities. Pete, however, insisted that such people were 'fakers' and labelled their leafy, affluent north London homeland a no-go area for anyone with credibility.

Later, Pete would identify this period as the time when he and Carl began to drift apart as they were drawn into different circles. Pete believed that, having become famous, the pair no longer needed each other as they had done when times were harder. 'All our dreams came true,' he noted later. 'We played every night for about a year and a half, started getting press, and then some of the reasons that I had needed him and he had needed me disappeared. Suddenly, he was the sexiest man in rock, so he didn't need me to tell him he was good any more, and I didn't need him to pull girls. So we lost each other.

Instead of following Carl into his new circle, Pete had developed a circle of his own that included people like the Wolfman (aka Peter Wolfe), who of course shared Pete's interest in hard drugs. Carl couldn't stand his bandmate's new crowd and hated the fact that his best friend had been taken over by the 'brown people', those whose friendship was based on taking heroin. He was also increasingly angry at Pete for inviting back to the Albion Rooms these people who would smoke crack in his bedroom and leave used syringes lying around. It wasn't as though Carl was a stranger to drugs himself, but he believed that Pete was stepping beyond the boundaries of what was acceptable, even in the world of rock 'n' roll.

That winter, the situation came to a head. One night, Pete, drugged out of his mind, found himself locked out of the Teesdale Street flat and chose to kick the door down. Now all kinds of people from the street could wander freely into the flat and squat in Carl's room. Carl couldn't take it much longer.

At around this time, Pete and Carl were booked to appear on BBC TV's flagship music show *Top of the Pops*. When they turned up to record their performance, scheduled to be aired on 24 January, Carl was unhappy with Pete's behaviour in the studio, in which he had once worked as a humble broadcast assistant, feeling that he was trying to steal the show by covering himself in pale make-up and bright lipstick and styling his hair in a huge New Romantic bouffant. He insisted that Pete had to abandon the outfit, complaining that it didn't fit with the band's image. Although Pete gave in to Carl's view, the incident was another example of the deepening rift between the pair, as Pete believed that the flamboyant gesture was exactly the kind of stunt The Libertines needed to make an impact on the world of mainstream pop. When Pete made a high-profile post-Libertines appearance on ITV two years later, where he spoke on television about Kate Moss for the first time, he adopted a similar, heavily made-up style.

The tension between Pete and Carl was eased in some respects by a frenetic touring schedule. When they were on the road, they were kept busy travelling and playing gigs all over the UK and Europe. During these periods, the disintegration of Pete and Carl's relationship was less obvious, and they continued their madcap antics. On the first Libertines tour abroad, in February 2003, there were reminders of the wacky days when Pete and Carl's friendship was at its best.

As the band played gigs in Sweden and Norway, the pair went on a series of typically eccentric nights out. In Sweden, they ended up in a foursome in a nightclub toilet. 'It was just girls, girls and more girls,' Pete recalled. 'We were fucking everything, everywhere. We had a great time.' Unfortunately, having a great time involved taking such quantities of drugs that Pete was on a knife-edge, which meant that his madcap antics easily gave way to full-blown addiction and self-destruction.

Pete's relationship with Carl was loaded with tensions that had been bubbling away for much of the previous year and finally erupted to the surface that February. At the *NME* Awards ceremony on 12 February 2003, Pete turned up in such a drugged-up state to collect the band's award for Best New Band that the magazine devoted a cartoon strip charting his progressively spaced-out appearance in its next issue. Carl and those present from Rough Trade felt he was so far gone that he had ruined a precious triumph.

Two weeks later, The Libertines were on the coach to King's Cross station, on their way to Germany to begin their European tour after wrapping up their winter on the road in the UK with a gig in the Rescue Rooms in Nottingham on the previous night. Pete was telling Banny how things were OK, how his drug-taking wasn't a problem, how the music was going well. His assertions didn't wash with Banny, however, who had just received a call from the band's third tour manager, who was threatening to resign. According to him, Pete was encouraging ever more violent stage invasions that were coming to represent a danger to the band's safety. Banny told Pete that things were not OK, that he was increasingly out of control and that he had to reduce his drug-taking.

Although he was perfectly aware that he wasn't easy to manage, Pete was in no mood to listen. As far as he was concerned, the stage invasions were all part of the plan. He wanted the audience to get involved with the gigs as much as possible, whether or not that was convenient for the tour manager and roadies. The ensuing row, begun over such a relatively minor point, escalated into an attack on his musical beliefs and way of life. 'Banny was hammering away at me,' he later remembered. 'She wouldn't let it go. I started to get a headache with all this stuff she was going on about. I had to get off that bus.'

Pete jumped off the coach at King's Cross, telling Carl he was off on an 'adventure' and begging him to come along. Everyone knew that meant Pete was out to score some crack. Still disturbed by the row with Banny and furious that Carl wouldn't join him, Pete left the bus and didn't come back. Instead, he blew a small fortune on drugs and spent the day getting high, smoking pipe after pipe. The band, contractually obliged to make the tour, had no option but to go ahead without him. Pete's dream of the boys being united in the band was rapidly disintegrating.

In the event, Pete bailed out of the European tour altogether, although during the earlier dates he had the option of catching a plane and taking up his position on the stage. The official version of events was that Pete was battling pneumonia and would join the tour the moment he shook off his illness. They expected him to fly out to Hamburg for a gig on 27 February at Schlachthof ('Slaughterhouse') with

Banny, who had stayed behind because of some other commitments, but again he failed to show.

The fact that The Libertines could and would carry on without Pete proved to be the shape of things to come. With hindsight, it was obvious that this solution had been several months in the making. He would never have believed it at the time, but the February 2003 tour of Scandinavia and Germany was the last that Pete would truly enjoy with The Libertines before they broke up.

Following Carl's return from Europe in March, the atmosphere between Pete and Carl was so tense that they could no longer put up any pretence of being able to live together. Since Pete had kicked down the door of the Albion Rooms a couple of months earlier, Carl arrived home to find that thieves had got in and stolen all of his gear. On top of the ever-present posse of crack smokers in his bedroom, that was the last straw. The following month, he moved out of the flat, selecting for himself his very own private flat in wealthy Baker Street. Pete felt that the move represented Carl's slide towards what was for him the dark side of the music business, the way of life of commercial and corrupt money men, while Carl quit the premises with a sense of relief, believing that he'd escaped the darkness of Pete's new friends.

Pete's commitment to the ideas behind the creation of the Albion Rooms commune was such that he couldn't understand why Carl wanted to leave. During the pair's early days there, they'd had a great time, both personally and professionally, having lived one long, continuous party while playing great gigs and writing great songs. Carl, however, felt he had to explain: 'We were a little bit like

Morecambe and Wise for a while, but I've always been really in my own space, and we didn't have that in the Albion Rooms. In the end, I had to get out because of Peter's new friends.'

Pete and Carl held one final farewell guerrilla gig that ended with Carl putting his fist through a window and the arrival of a vanload of police. In a brilliant final hurrah, the lads serenaded the boys in blue with a version of The Clash's 'The Guns of Brixton'. The song asks the listener whether they would go quietly when the police come knocking at the door, or if they would point a gun at them instead.

Pete's behaviour became increasingly unstable, and during The Libertines' foray to Japan in March 2003 his madcap antics gave way to pure destruction. The band went down well in Japan, playing at a series of packed venues and even appearing on a mass-audience TV show, *Battle of the Bands*, with Japanese indie group Mo'Some Tonebender on 15 April, but the pent-up tension in the group erupted during one telling incident in Sapporo. On that occasion, Pete, who was having difficulties getting hold of enough drugs to stave off withdrawal symptoms, suddenly felt an urge to smash up the set while the band were on stage. He trashed John's amp and Gary's drum kit before storming out and going for a shot of sake in the bar across the road.

One tour that Pete did want to go on, meanwhile, was the two-week trip to the US in April–May 2003. Although by now considerably well travelled, Pete had never been to New York or California and was keen to have a look at both. As it turned out, he had to postpone his arrival by a day because of the death of his maternal grandmother, and his mood on arrival in Los Angeles was consequently somewhat subdued. Pete's loss and subsequent late arrival also meant the group had to cancel their first date on 24 April, in San Francisco. When he arrived to play at the Coachella Festival in Indio, California, two days later, things got off to a shaky start when technical difficulties meant that the plug was pulled on The Libertines after only two songs. Pete cheered himself up by racing a couple of golf buggies with Carl.

After three days in the west, Pete and the band were off to New York where they were lined up for a recording session, a series of gigs and an appearance on the famous *David Letterman Show* on TV. Their first date, a sell-out gig at the tiny but trendy Luxx Club in Brooklyn, was a resounding success; the packed crowd gave the band an enthusiastic reception and Pete left the place in a triumphant mood, heading back to his hotel Off Soho Suites for an all-night celebration. Pete and Carl ended up in a hotel room playing Chas 'n' Dave numbers on their guitars in front of a small collection of new friends. The next day, the band were due in the recording studios, and that was where things began to fall apart.

Pete would later boast that on that trip he'd picked up a crack dealer within two hours of landing at New York's John F Kennedy Airport. Carl remembered witnessing Pete's new method of scoring and the consequences that followed. 'Someone had told Pete that, if you wanted crack or brown outside of London, you simply had to ask a homeless person. To him, that was "Bingo!" To me, that was, like, "Dur, why do you think they're homeless?" All of sudden, Pete's crying in my room, saying, "I've got all these people in my room." I had to go down to his room and kick them out. They're sitting there, getting their free hit, and Pete's upstairs crying. I'm thinking, Where is this going?'

Pete suddenly found himself with a group of new, homeless, crack-addicted friends, some of whom were young, female and willing to accept more than just free drugs. They were so loyal that they wouldn't be parted from Pete for a moment, and insisted on accompanying him to the studios. Carl remembered, 'There was Pete and his new friends having their little crack fun. They were singing this song – which is my tune – adding and changing bits. Then a girl says, "Come and sing. It's fun. Shall I teach you the words?"' Carl left the studio in disgust.

The recording session that was supposed to take place in New York was never finished. However, Pete and Carl did manage to make a good impression on *Letterman*, which had an audience of 60 million people. The pair arrived at the studio in the Ed Sullivan Theater on Fifty-third Street to discover that Marilyn Manson was also putting in an appearance on the same programme. Typically, Pete and Carl were completely undaunted by his presence and decided to make fun of him, calling him by his real name, Brian, while after the recording, on the steps outside the building, Pete pretended to Manson's fans that he was the star's stepbrother, donning a hat and sunglasses and speaking with a slow, drugged-up American drawl.

Earlier, in front of the camera, Pete and Carl had worn their trademark red guards' jackets and given a sound performance of 'I Get Along'. Pete had been thrilled to play in front of such a massive new audience, his only disappointment being that he didn't get to sing on the show; only Carl had a vocal part on the track.

The *Letterman* experience meant a lot to Pete, and two other gigs in New York also went down a storm, proving just as popular as the first one at the Luxx. However, he infuriated Carl, Gary and John during a performance at the Bowery Ballroom by inviting his crack dealer on stage to do a song. The audience was oblivious to the significance of what was happening, however, and interpreted it as a generous gesture to a random member of the public.

Pete turned up five minutes before the start of each of these gigs, and left immediately afterwards to hook up with his New York drug friends, who were in the process of introducing him to a whole new range of experiences. He learned how to inject heroin and smoked crack with gangsters in the city's vast, forbidding tenement Projects. By his own admission, the ten days Pete spent in New York were a dark period full of sinister and frightening elements, during which he found his levels of aggression were spiralling. Carl could see that Pete was going off the rails and suggested that Pete 'take it easy' and take a break from touring with the band.

Pete did not listen. He was frustrated with Rough Trade, feeling that the label sent him to the US on another promotion drive when all he wanted to do was create some new music. The anger, cranked up by the drugs, exploded into rages that were more extreme than any of Pete's previous temper tantrums. Evicted from Off Soho Suites, he smashed everything in his new room at the Chelsea Hotel, then turned up at Rough Trade's New York office demanding to use the computers in order to access the internet. The staff were suspicious of this haggard youth they'd never met before, who stank of alcohol and crack, and their response was to attempt to get rid of him. Pete was furious, screaming at them that he was a millionaire and the new owner of Rough Trade, before flinging a computer to the floor and smashing a bottle of red wine against the wall.

For all the thrills of the Big Apple, Pete felt a wave of relief wash over him when he stepped off the plane at Heathrow Airport. Back in London, he wasted no time in getting stuck into what was becoming by far his favourite musical activity: staging guerrilla gigs. At the end of May, Pete held a soirée at Wolfman's flat in Gunter Grove. The other Libertines opted to give the event a miss, largely because of Wolfman's involvement, but nevertheless more than a hundred fans turned up to the cramped basement flat, to be treated to Pete's solo efforts. The event came to an abrupt end as the police were called and a fight broke out, but it was still given a write-up in the *NME*.

Pete was delighted with the reaction he was getting from these gigs, but he was disappointed that Carl didn't turn up for them. He was desperate for Carl to get more involved, for a return to the spontaneous knees-ups they had created at the Albion Rooms, and so he organised another guerrilla event on a rooftop in Whitechapel and tried to push Carl into coming along. The day in question happened to be the same day as Carl's twenty-fifth birthday party, and he was due to celebrate it by going out for a meal with his family and friends. Pete, however, wasn't having any excuses; for him, this gig was what The Libertines had come to mean. It would be an event of pure performance and communion with the fans in which they could put all the troubles of the European and US tours behind them. Over a meeting in

Regent's Park, Pete enthused about the guerrilla gig project, telling Carl how fans would turn up from all over the country, die-hard fans who would follow The Libertines whether or not they did what the record label wanted. Pete's insistence was such that Carl agreed to turn up as soon as his birthday dinner was over.

The night arrived, and a crowd of fans came to Whitechapel to see The Libertines perform a gig on top of a roof. The atmosphere was terrific, with the crowd singing along to Pete's numbers; everyone there knew the words. But the minutes ticked by and Carl didn't show. Barât had made the decision that the evening with his family was more important than a small-scale event that couldn't even boast a proper venue. Carl's family and friends did not want him to leave, and he didn't want to leave them. He was faced with the question, why should he sacrifice the rest of his birthday for Pete's project and the demands of a small number of fans?

Pete had such a belief in what he was doing that he couldn't understand the terms of this question, let alone Carl's decision not to come. In his view, it was fine to drop out of whole tours, because all they were about was making money for the music businessmen, but dropping out of a guerrilla gig was a much more serious crime, as it meant letting down people who really loved the music. He'd invested so much of himself in the idea of being a people's minstrel that he saw Carl's failure to show as a flagrant snub of everything he stood for. 'He didn't show and he didn't even fucking call,' he said after the event. 'I needed him there. He broke my fucking heart.'

Inflamed by what he saw as Carl's betrayal, Pete hit back

by refusing to accompany the rest of the band on their summer tour of Europe. The truth was that he didn't want to go anyway. He'd had enough of promotions, PR stunts and going on the road for weeks, playing gigs in strange places where he didn't want to be. To Pete, touring had become a chore rather than the pursuit of the increasingly marginalised Arcadian dream. Pete wanted to be in what he'd made his home city, surrounded by people who knew and admired him and his music, with easy access to his usual crack and heroin suppliers and friends who shared his habits. He'd created a lifestyle wrapped up in an ideas system, and the result was such a powerful force that it swept away other considerations like the things Carl, Banny or Rough Trade wanted him to do.

Carl's take on this situation was that Pete had been taken away by 'dark forces', forces that were certainly powerful enough to separate Pete from his band. While The Libertines played on across the continent without him, Pete was performing a bewildering series of guerrilla gigs in all kinds of venues, from the back streets of Whitechapel to the Red Rose Labour Club on the Seven Sisters Road. He was developing his breakaway band Babyshambles, a project that he regarded as his very own, beyond the control of Banny and Rough Trade and anyone else who wanted to limit him. In June 2003, he set up the website babyshambles.com, which would publish news of his guerrilla gigs and his online diaries.

Although Pete claimed that he could live perfectly well without The Libertines' support network around him, in reality he was going through a difficult time. On top of what he saw as Carl's betrayal in not turning up to play at his guerrilla gigs, Pete's policy of opening up to his fans and inviting them into his home had finally revealed its dangers; someone had accessed his precious email account, he had attracted several stalkers and he had even begun to receive death threats. What was more, his passport seemed to have disappeared. Worst of all, another of his relatives, his aunt Lil, had died.

By mid-June 2003, Pete had become completely immersed in a dangerous world of drugs and self-destruction, sleeping in the homes of the new friends with whom he had surrounded himself. One experience he had at the home of a female fan was typically disturbing. When Pete tried to leave her house, she became hysterical and locked herself in the bathroom. Pete kicked the door down to find her slicing at her arms with a razor blade. Rather than attempt to calm her down and seek medical help, Pete's actions were equally alarming: he began slashing at his own arms. As Pete remembered, 'In a blind rage I seized the blade and, well, it is all rather disturbing the action I had to take to shut her up – ie show her that two could play at that game.'

At this point, however, Pete remained in a state of complete denial, refusing to accept that he had a drugs problem or that his behaviour had become in any way unstable. At the time he wrote, 'I am not (nor ever have been) addicted to heroin, crack cocaine, sodomy or any of the other lot currently dripping from my name like doppily glew.'

He'd decided that he'd had enough of being bossed around and forced to go on tour when he didn't want to. He wanted to be at home in London, where he had a lifestyle to lead and the funeral of his aunt Lil to attend. He thought that the rest of the group would forgive him for not turning up, not believing for a moment that there was any chance of them not allowing him back.

Also, Pete wasn't entirely satisfied with the line-up of the band. Despite their invaluable contribution, he had doubts about John and Gary's involvement, being unsure they were true Libertines and true believers in the Arcadian dream, rather than just seekers of fame and fortune. He was starting to believe that his and Carl's ideal had been warped into nothing more a money-making machine. 'It was just a case of "Let's get the best-looking people and be as much like The Strokes as possible,"' he said later. 'That was the idea at the time.' Not for a second did he suspect that *his* place in the band was in jeopardy – after all, he and Carl *were* The Libertines. He thought that they were touring without him purely out of contractual obligations. At the time he wrote, 'The Libertines is an ever-changing, swirling, unpredictable monster of a band, and line-ups change as often as I do brogues... not every week but "Don't ever get too comfortable if you're not Carlos or Myself", basically, is the rule of things. The boys are not playing Libertines gigs; they're doing their best not to get Banny sued for breaching European gig contracts.'

While The Libertines were limping onwards to Paris in mid-June, Pete called Banny to tell her that he was on his way. She told him not to bother, saying that even Carl didn't want him any more. Pete couldn't believe it; he said he thought it was a 'sick joke' and told Banny his old friend would never turn him away from a gig. She in turn said that he should ask Carl himself.

Minutes later, Pete received a call from Carl. What followed was a key scene in the demise of The Libertines, a scene that Pete would always regard as a terrible betrayal. Forcing himself to utter the words, Carl said that Banny had been right. It had been decided that Pete shouldn't return to the band, and it was down to Carl to tell him. 'It was the hardest phone call I've ever made,' Carl remembered. 'I phoned him from Paris and said, "Don't come." He was gobsmacked. I don't think he thought I was capable of it. I think he knows why I did it, but, in a childish way, he won't forgive me.'

Pete had let the group down, and he was no longer wanted in Paris. They could get along without him. Carl explained it was down to Pete's 'condition', that his drug-taking was simply out of control and that Pete wasn't capable of going on tour until he tackled the problem. The tone of his voice was deadly serious, and Carl said his piece without any trace of the humorous banter with which he usually spoke to his friend. 'It was like it wasn't him,' Pete recalled. 'His voice was really far away, like it was a different person. I just couldn't get my head round it.'

Pete realised that Carl, Gary and John felt that he'd let them down badly. He admitted he was at fault, but believed that his punishment was way beyond what he deserved. He'd suffered family bereavements, after all, and he felt that the rest of the group hadn't been sympathetic. They hadn't taken into account problems such as the loss of his passport, and were instead determined to blame everything that went wrong on his drug habit. Pete simply couldn't understand why he was being excluded from his own band. Although he realised what Carl meant by his 'condition', he felt the suggestion that his drug addiction was out of control was overblown.

Pete's reaction was to devote still more of his energy to his breakaway Babyshambles project, his mood one of defiance. He told fans on an internet message board, 'I'm getting on with things without any of them, though God knows I love him. It's not happening any more and it's the way it is. Fuck 'em. And fuck all you who sit back typing self-preening, running me down. Carlos asked me not to play, that he didn't want me, so that's that.'

Pete believed that, by excluding him from the band, The Libertines had betrayed everything they stood for. It was as if the scales dropped from his eyes and, in place of the hedonistic, decadent group he had founded, he saw nothing more than a commercial enterprise, a job of work that needed to be done to make more money.

One of the reasons why his rejection came as such a shock was the wider significance he ascribed to it. Pete felt that he was the only one left who believed in the ideals on which The Libertines were based. By insisting that he did whatever tours and promotions Rough Trade wanted, the other members of the group had, in his view, reduced his artistic vehicle to merely a part of the music business.

In a rant he posted on a fan forum, Pete railed against what he saw as the belittling of his creation. 'The Libertines is more than a four piece band you read about in the *NME*,' he wrote, 'just as *Up the Bracket* is more than a Rough Trade album. It is a now eight-year-old blueprint for life, and an uncustomised illegal/illicit manoeuvre in the Arcadian hinterland. We have been forced to operate in this manner in order to grab your children's attention, in order for the real show to start, in order for justice to be done. There is no such thing as a backstage pass or hospitality tent in Arcadia. Do not be conned. Music is free; come and get it. Roll up, roll up, donations welcome...'

Although The Libertines had thrown him out, the Arcadian project that the band represented would live on. Pete was determined to see to that; his ideas had been trampled on only to be reincarnated in another form.

Spurned by the rest of The Libertines, Pete responded by withdrawing into a world that the rest of the band had little to do with, voicing an intention to seek out more understanding companions. He felt rejected even by his fans, who had expressed disappointment at his failure to go on tour. 'The recent responses from Libertines fans have made me a little bored and weary,' he related. 'I think a sensitive, more open-minded crowd of ears awaits me.' Such statements were interpreted by many who knew Pete as a coded way of saying that he was heading still deeper into drugs, while some were starting to suspect that music and drugs had become so intimately linked in his mind that his real motive for carrying out guerrilla gigs was a desire for instant cash in order to fund his habit.

That accusation, made by several in the music industry, infuriated Pete. 'If I want drugs, I don't have to do a gig to get them,' he argued. 'I do a gig when I feel shit, because I need to be playing. There's no drug in the world that can compare with playing music.'

Even when The Libertines arrived back in the UK, Pete remained estranged. The band played without him at the Forum in Kentish Town and at the Glastonbury Festival. Then, later that summer, they went on to perform at the Reading and Leeds Festivals, major venues with large crowds, all without Pete.

…herty's relationship with supermodel Kate Moss garnered acres of newspaper coverage.

Top: The Libertines appeared on *Later with Jools Holland* in October 2002.

Bottom: Noel Gallagher reportedly told record producer Alan McGee (*left*) that the Libertines were the next Oasis.

p: Doherty and Peter 'Wolfman' Wolfe released their single 'For Lovers' at the Virgin egastore, London in April 2004.

ttom left: Doherty's relationship with Carl Barat was often stormy.

ttom right: Kill City vocalist Lisa Moorish (*left*) is the mother of Doherty's son Astile.

Top: The Libertines picked up the NME Carling Awards for Best New Band in 2003. Doherty, who had been sacked from the band because of his drug problems, was sentenced to six months prison on 8 September, after pleading guilty to burgling Barât London flat.

Bottom: Doherty was given a four-month suspended prison sentence in August 2004 fo possessing a 4-in flick-knife. He arrived at the court singing the Oasis song 'Whatever'.

n June 2004, Doherty spoke frankly about his heroin addiction to reporters at his
London flat (*above and below left*).

Bottom right: Still in trouble with the law, Doherty was embraced by fans after
appearing at Snaresbrook Crown Court on charges of robbery and blackmail in
February 2005.

Top: Babyshambles pose for the cameras before going on stage at the Nokia Isle of Wight Festival in June 2005.

Bottom left: The group had played at the second Children of the Tsunami Concert at the Garage, Islington earlier in the year.

Bottom right: Doherty was engulfed by fans in Trafalgar Square during the Unite Against Racism concert on May Day 2005.

Top: Elton John and Doherty kiss during their performance of 'Children of the Revolution' at Live 8.

Bottom: The video for Babyshambles' second single 'Fuck Forever', released in August 2005, was filmed at London's Spitalfields Farm.

Several UK newspapers described Doherty's performance with Babyshambles at Live 8 as 'shambolic'

Whereas Pete had felt stung when Carl said the band didn't want him in Paris, by this point he really didn't care about being left out. He shut out any thoughts about what the band were doing, immersing himself totally in his new scene, consuming ever more vast quantities of hard drugs.

For Carl, meanwhile, touring without Pete was an extremely difficult experience. He was carrying a huge responsibility on his shoulders, and felt like he couldn't win the battle for media approval. 'A while ago, a French journalist talked about the gig we played in Paris, Elysée–Montmartre,' Carl recalled shortly after the tour. 'The guy told me that the gig had been crap. That's normal: I was tense; I couldn't stop trembling. I felt so lost that I puked up before going on stage. And for what? The media and even fans began slating the band: "Without Peter, without the poet, blah blah blah, The Libertines are dead. Carl Barât is a wanker!" Things are more complicated than that. Pete is my friend, and I can't imagine that band without him, but at the same time I'm not sure that, if he was touring with the band, it would calm him down. He needs treatment first.'

The one piece of Libertines business that Pete managed to get involved with that summer was the recording of the single 'Don't Look Back into the Sun'. He knew that he was in trouble straight away, however, when he discovered the track was being produced by Bernard Butler. He deliberately kicked against Butler's commanding approach by flaunting his crack pipe in front of him in the studio, and on one occasion he arrived so late and so drugged up that Butler sent him home. Pete believed that he was in a process of creation that couldn't and shouldn't be fitted in to a nine-to-five schedule – which, given the state he'd got himself into, was a convenient idea. He screamed at Butler and threatened to batter him unconscious before spinning unsteadily on his heels and walking out.

Following this row, Pete hit back by becoming even less reliable, hardly ever turning up to the studios. In the end, Butler was forced to play Pete's guitar parts himself, while the band just managed to get enough of Pete's vocals recorded to enable them to finish the track.

Making the single – a song that he and Carl had written in Paris – had been a miserable business, and Pete had barely enjoyed any of it. He was pleased with the song's lyrics, though, feeling once more that they'd captured in words what The Libertines were about. They were the renegades on the run, like the soldier-deserters of Pete's imagination, the comrades in crime who liked living outside of society's rules. Given that Pete was now using heroin up to five times a day, there was a certain sharpness to the lyrics, which spoke of having a preference for 'living strange'.

When the single hit the streets on 18 August 2003, the fans greeted it as another glorious affirmation of The Libertines myth. It received enthusiastic reviews in the music press and reached number eleven in the charts. The problems during recording were widely known but little cared about; the track was being pumped out by every radio station, attracting a mainstream audience for the band in greater numbers than ever before. The shift into mass-market appeal was ironic, given that Pete was at the time renouncing all that in favour of cult status in the London music cliques.

Worse was to come. The Libertines were booked in for another tour of Japan in July, a contractual arrangement that, if broken, would result in severe financial penalties. The Libertines were doing very well, commercially, in the Far East, even outselling what some saw as their American counterparts The Strokes. From a business point of view, it would have been madness not to go, but, by this stage, Pete really didn't care what the money men wanted. He refused to see their logic, and the only explanation they could find for that was his drug habit.

There was no denying that Pete's addiction to crack and smack had grown into a monster. Those close to him started to suspect that his ideals were beginning to be formed by the strong physical need for a fix. Whatever the reality, in Pete's mind there was no truth in this whatsoever. He didn't want to go to Japan because he didn't believe in it; that had nothing to do with the drugs. According to Pete, heroin and crack were part of his process of creation. They didn't influence his opinions about the money-making business of music. He hated that regardless, whether he was on drugs or not.

To his management, Pete was a man in denial; to the fans who turned up at his guerrilla gigs, he was a misunderstood idealist. In fact, he was probably a mixture of both, but his conception of the circumstances in which he found himself would once more prove a formative influence on events. Rough Trade decided not to push Pete on the matter of Japan. Instead, the label decided that it would put him into an addiction rehabilitation programme to rid him of the substances that stopped him from seeing sense. In the lead-up to Pete's first stint of rehab at Farm Place, near Dorking,

Surrey, the label hired a pair of security guards to protect him from himself. They then moved him out of his squat, put him in a safe house and followed him wherever he went.

Pete detested the scheme; he was being controlled, and he'd never enjoyed that. The minders were a large, powerfully built pair who had a habit of dressing in black. They didn't chat and they wouldn't be persuaded to do anything they weren't supposed to do. Pete became so desperate to get away from them that he tried to escape from them the first chance he had. This occurred while he was being driven by the minders down Essex Road in Islington. When they got out of the car to use a public phone, Pete jumped into the driver's seat and put his foot down. Unfortunately, it had been some time since Pete was last behind the wheel, and he didn't have a driving licence. He'd also forgotten about changing gears. Over-revving the vehicle in first, he blew the gearbox. The minders dragged him from the car by his heels as smoke billowed from beneath the bonnet.

That June, Pete was admitted to Farm Place, but didn't believe he really needed any kind of rehab. He felt he'd been pushed into the programme by the record label, just because he wouldn't do what it wanted. Given this, it was unsurprising that he was out after six days, on the bogus excuse of attending Wolfman's fictitious wedding.

Pete felt under huge amounts of pressure during this period. One of his girlfriends, Lisa Moorish, was about to give birth to his child. The baby hadn't been planned; indeed, the responsibilities of fatherhood had been the last things on Pete's mind at the time Lisa conceived. In his diary, Pete drew a telling picture of the situation, showing himself hijacked on a plane with the words 'Moorish Air' scrawled across the fuselage. He felt that the baby was something that had happened to his life that was beyond his control. He was flying into fatherhood under Lisa's direction, with no option to bail out. For a man who liked to dabble in love and avoid responsibility, it was a terrifying prospect.

Despite the vortex of emotions that raged inside him, Pete turned up to see the birth of his baby son, Astile, in July 2003. He'd spent the previous day pickling his brain in huge quantities of drugs and was in a physical state that bordered on the medically sedated. The birth left him deeply moved, but no less disturbed, and he followed it by disappearing for six days on a drugs binge. Lisa was beside herself with anxiety over Pete's condition, blaming his vanishing act on the drugs. She believed that he'd become so hooked that he couldn't do anything other than get out of his mind every minute of the day.

Not for the first or the last time, Pete discovered that people couldn't believe his acts had any motivation other than crack and heroin. Pete was under pressure from demands of the band, his girlfriends and the mother of his child. Banny and Carl feared for his safety. Former girlfriends believed that 'something really bad was going to happen'.

It did.

CHAPTER 10

Can't Stand Me Now

'IT ISN'T DRUGS THAT I NEED TO GET RID OF; IT'S THE
DEMONS THAT FILL MY HEAD.'
– *Pete Doherty*

It was 25 July 2003, less than a week after the birth of
Astile, and Carl was away with the remaining
Libertines on tour in Japan. Pete turned up at his best
friend's door. He knew Carl wasn't there but he rang the
buzzer just to make sure. Carl's sister, Lucy, had been
staying at the flat, although Pete was not aware of that.
Getting the lack of response he expected, he started kicking
at the door in a frenzy. After several efforts, he succeeded
in booting the door down – and proceeded to ransack the
place. He stole a guitar, laptop, video recorder, harmonica
and CD player, loading the loot into a car parked outside
in Baker Street. Pete made no attempt to conceal the
burglary, kicking the door in noisily, wearing nothing to
disguise his features, staggering around in the busy street,
carrying out the items of music equipment one by one. He
was so high on crack that he didn't even notice the passers-

by staring at him as he got into the car with the booty of his crime. It was an appallingly amateurish effort.

Hours after carrying out the burglary that Friday, Pete answered the phone to Lisa for the first time since Astile's birth. He told her what he'd done, adding that it meant he might not be around for a good while. Already in a state of emotional turmoil, Lisa was plunged into shock by what she heard. She felt she had no choice but to call the police, believing that Pete had become so out of control that he had to be locked up, as much for his own sake as anyone else's. His behaviour was becoming so extreme that she feared the next step would be still more destructive, possibly suicidal, and so found herself in the curious position of reporting the father of her newborn baby for burglary.

Down at the station, police doctors found high concentrations of crack and heroin still circulating around Pete's bloodstream. From their point of view, Pete was among dozens of thieves driven to crime by a need for drugs money, and indeed there was an element of truth in their assessment. Pete was addicted to hard drugs and was short of money, being at that point around £300,000 in debt. He did need cash for his next fix and, if he'd got away with his crime, he'd almost certainly have sold Carl's gear. However, he could have chosen to burgle anyone's flat, yet he'd selected Carl's as a target, not just because he wanted money but because Carl wasn't there to give it to him. His former companion had gone off on tour without him, was running The Libertines without him, and the closed door of his new flat was for Pete a symbol of that rejection.

It didn't matter to Pete how much his own actions had contributed to the estrangement; on that day, high on drugs

160

and in a state of emotional turmoil, Pete wanted Carl to be there but he wasn't. He would later struggle to explain his course of action, arguing, 'I went to speak to Carlos about how I had a drummer and bass player living on my floor. They're on the dole and I needed to pay them because they're musicians. I was going down to Carlos's to say I couldn't pay them out of my own money, and I found myself shouting at him. It turned out I was arguing with my reflection. When I realised this, I booted the door in. I was engulfed by complete misery and despair. It wasn't revenge. It was more, "Why are you ignoring me?" – a cry from the darkness. I do feel remorse. I feel sick.' Pete also tried to justify the burglary by claiming the goods he 'stole' were his own. It was a particularly bohemian robbery, but a robbery all the same. None of the excuses really washed.

For once, Pete was eager to place as much blame as possible on the drugs, telling a crowd of reporters, 'Yes, I'm a heroin addict. Yes, I'm addicted to crack cocaine, and I don't know what to do. I'm all cut up, unsure. I don't know what I'm doing. I need a good kicking and I need some help.' All of a sudden, the drugs provided a useful excuse.

However, the mind-bending substances that induced Pete to row with his own reflection were only a part of his motive for the break-in. Gary had his own take on the cravings. He believed that these feelings Pete struggled with were as important as heroin or crack: 'It was Peter once again crying out for attention, and the only way he could do that was burgling his best friend. There were millions of people he could have done that to. He chose Carl.'

The target of Pete's need for attention found out about the burglary as soon as his plane touched down from

Japan, when he discovered a message from Banny on his answerphone warning him about what had happened. On listening to it, Carl said he felt himself 'descend a bit deeper into this very painful world... To begin with, I was shattered. How could my best friend dare go into the privacy of my home while I was away? I was sharing the flat with my sister. She had serious health problems. When I learned that Peter had burgled my flat, I immediately thought that, had my sister been there, she could have had an attack.'

Although at times he skirted the issue of his need for Carl, Pete made a characteristically full and frank confession of the burglary at Horseferry Road Magistrates' Court, in Westminster. He then checked into the Priory in an attempt to rid himself of the addictions that almost everyone blamed for this act of desperation. Alone in his room in the clinic, battling the pangs of withdrawal symptoms, Pete felt swept away by guilt for the betrayal of his friend. In a message posted on a fan website on 16 August, he wrote, 'Carl. I'm sorry. I'm so sorry, so truly, and I love you and I'm here.'

On 8 September, Pete returned to Horseferry Road to be sentenced. By this stage, he'd convinced himself that he wouldn't be jailed, turning up in a mackintosh and trilby and smiling confidently for the benefit of the assembled TV crews.

Judge Roger Davies, however, didn't see anything to smile about. He said, 'Doherty was suddenly earning too much money for his age and began behaving irresponsibly. Unlike most of us who have to study and work hard, they suddenly acquire wealth. He continues to pursue a hedonistic lifestyle which involves the heavy use of drugs.' He sentenced Pete to six months in jail.

Pete's show of bravado was flattened by the decision. He was in shock, his mood instantly deflated into one of depression and downright terror. He knew himself well enough to realise that prison would be difficult at best for him. He already felt imprisoned enough by the mental manacles of society; how, then, could he cope with a real metal-and-brick cage?

When he arrived at Wandsworth Prison in south London later that day, it was as bad as he'd expected. The grim Victorian structure built of London brick stained black with grime was crowded, cramped and notorious for its tough regime. The officers were stern, the prisoners even more so. Pete was constantly frightened of both, later admitting, 'I was scared all the time, totally paranoid. I thought any one of them could do me at any time. It was a real shock.'

Pete found that he could easily get hold of heroin in Wandsworth (though crack was harder to come by), but his encounters with the prison dealers left him in a still more perilous position after one of his friends on the outside failed to deliver cash to the required address. On that occasion, Pete thought he was about to get a battering – or worse.

For a few days, he was moved to Standford Hill Open Prison, on the Isle of Sheppey, Kent, where he received a visit from his mother, grandmother, Lisa and baby Astile. He felt ashamed to be seen by them in these circumstances and was glad when they'd gone. Later that week, Carl also turned up for a visit, only to find that Pete had been moved back to Wandsworth because his solicitor was filing an appeal.

Pete had plenty of time to himself in jail. He found that the only positive aspect of his incarceration was his once-weekly access to the prison library, where he would stock up on five or six books at a time, inspiring his own writing and throwing himself into words. It felt, he said, like a lifeline.

Apart from that, the hours dragged on, and he spent many of them mulling over what had happened between him and Carl. He felt painfully guilty about the break-in, to the extent that he could deal with it only by trying to blot the memory from his mind. After all, it was supposed to be a bit of a laugh. Never did he think he would be held to account for his actions. Pete had thought that he could rely on Carl through thick and thin, and, even though Carl had nothing to do with Pete being arrested, Pete couldn't help but feel that he'd been let down and abandoned. 'I couldn't equate it with even the slightest idea I had of reality,' Pete confessed later. 'Things like going to prison are so horrendous, I think it's going to take me some time to talk honestly about how I feel about it. I'm managing, so far, to shut it out pretty well. I've never been to prison. That's the way it has to be.'

Although Pete was a sexually liberated man outside prison, one of his biggest fears inside was being molested by a fellow inmate. He was quite prepared to experiment with consensual homosexual acts, but being raped by a convict was another matter entirely. Luckily, he avoided any such ordeal, but there were times when he felt perilously close to suffering it. Inside Wandsworth, he found what he described as 'Individuals that you happen to be put in a cell with, someone who you really don't want to be in a cell with. Some nasty piece of work, getting his dick out all the time and saying, "Is this normal, Pete?"'

Much to Pete's relief, at a hearing at Middlesex Guildhall Crown Court, his solicitor, Richard Locke, managed to get his sentence reduced to one month, securing his release for 8 October. The news spread rapidly among Pete's fans, sparking frantic message-board attempts to get him lined up for his first guerrilla gig. The event, which would become known as the legendary 'Freedom Gig', was organised by a Libertines fan called Dean following a phone call and letter from Pete the week before his release and was scheduled to take place at the Tap 'n' Tin pub in Chatham, Kent, on the evening of the day that Pete got out. The tickets, priced at £10 each, were sold out in a matter of hours, even though the unpredictable nature of being released from jail meant that it was impossible to promise that The Libertines would definitely arrive.

As excitement about the show buzzed across the internet, the big question remained: how would the other members of the group, and Carl in particular, react to the freed Pete? It was certainly a question that occupied Pete's mind, and Carl, too, spent a lot of time thinking about what he should do. He'd taken the news of Pete's jail term hard, feeling responsible for the fact that his best friend had been locked up, although in reality there had been little that Carl could do to stop the wheels of justice from turning. Pete was charged by the police, and the case against him was brought by the Crown Prosecution Service. Contrary to some fans' belief, Carl had nothing to do with it, and yet the facts of the case didn't stop Carl from blaming himself. 'When I heard Pete was going to jail, I broke down,' he remembered. 'It's a stupid reaction, but I thought, I've jailed my friend. It was bollocks, but I couldn't help it.'

That Wednesday morning, Carl got up at 6am – a time of day that was uncharted territory for a libertine – and made his way to the gates of Wandsworth Prison. Many of those he knew advised against making the gesture, but he told them he was going to meet Pete because he didn't want 'the bad guys' to get to him first. He arrived at the prison gates at 7.30am, whereupon he hung around with a few fans and reporters.

Eventually, at 11am, the huge heavy doors swung open and Pete came walking out with a plastic bag inscribed 'HM Prison Service' slung over his shoulder. He was surprised and delighted to find his old friend waiting for him. The strife that had landed Pete in prison was forgotten in an instant, and he and Carl were hugging each other in front of the cameras. Pictures of the meeting say more than either Pete or Carl has done on the subject, showing the pair striding away from the jail with their arms wrapped around one another, Pete clasping the bag full of his belongings. Relief and joy at seeing each other is written all over their faces. Waving to the fans, Pete shouted, 'Up The Libertines!' before jumping in a car and heading for central London.

In the West End, Pete made for his accountant's office to get some money, then went straight to the nearest pub. He and Carl knocked back whisky mixed with ginger beer and got drunk as rapidly as possible. They were chatting and joking just as they had in the days before they'd made it big and were soon the closest of friends on the loose in London once more. 'That afternoon was pure elation,' Pete remembered. 'It felt fantastic to be out.'

As the afternoon turned into evening, Pete and Carl staggered forth to find their way to the Freedom Gig. Carl caught the train from Victoria station, while Pete went off to see his sister Amy Jo in Lewisham, stopping off to buy some crack and heroin on the way. The duo converged again on the Tap 'n' Tin pub in Chatham, a town that neither could remember having been to before. They were greeted there by an ecstatic crowd of 200 people – fans who had made it to Chatham via train, bus and car from all over the UK. The atmosphere was one of raw, unadulterated elation as Pete, Carl, Gary and John reunited in the back room to belt out Libertines numbers like there was no tomorrow. It was what the *NME* described as a 'once-in-a-lifetime gig'.

Pete and Carl gave a performance of incredible energy, considering that both had been drunk to the point of leglessness earlier that day, and performed some of what had become their classic tracks. Songs like 'Boys in the Band', 'Time for Heroes' and 'Good Old Days' were played with such raw emotion that some of the lucky 200 fans later referred to that gig as the best night of their lives. In the end, however, the alcohol caught up with Carl as he attempted one leap too many and landed on a bollard, falling over and slicing his chin open. Pete rushed to his aid, grabbing a mobile phone and calling 999 for an ambulance. The Freedom Gig finished with Pete playing the nurse to his friend, holding him in his arms as they waited for the paramedics to take Carl to hospital.

The feelings of unity and tenderness that enveloped that

night in Kent could have spelled a new beginning for The Libertines. Indeed, that was what everyone in the band was hoping for: the chance to start again. Just as Pete was looking forward to getting back on track, however, Banny resigned. She simply couldn't take any more, after the débâcle of the burglary, and washed her hands of the band, despite having been the woman who'd formed it. It was a hard thing to do, throwing away a group and a style of music that had been built on her ideas, and her decision to pull out just as the band were becoming a mainstream name cost Banny serious injury to both her pride and her bank balance. It's a measure of how difficult The Libertines were to manage that someone as determined as her couldn't stick with them any further.

Banny had prepared the band for the bad news during the summer, telling them that they'd have to find someone else to sort out the second album, so Gary approached Alan McGee at the Reading Festival and asked him to take over, after Pete had already got in touch with him by phone. McGee's decision to accept the challenge should have meant that things were looking up for The Libertines; the veteran of bruising periods at the helm of Oasis, Primal Scream, My Bloody Valentine and The Jesus and Mary Chain, McGee obviously had what it took to deal with the most chaotic and difficult artists. If he couldn't turn The Libertines around, nobody could.

The timing of the takeover, just after the Freedom Gig, meant that McGee was starting off when the band were on a high. He decided that what was really necessary was for Pete and Carl to go somewhere quiet, spend a few days together and thrash out their differences, and he chose his country home near Hay-on-Wye on the Welsh border as the location for this love-in.

McGee invited Pete and Carl to stay in his picturesque stone Victorian house, surrounded by the Black Mountains, in mid-October. The environment there was suitably atmospheric and Arcadian for Pete, with a springy, rusty old brass bed in his cold room, an antique reading couch and a bandy-legged desk. He and Carl set up a miniature studio in the echo-filled library using a digital recorder and amps.

At first, the duo got on relatively well, squabbling slightly, writing the lyrics to 'What Became of the Likely Lads?'. Then, one night when they had been drinking heavily, a row broke out. Pete couldn't remember exactly what had caused it; they'd been talking about the past, about the drugs they had taken. Whatever the origin of the dispute, however, the effects were unexpected and disastrous. At four in the morning, Carl leaped from his chair in a fury, stalked into the bathroom and repeatedly smashed his face against the sink.

Pete was astonished by the scene, but in his anger and drunkenness he did nothing to intervene. It was as if Carl was acting out his hatred for him, and Pete didn't want him to stop. It was only in the sober light of the next day that Pete realised just how much damage Carl had done to himself. His face was completely mangled, requiring dozens of stitches. He'd almost lost the sight in one eye and needed repair work to the surrounding socket to make sure the eyeball stayed in place. Carl was taken to the local hospital, then to an eye specialist, where he was fitted with a patch to conceal the damage, but it would be a month before his injuries were sufficiently healed for him to be able to go out and walk the streets.

Pete's shock was shared by the new manager, who, as Pete put it, found that he had on his hands 'a genius songwriter with a penchant for crack and a sex symbol who likes to beat himself up'. McGee came to the conclusion that The Libertines were the most extreme band he'd ever encountered, their volatility exceeding that of Oasis or any of the others by a country mile.

Pete spent the afternoon of 24 October waiting for Carl to return from hospital, ploughing through McGee's video collection in an attempt to take his mind off the situation. He got through footage of The Jesus and Mary Chain, Morrissey, The Who and Bob Dylan before Carl turned up, looking like a pirate with an eyepatch strapped to his face.

Following Carl's return, the atmosphere in McGee's house was tense. That night, the three of them – Pete, Carl and McGee – had dinner together in an evening punctuated by embarrassed silences while Carl, still drowsy from the effects of his anaesthetic, struggled to make conversation. That night, Pete tried to comfort his friend, accompanying him to his room. 'I told him he was my best friend and I cared for him so much, was worried about him and loved him,' Pete remembered. 'He held me and said, "Its been a long time since you said that."'

Pete felt guilty that he hadn't tried to stop Carl from hurting himself. The sense that he was to blame for Carl's injuries was reinforced when he received an anonymous text message that read, 'Peter, you are an evil, manipulative, jealous bastard. You've hurt Carl one too many times.' The unnamed messenger was the first of many to blame Pete for Carl's moment of self-destructive madness.

Because of Carl's injuries, the recording of The Libertines' second album – which at that point was due to be produced by Bernard Butler – had to be put off for five months. In the meantime, the band carried on performing, with Carl wearing an eyepatch.

On 19 November, 150 fans squeezed in to watch a gig at the Duke of Clarence pub in Islington. Even Mr Razzcocks made an appearance, joining in when the band played songs from the early days such as 'Love on the Dole', 'Bucketshop' and 'Seven Deadly Sins'.

Once Carl's face had healed up, towards the end of November, The Libertines took to the stage for three sell-out dates at the Kentish Town Forum. The shows received a rapturous response; Carl's performance seemed to have acquired a newfound confidence, while Pete just looked delighted to be back playing in his band.

The relaunch of The Libertines, complete with Pete, was an emphatic triumph. However, developments behind the scenes reflected a disturbed atmosphere. Having witnessed events at Hay-on-Wye, McGee hired security guards to protect Pete and Carl from each other, and from themselves. The burly heavyweights, whose wages were paid by the band, were nicknamed 'the Twins'. McGee claimed that they were a necessary precaution to stop Pete and Carl from killing each other.

Under an uneasy peace, The Libertines were able to throw their Christmas party at the Whitechapel Rhythm Factory with thirteen other bands, having scraped through 2003 just about intact. The end-of-year event, held on 23

December, was a riotous all-night affair, providing a bill consisting of all the band's close complex of allied friends and performers, organised by The Queens of Noize DJs, Mairead and Tabitha. The hundreds of attendees, late onstage timings and three bars in close proximity to one another resulted in yet another memorable evening. On this occasion, however, The Libertines' euphoria was inspired by a sense of relief that they'd made it through the year rather than the uncomplicated exuberance that had underlined similar events in the past.

During this period, Pete found that he was enjoying the gigs much more than he had in the months leading up to his arrest for burglary and, as soon as the festive season was over, he went with the band on a sell-out tour of venues in Glasgow, Manchester and Birmingham. This time around, life on the road didn't seem so stifling. However, the tension with Carl was to resurface at the end of that winter UK tour.

In February 2004, The Libertines were booked to play three nights running at the Brixton Academy. On the last night, Pete felt a wave of self-disgust engulf him as he and Carl were singing 'Can't Stand Me Now'. Pete explained, 'It had taken six, seven years for him to say it, to say the truth: can't stand me now. He sang it to me and I thought, You're right. We've used each other, got here, but, underneath it all, you're not my mate. So I kicked his amp over, smashed his guitar and cut myself up.'

Pete stormed out of the club and indulged in his habit of expressing his self-hatred by cutting himself, this time slashing open his chest with a razor blade in the street outside the door. In this case, he'd found his hatred reflected in Carl, who later insisted that he'd been singing with no more feeling than normal. Others put Pete's reaction down to paranoia caused by tiredness at the end of the tour, exaggerated by drugs. In Pete's mind, however, when Carl had chanted the words 'can't stand me now' that night, he'd really meant it.

Ten minutes after experiencing this surge of emotion, Pete reappeared on the stage with lines of blood crossing his chest. He was greeted with a deafening cheer from the fans, who took it all as part of the theatre, while, in fact, his angst was real and verging on the dangerous.

Later that night, bandmates and friends waited outside the dressing room. The atmosphere was fraught – no one was sure what might happen between Pete and Carl – but, when the door was finally opened, there was no strangeness. The pain had been buried once more. 'The worst thing they did,' Gary said, 'was ignore the fact that things have gone wrong between them. They've never once tried to sit down and talk to each other.'

The continuing turbulence between Pete and Carl prompted their manager to attempt a repeat of the peacemaking getaway to his home in the Black Mountains, and the pair were sent for some recreation, this time to Paris. This was partly to remove Pete from his habitual surroundings of London crack dens, while he and Carl also hoped to relax sufficiently to create some new songs. They stayed in the red-light district of Pigalle, in a hotel next door to a shop called Le Sexodrome. Typically, the duo embarked on a drinking binge, running up a huge bar bill that they couldn't afford to pay, and were compelled to play a series of free pub gigs in compensation.

The following month, the band, accompanied by their security guards, started to record their second album. Pete found it a difficult business, his relationship with Carl growing worse seemingly by the minute. During the very first session, the pair had another scuffle on the set and had to be forced apart.

Carl, Gary, John and the management had all made an effort to keep Pete happy in one respect, having gone along with his wishes to replace Bernard Butler with Mick Jones as producer of the album. Pete's dislike of Butler, however, ran contrary to the opinions of others in the band. Carl, for example, believed that Butler could get The Libertines to number one in the charts, although after the disasters of 2003 he was willing to compromise. 'I like Bernard,' Carl admitted. 'He's a nice bloke. He'd already produced the singles "What a Waster" and "Don't Look Back into the Sun". I think he did a hell of a good job. There's only one problem with Bernard: he is, let's say, a tiny bit strict. He can behave like a dictator or a policeman. I don't mind but Peter hates authority. It reminds him of his father. At the beginning of the sessions, Bernard and Peter never stopped having rows. Peter refused to work in that atmosphere and ran away. To make him come back, we had to find a compromise. It was Mick Jones.'

Jones was Pete's favourite producer, following the success of their studio partnership during the recording of the first album. The ex-Clash man had the ability to work with Pete's unpredictable, flamboyant nature, managing to control him without appearing to be authoritarian. Jones would sit for hours while Pete screwed himself up into performing mode, seeming to possess a limitless patience, and, despite the interludes between Pete's bouts of creativity, the recording was done at a furious pace. In effect, the band played live and non-stop for three weeks, the urgency of the moment ultimately reflected in the album's dirty, rough sound.

Pete and Carl managed to overcome their differences for most of the recording sessions, but the atmosphere between them was tense and cold. They seldom spoke to each other about anything other than the business in hand, the co-operation between them being limited to what was necessary in order to get the job done. Wherever they went, they were shadowed by the security twins, after McGee had instructed the bodyguards to make sure that Pete and Carl never ended up in a room together without them. The measure appeared overcautious, but in the event it proved justified. Under the thin veneer of ice-cool civility, Pete was struggling to keep a lid on his anger, while Carl, too, was ready to explode at the slightest opportunity.

The inevitable flashpoint came when Pete told Carl that he wanted to apologise to his sister Lucy about the break-in. There was no doubt that Pete was sorry the burglary had scared her; he hadn't known she was living in Carl's flat at the time. Carl replied that Pete couldn't go near his place until he'd got himself clean, that he was still on heroin and everybody knew it.

Pete snapped. He jumped on to a glass table that lay between them and launched himself from it, landing on top of Carl with his fists flying, pummelling Carl in a fury while his more solidly built bandmate began striking back. The twins stepped in to drag them apart, and the fight was over in less than a minute, but its viciousness had been evident for all to see. 'I wanted to kill him,' Pete admitted. 'If the twins hadn't got in the way, I'd have done for Carl or he'd have done for me. It was that bad.'

The results of their fractious time in the studio, however, were worth it, making the overused 'difficult second album' cliché appear laughable. With their self-titled follow-up to *Up the Bracket*, the brawling Libertines managed to produce one of the most honest and introspective offerings in recent rock 'n' roll history. Although not as raw as its predecessor, *The Libertines* told the true story of the band, laying bare their fights, their disasters and the threat of their impending demise. The drug-fuelled merry jaunts through the streets of London referred to in their debut were replaced with a tone of regret that spoke of overindulgence and withdrawal. From the moment that Carl followed the fading chords that opened the album, singing of a love so strong that it became destructive, it was clear that this was going to be a very special record. In 'Can't Stand Me Now', Carl and Pete revealed their feelings about the drugs, the burglary, their friendship and the rows to anyone who wanted to listen. The song brought tears to the eyes of many fans.

At the other end of the album was the moving sister track to 'Can't Stand Me Now', 'What Became of the Likely Lads?', featuring more sharp references to the band's troubles and confirming Pete as Britain's best lyricist since Morrissey. The lads talked of forgiveness and of being 'thick as thieves', Pete sung the characteristically punning and punchy lyrics and the pair bounced off each other like a comedy double act. The story was honest but optimistic, harking back to days when it was Pete and Carl against the world. While the song suggested both would like to reforge that bond, it was obvious to listeners that their relationship had disintegrated beyond repair.

Elsewhere, the aptly named song 'The Saga' was Pete's most explicit discussion of his addiction on the album. Sung in a desperate snarl, Pete admitted on the track what he'd rarely confessed to his closest friends, singing of the lies and deception that drug addiction lead to, acknowledging that you know you've got a problem once you start lying to those close to you and deceiving yourself that you are okay. However, in a break in the track, he found time to mutter words more familiar to those who tried to talk to him about his habit, accusing them of being the ones with 'the problem'.

In his retort, 'Road to Ruin', Carl admitted that he was 'sick of it all' but encouraged Pete to trust in him and take him by the hand.

The album wasn't just made up of new songs; the band also drew on an impressive library of finely polished pieces that hadn't found a place on the first album. Old and new were placed side by side: 'Don't be Shy', 'Music When the Lights Go Out' and 'What Katie Did' all reflected the band's sensitive side, while 'The Ha Ha Wall' and 'Last Post on the Bugle' had a classic Libertines sound and showed the band at their energetic and chaotic best. Pete would later exploit his long catalogue of unreleased songs to full effect with Babyshambles.

'The Man Who Would Be King' was one of the most accomplished and polished works the band had ever produced. The better-educated big brother of *Up the Bracket*'s 'Tell the King', it's a masterpiece that took the band beyond the brilliantly raw punk sound of their debut, betraying Pete's obsession with classic films and TV programmes. In the cult 1975 British film of the same title, Michael Caine and Sean Connery play two soldiers who abandon their careers of serving Queen and country and travel to remote Afghanistan to set themselves up as rulers. Connery joins some renegades in an attack on a nearby city and, during the ensuing fighting, is struck in the chest by an arrow, but miraculously survives uninjured. The arrow had in reality hit his cartridge belt and failed to penetrate his flesh, but the Afghan natives believe he is a god. Connery then attempts to make them give up their riches to him.

Pete saw something of himself in Connery's character, in his abdicating from what he saw as conventional life with the intention of entering a creative, imaginative arena in which he would be monarch of all he surveyed. In 'The Man Who Would Be King', Pete sings about being able to live his dream. However, he did acknowledge the potential pitfalls of pursuing his dream, and this was also made clear in the film, when Connery eventually falls into a self-deluding arrogance, starting to believe his own lies rather than leaving with the treasure he has collected.

With Mick Jones back at the helm, *The Libertines* had traces of the raucous sound of *Up the Bracket*, but it was more polished and poignant than its predecessor. For most fans, The Libertines' first album was a life-changing work, but their second confirmed exactly why the band changed their fans' lives in the first place. Critics had accused the band of being a fraud, of making a soap opera of their troubles as a marketing ploy, but what they didn't understand was that, for those who had tuned in from the first episode, the music was the soap opera and the soap opera was the music. The fights, the burglary, the drugs, the facial injuries, the emotions – they were all real and the band were prepared to explain them in song.

The recording of the second album was, by Libertines' standards, a professional, focused affair. The sessions took place over two months but, in terms of actual time spent in the studio, the project took three weeks to complete. However, the friction between Carl and Pete meant that it had to be cobbled together to a certain extent, with songs that had been in Pete's locker for years being wheeled out to make up the numbers; 'Music When the Lights Go Out', for example, was on the band's demo, *Legs 11*, which had helped to get them signed, but hadn't been included on the first album. Such a blend of older and newly written songs actually gave the album immense depth; nobody could accuse the band of having thrown together a bunch of half-finished songs. In reality, much of the album had been several years in the making, and it showed.

The autobiographical feel to *The Libertines* was captured in the front-sleeve picture, a shot of Pete and Carl taken at the Freedom Gig that the band had played immediately after Pete's release from prison, with the pair displaying their matching Libertine tattoos. In the picture, Carl is bronzed, beautiful and staring square into the camera, while the pallid Pete's eyes are downcast. While Carl looks muscular and protective, Pete appears withdrawn and fragile, his pose suggesting that he was preparing to inject more drugs.

Pete, who had always taken an enthusiastic interest in

the band's artwork, later claimed that he had no say in the cover, slamming it as being 'irresponsible' for its glamorisation of drug use. In fact, the image, like every other aspect of the album, told the story of Pete and Carl, of their friendship and its betrayal, with an honesty that left nothing concealed or glossed over. 'We didn't hide any detail,' Carl explained. 'Drugs, treacheries, reconciliation – everything's in it. *The Libertines* is the most auto-biographical record in the world. The day we entered the studio, it was clear: we knew this record could be our catharsis. We'd accumulated too much dirty linen. We had to pour out everything.'

Carl was absolutely right about the breathtaking honesty of the album and the story it told. Sadly, he was wrong in predicting that its creation would have a cathartic or therapeutic effect. Rather than purging The Libertines of their capacity for self-destruction, the album served only to chart that demise and capture it for posterity. By the time it was on the shelves, Pete was out of the band – this time, it appeared, for good.

CHAPTER 11

Clinical Melancholy

'I DON'T WANT TO TURN INTO PETER LIBERTINE,
THE REHAB KING.'
– Pete Doherty

With his spectacularly erratic behaviour, followed up by his frank confessions, Pete was fast becoming the most famous drug addict in Britain. By the end of 2004, everyone knew about his chemical appetites; even people who had never heard a Libertines or Babyshambles track identified Pete with heroin and crack.

It was a state of affairs to which Pete had never aspired, being one that perhaps reflected the interests of the public rather than his own intentions. He wanted to concentrate on the music and, beyond that, the ideas. The hedonistic beliefs that guided Pete's life portrayed drugs as part of the creative process, not an end in themselves, but the slippage – from drugs as a sideline towards drugs taking centre stage – seemed irrepressible. In keeping with the pattern of Pete's life, in which reality appeared always to follow on from fantasy, this public perception was mirrored by a private situation in which drugs were becoming more and more central to Pete's own view of himself.

First of all Carl, then the record label, then the general population developed the opinion that Pete had gone way off the rails. They fitted him into the stereotypical rock-star story in which the drug-addicted artist destroys himself and the band, a case of 'He had it all and threw it all away'. The script was oversimplified, however, and rode roughshod over many facts that didn't fit. For instance, Pete's heroin addiction was well under way before The Libertines had signed their first deal; it didn't hinder their rise to stardom, so why should it be guaranteed to precipitate their demise? And, at times when Pete was supposedly too drugged up to be in The Libertines, he was perfectly capable of performing gigs for his breakaway band Babyshambles. Indeed, several of Pete's acts that had been blamed on the drugs' influence, such as the burglary of Carl's flat, were in fact driven by severe emotional disturbances, feelings of isolation, hatred and envy. Pete's reliance on narcotics was a symptom as much as a cause of these other problems, but the complexities were rounded off in the image of 'Junkie Pete' that was propagated in magazines and newspapers.

When Rough Trade first sent Pete into a rehabilitation clinic, in June 2003, he regarded the move with something akin to a sense of injustice, feeling that he was at the time being forced into rehab when, in fact, he didn't want to give up crack and heroin. He was in denial about his medical condition; although in his heart he knew that he was hopelessly addicted, he maintained the fiction that he was still taking drugs from choice – the classic mental strategies of an individual with a serious problem.

The situation was made worse, however, by the mythology that sprang up concerning Pete's time in rehab. The implication was that Rough Trade was sending him to a clinic because his addictions were responsible for his failure to perform. In fact, it was more the case that Pete didn't want to perform the way the label wanted him to. He'd had enough of promoting records and going on tour, and now just wanted to write songs and play them for his fans, which was why he kicked against the disciplines of the music business.

At the time, of course, such explanations were overshadowed by Pete's habit, which transformed the public's perception of the situation into one of Junkie Pete screwing up. The manner in which the label was misaligned with the facts actually made it easier for Pete to maintain a state of denial about having a problem with drugs at all; he could point out that the difficulties with the band were down to other matters, accuse everybody of twisting the story and dismiss rehab as a sham.

Pete's sojourns at rehab would gradually strip away the convenient fiction about his habit destroying the band, revealing the reality of a personal medical problem of life-threatening proportions. Pete would never be convinced that the break-up of The Libertines was all down to drugs, but he would eventually come to see that he had to get off them, or at least to reduce his intake of them if he was to survive.

When Pete was taken to the Farm Place rehabilitation clinic in Surrey in August 2003, his medical problem was obvious. He was spending up to £1,000 a day on heroin and crack. He was smoking or injecting heroin five times a day and smoking dozens of crack pipes during a session. He was spending whole days and nights in crack dens, surrounded by the desperate and homeless with their debris of pipes and needles, all of them out of their minds. At times, he was so high that he would hallucinate, seeing the air in front of him dissolve into a sea of locusts. He would develop rashes all over his body. His eyes were sunken. If he couldn't get a fix, he would be shaky, anxious and sometimes furiously angry.

Pete arrived at the clinic after Rough Trade lured him out of hiding by promising to discuss his Babyshambles project. During the meeting, he was persuaded to give rehab a go and was whisked away to Surrey in a car. The move was so sudden that he didn't even have a change of clothes.

When he got there, Pete hated the place on sight. The moment he arrived, he felt depressed and sick. Isolated in a manor house surrounded by ten acres of parkland, Farm Place was claustrophobic, with room for only nineteen people. Pete was horrified to see himself bundled together with other drug addicts and alcoholics, most of whom were more willing to accept the fact that they had a condition. The calm words of psychiatrists, doctors and counsellors filled him with dread. Hard days of withdrawal stretched ahead of him, and he tried to pass the time by posting lengthy emails to his fans. His commitment to weaning himself off drugs was belied even in the detail of his chatroom nickname, 'Heavy Horse', suggesting copious heroin use. One typical message saw Pete describing himself as the 'lamb in the land of the leper'. He regarded himself as an innocent being demonised, made into an outcast suffering from a lethal, contagious disease.

Pete's misery was compounded by dwelling on thoughts about his burglary of Carl's flat. He spent his days crying, occasionally trying to distract himself from his pain by the incongruous act of bursting into song. He sought relief by confiding in a maternal, middle-aged Irish nurse, who he felt was sympathetic to his view that the people who had brought him to Farm Place didn't have his interests at heart. In his diaries, Pete described the nurse telling him there was a 'hallful of bastards' waiting outside, pretending to be his friends.

Pete didn't want to be in Farm Place. He didn't believe in what he was there for and wanted to get out. To this end, he called his friend Wolfman and asked him for help.

Their escape plan was simple and effective. Wolfman rang the clinic, telling them that Pete was expected at his wedding. Six days after arriving at the centre, Pete left in the back of a taxi. The 'wedding' turned out to be the marriage of a syringe full of heroin and a crack pipe. He wouldn't be going back.

It was almost a year before Pete made his next attempt to get off drugs. In the meantime, his life had shown ample evidence of their destructive influence as Pete had plunged headlong through jail, absentee fatherhood and a string of failed relationships. He had almost been pushed out of The Libertines the previous summer, having been replaced for a period by New York rocker Anthony Rossomando.

By 2004, with new manager Alan McGee in charge and the group's second album to record, Pete had reasons of his own for wanting to clean up. He entered the Priory clinic in Roehampton, southwest London, with trepidation and under pressure from his management, but this time he didn't have to be kidnapped.

The Priory is an imposing sight, set in the white Gothic building of a Victorian hospital. Not just a rehab centre, it's also a psychiatric hospital, treating all manner of conditions, from anorexia to schizophrenia. It has been the haunt of so many troubled stars that it has rarely been mentioned except in the company of words such as 'exclusive' or 'celebrity'. Those who have undergone treatment at the Priory include Richey Edwards of The Manic Street Preachers, snooker star Ronnie O'Sullivan, footballer Stan Collymore and even Pete's future love, supermodel Kate Moss.

When he arrived at the Priory on a Friday afternoon in mid-May 2004, Pete was in a state of totally unrestrained addiction. Apart from a short break from crack during his month in prison the previous autumn, he'd been smoking it constantly since his six days in Farm Place, eleven months earlier. During the same period, he'd been taking heroin without any pause at all. If anything, his usage had increased to even more epic proportions. Doctors at the Priory told him that he'd taken enough drugs to kill most people and that his survival meant his constitution was a scientific marvel.

Pete took a grim pride in the resilient qualities of his mercilessly abused body, struggling to keep his spirits up by resorting to black humour about his condition, communicating with his fans through messages uploaded to his Babyshambles website. In one entry, he spoke of the large amounts of medication the doctors were giving him to ease withdrawal symptoms: 'The detox programme I'm on is capable of bringing the entire Russian Olympic team to its knees. They have whacked me on loads of medication, sixteen different colours of pills. I have a very deranged and murky recollection of the last few days.'

Indeed, Pete found himself in a zombie-like state for much of his time at the clinic. The diary entries from this time often have a surreal quality, speaking of periods of unconsciousness or dreams that appeared to merge with reality. Another passage reads, 'A gaggle of nurses around my crinkly bed. They all jump as I wake up and yelp something about jelly. Then I notice a needle sticking out of my arm and spots of blood. Vomit and shrieks, some girl warbling down the corridor in a towel. At least my laptop is here still. The only one who ever stood by me.'

As that last sentence shows, Pete felt desperately lonely in the clinic, cut off from all his friends, family and fans. His sense of isolation was a painful reminder of the long, lonely days of his childhood. It was broken briefly with the arrival of Carl on a visit, but Pete did not find that a pleasant experience. Carl's appearance was well intentioned; he'd come to give his old friend some support, despite the fact that in recent times they'd barely said a civil word to each other. He'd gone to the trouble of visiting Loftus Road and bringing photographs of himself outside the QPR's home ground, and he'd also brought Pete a pair of QPR swimming trunks and suggested that the two of them could go for a dip.

Carl's gestures of friendship, however, were muted by circumstances; he was accompanied by one of the eighteen-stone security twins, and it turned out that the swimming pool was shut. For Pete, all Carl's visit achieved was to remind him of the relationship he'd lost.

The messages of loneliness Pete sent out from his laptop inspired a group of his fans to turn up at the Priory, pretending they were his brothers and sisters. Like Carl, however, they failed to cheer him up; Pete was so removed from his surroundings by heavy medication that he could barely register their presence in his room. His feeling of having been abandoned was made worse by a depression brought on by the chemical effects of coming off heroin and crack, one of the psychological consequences being a slowing down of time, so that the minutes seemed to take forever to tick by.

Pete was initially checked into room eighteen at the Priory, before moving to room seventeen a few days later. His programme of heavy medication was gradually decreased as the withdrawal symptoms began to ease, and his diet of various pills was supplemented with warm milk and liquorice sweets. Despite the treats and the medicine, he was gripped by fits of severe anxiety and felt too distressed to read much of the mail sent in by sympathetic fans.

Pete stuck at his programme at the Priory for a week, although it felt to him like a year. Then he just left, telling staff that he was off to see the FA Cup final after a friend had bought him a ticket. It was less transparent and more truthful an excuse than Wolfman's bogus wedding had been; Pete really did watch the game, but he also went straight to his dealer and bought some heroin and crack.

At this stage, Pete was in the middle of recording the second Libertines album, and McGee had imposed a spending limit on him in a bid to prevent him from buying drugs, at least until the record was cut. So Pete sent online messages to his fans, begging for funds. One post ran, 'Will someone lend me £1,000 until the album comes out? I'll do a one-on-one, any song you like. Or gig for the cash on the nail.'

Pete eventually raised some money by giving an interview to the *Sun*, in which he spouted a string of lies claiming he'd left The Libertines, smoking crack all the while he spoke to the newspaper's showbusiness reporter. Pete was no stranger to embellishing his stories and liked to play a few games with those who wanted to interview him, but his disturbed appearance on this occasion reflected more desperation than playful mischief. In tears, he launched a public swipe at Carl, saying, 'It's got to the point where Carl and I don't speak except on stage. It breaks my heart. He treats me badly and every time I come running back like a battered housewife. I feel like I'm seeking the ghost of a former friendship, but Carl gave up on me years ago.'

The bitter complaint was a sign that the isolation Pete had felt at the Priory had really got to him, and his feeling of being marooned had been exacerbated by his estrangement from his parents. The separation from his mother, Jackie, and father, Peter Sr, had been in place for years. He'd hardly spoken to his father since leaving home at the age of seventeen. As a child, he'd been much closer to his mother, but he'd seen little of her since The Libertines were formed, filling the void left by the absence of his parents with his intense friendship with Carl and numerous girlfriends.

As Pete faced up to his crisis, Jackie and Peter Sr were living on an army base hundreds of miles away in Germany. The public revelation of his drug habits had been the final straw for his father, who had told everyone in the family that he was disowning his son. Jackie was more sympathetic to his plight, but Pete hadn't given her the chance to communicate with him, let alone help him. Now, at the age of twenty-four, barely on speaking terms with Carl and battling with rehab, Pete missed his mother like never before. 'I've broken her heart,' he mourned.

As soon as he'd come down from his post-Priory binge, Pete called Jackie at the army base. He'd been a fool, he said. He wanted to stop the drugs, and he needed her help. It was a plea that Jackie answered immediately. She'd been keeping track of Pete's life through his older sister, Amy Jo, and was beside herself with worry about his precarious state. A plan was hatched for Pete to drive in the company of his current girlfriend, Irene, to Paris, where his mother would meet him and take him to another rehab clinic in the city.

When Pete arrived in France at the beginning of June, his reunion with his mother turned out to be an emotional occasion. Both were in tears, and Jackie promised that she would help see him through his addiction. She told him she was very worried about his health, that the stories of his drug abuse were so distressing that she couldn't sleep at night. However, she'd had bad news of her own, having discovered a lump in her breast that she feared might be cancer. She vowed to get it checked out and treated, as long as Pete would do one thing for her: go to the Thamkrabok Monastery in Thailand, known as the toughest drug rehabilitation clinic in the world. Pete couldn't refuse. 'I think that was unfair to put so much pressure on me,' he remembered, 'but I went anyway to prove I would do it for her.'

On his admission to the French clinic, Pete was fed a

daily cocktail of strong medication comprising Zopiclone, a sleeping tablet intended to combat the severe insomnia brought on by withdrawal symptoms; Lorazapan, a drug which dampened the fits of extreme anxiety he was suffering; and Olanzapine, prescribed to stop him from developing psychotic symptoms under the strain of coming off crack and heroin. During his time there, he tried to occupy himself by watching the England football team play Japan and by listening to the mixes from *The Libertines* album that had been sent to him by Mick Jones, while his craving for crack and heroin was so strong that he kept counting the hours since his last fixes, writing the times repeatedly in his diary. His mother was present at his bedside for much of this time, removing his stashes of cannabis and making sure that he didn't abscond.

Pete spent a week in the Paris clinic, then headed back to London for a day's break, which he spent at Carl's new West End club night, Dirty Pretty Things. The following day, he boarded a plane bound for Bangkok. He had no idea what he was letting himself in for; he'd been suffering from the shakes and vomiting throughout the previous week as he withdrew from crack and heroin and hadn't felt able even to research the monastery on the internet. He had a vague idea that the regime there was strict, although he assumed it would be more or less the same as the Priory but in a warmer climate. He couldn't have been more mistaken.

The Thamkrabok Monastery, owned by the *EastEnders* soap actress June Brown, prides itself on succeeding with addicts whom other clinics have failed to help. The Buddhist settlement, located in the mountains of the Saraburi province of central Thailand, has been treating

191

long-term addicts since the 1960s. Sprawling over 784 acres, the centre deals with an average of 500 addicts each month, a third of whom come from abroad, like Pete did. The residents there are placed under twenty-four-hour armed guard in case the withdrawal process leads to any violent behaviour. Their programme consists of five days of rigorous cold-turkey detox, after which patients are put to work around the monastery. Addicts aren't given any drug substitutes to soften the withdrawal, and on occasions Pete could hear them wailing in pain. They are made to sing the Thai national anthem every day.

Once a patient has overcome his addiction at the monastery, he or she is required to sign a vow never to take drugs again before leaving. The monks who run the centre include Phra Gordon, otherwise known as Gordon Baltimore, a former US Marine from Harlem, who explained the regime as follows: 'The patient is nothing but a robot. We push the button to decide when he eats and when he sleeps. Once someone starts his programme, the only way he can quit is when he's dead. The method of punishment is the bamboo stick.'

On 9 June 2004, Pete arrived at the monastery, where he was met by a monk carrying a pair of red pyjamas. These were to be his uniform during his treatment; he would not be permitted to wear anything else. The monk showed him to his quarters – a bare bunk bed in a room containing fifteen shattered-looking fellow residents – and, after a restless night during which the sound of chanting monks was played constantly through speakers in the ceiling, Pete woke up the next morning to find that there was no breakfast. Instead, he was given a shot-glass of a resinous, bitter-tasting black liquid made of 108 seeds, leaves and tree bark, then made to drink several pints of water. The mixture was intended to make sure that Pete spent the rest of the day vomiting – and it worked. He threw up until there was nothing left to expel, until he felt so sick he could barely walk or talk.

The aim was to get rid of any residues of heroin and crack as quickly as possible. In further pursuit of that goal, the monks put Pete, along with nine other addicts, into a giant steam bath. Scalded on the outside, scoured on the inside, Pete felt like he was in Hell on Earth.

June Brown had given Pete a free ticket to be treated at the monastery, without which he would have had difficulty making the trip, still being heavily in debt after spending around £300,000 on drugs in the past year. He was hoping that the proceeds from the new Libertines album – currently being finished in his absence – would soon lift him back into solvency. However, although the monastery was an ideal choice financially, in every other respect the place was far from being well suited to Pete's temperament. His one source of comfort was the sound of The Strokes' *Room On Fire* album, which a Swedish addict staying in the room next to Pete's played continuously. Apart from that, Pete could find nothing to alleviate the unremitting torture he was going through.

Pete had been booked in for a course that was supposed to last ten days. Instead, after just three days, he had a miniature nervous breakdown, collapsing in a flood of tears. He simply couldn't handle the degree of discipline imposed by the monks. In his diary, he wrote, 'Thamkrabok Monastery have done everything they could to help me, but

I am not strong enough for this treatment.' He went on to explain, 'I wanted to go home so badly. I was crying in the night and the afternoon. I had a breakdown.'

Pete demanded to be let out. Although the monks protested that he hadn't finished his treatment, he couldn't stay in the centre a minute longer. He grabbed his passport and luggage and headed for the cheap heroin of Bangkok.

Back in the Thai capital, Pete found a hotel that handed out a drugs menu to residents when they checked in. 'They offered room service of heroin with my bacon and eggs,' he recalled. 'I told them I had no money, but they said I could have it on tab. I notched up a £280 bill in three days. If I'd done the same amount of brown in England, it would have cost me thousands.'

By this stage, of course, Pete was totally broke; he couldn't afford the air fare home and was in danger of getting stranded in Thailand. Again, he found that the only solution was to throw himself on the mercy of his fans, sending out a message-board plea for £1,000 to pay for his ticket. The request was granted within hours.

Pete returned home with a sense of relief but little elation. He knew that he'd disappointed Carl and the band, the people at Rough Trade and his fans – and he'd failed once more to live up to the wishes of his parents. He called his mother – who had been given the all-clear about her breast lump – to find her furious, threatening to disown him. She passed the phone to Peter Sr, who told Pete he'd made his parents ashamed of him. 'My dad told me I'd broken my mum's heart,' he confessed. 'He said I represented everything he hated about humanity: a liar, a thief and a junkie. That really got to me. But after five minutes – five days, maybe – I cut myself off from him completely. We hadn't spoken for years anyway.'

Days after returning to London, Pete was stopped for speeding by the police, who on searching him discovered a flick-knife. He was charged with speeding, driving without a licence or insurance, and possession of an offensive weapon. With Pete having failed to get through rehab and yet another court case pending, Carl, Gary, John, McGee and the bosses at Rough Trade all decided they'd had enough. The second album was done; they didn't need Pete for any imminent recording and didn't want the aggravation of dealing with his antics on the road. The statement that finally dumped Pete from The Libertines was carefully worded to make it sound sympathetic to his problems, but no amount of artistry could conceal the brutality of what it meant.

When Pete heard the news, it hit him like a hammer. To say that he was shocked doesn't convey the impact the announcement had on him. He never believed that Carl could turn his back on him like this. Suddenly, no quantity of drugs was enough to ease the pain. 'I tried to calm down with a smoke,' he recalled, 'but, as I was cooking up, I looked at the brown and screwed it up. There wasn't a drug in the world that could make me feel better. It made me feel dirty, and I realised, "This is why I can't play. I've got to start getting clean."'

The realisation that the drugs weren't working for him was momentary and short-lived. Within days, he was back on crack and heroin, taking huge quantities of both with a vengeance. During this period, he even began to justify his binges by using the excuse of being thrown out of his band, while telling many people that the actions of the other Libertines had driven him further into the world of drugs.

By September 2004, Pete's problem had become so severe that he sought direct help from his parents, who had by now moved from Germany to a house near the Blandford Forum Army Base in Dorset. He went home and was promptly locked in a room by his mother and father, who decided to put him through their own programme of cold turkey in the manner of the heroin-addict character Renton in the cult film *Trainspotting*. Like the Edinburgh addict portrayed by Ewan McGregor, at his parents' house Pete endured agony. He confessed to friends that he'd hidden secret stashes of drugs all over the house – under his pillow, in the bathroom, beneath the carpet – but Jacqueline discovered these secret supplies one by one and quietly disposed of them.

Gradually, Pete slipped into the ordeal of cold turkey, shivering and sweating so much that he soaked two duvets. In his diary, he described becoming in turns hot and cold, shaking and struggling to sleep. He fantasised lovingly of his favourite crack house in New Road, east London, imagining every detail of the squalid flat, with its scattered needles and pipes. At one point, the temptation of the image grew so strong that Pete made a bolt for the front door, only to be rugby-tackled by his father in the hallway.

Pete's attempt to overcome his addictions at his parents' home failed after a week. Two months later, during a conversation in Soho's Colony Room on 3 December, he explained his predicament with characteristic honesty: 'I don't want to die, and I'll take every precaution to avoid death. Probably, for the way I am and my state of mind and the state of my life, it's best to avoid heroin – and it's certainly best to avoid crack cocaine. It's having the right people around me and the love of my family and the people I'm closest to. I've got that strength. I've got to find it yet, but I've got it. It's like having an untidy room. It's there somewhere.'

Pete's wavering determination to rid himself of his addiction to drugs emerged again in February 2005, when he was back for another spell of rehab. This time the counter-narcotic drug Naltrexone was implanted in the top of his leg to neutralise the effects of heroin. The need for a chemical block to stop him getting the high he craved reflected both an intention to give up and a further failure to overcome his addiction. There was still that part of him that kept believing that the drugs might work. As he expressed it in a defiant moment, 'They think I'm a junkie scumbag. All right then, I'll show them what a junkie scumbag is.'

Pete's attitude on the subject of drugs seemed to waver, depending on his mood or level of consumption at the time of being asked. This vacillatory behaviour was unusual for him; on other matters, he had fairly established, well-thought-out ideas. When talking about crack or heroin, however, he increasingly seemed to blow hot and cold, to be one minute believing in the old mythology of the creative powers of opium and the next spouting something that could be taken from the lips of a doctor at a detox clinic. Shortly after returning from his failed rehab in Thailand, he asserted, 'I'm not scared about death. I don't care if everyone says I'm going to die if I carry on taking drugs. I'm more terrified for others – my mum and friends

197

who are worrying themselves over me. Sometimes I'm convinced I do want to be free from the drugs – but I don't feel a lot of people's worries justify it. I know people who take more drugs than me and they're still here.'

On other occasions, Pete would revise his opinion, adopting the view that drugs could damage him, could even kill him. 'It is impossible for things to go on as they have done,' he admitted on one occasion. 'I will end up six feet under, particularly with the crack. It just spirals into the darkest, saddest melody. But there is something irresistible about it, something like waiting for the perfect wave that never comes. But it is awful if it destroys anything that is good.'

Even after losing the band he loved, Pete couldn't bring himself to believe fully and truly that heroin and crack had been the cause. They had stopped him playing and, as he put it in the lyrics to 'Can't Stand Me Now', blamed it on heroin. He was still out there, showing that they were liars, proving that he could perform, on stage with Babyshambles. Nevertheless, there was this fleeting thought that, whether his eviction from The Libertines had been merited or not, his addictions were certainly not helping him. The realisation came and went like the wind, but there were times when he could see that life without drugs would be better. The feeling he'd had when he'd heard the band had turned him away, the feeling that heroin couldn't help him, represented a huge shift from where he'd been on the day he first walked into the Farm Place clinic. It also represented a glimmer of hope for Pete's future.

CHAPTER 12

She'll Never Forgive You But She Won't Let You Go

'A LOT OF PEOPLE FELL IN LOVE WITH HIM,
AND HE FELL IN LOVE WITH A LOT OF PEOPLE,
SO I HAD NO MONOPOLY OVER HIM.'
*– Tabitha Denholm, The Queens of Noize DJ
and former girlfriend of Pete Doherty*

Pete's well-publicised drug habit wasn't his only addiction; he was also addicted to love. His most famous conquest would be the supermodel Kate Moss, but she was far from being the first woman that Pete had serenaded into bed. Many women fell for him and tried to save him but eventually drove him away. Each love was heartfelt, romantic and sacred, like his music, but ended as suddenly as it began.

Pete's relationships with women were at once profound and fleeting, following a pattern in which he would fall madly, deeply in love with each one, then cheat on her and later walk away. Although he had been shy as a teenager, by his early twenties he'd grown up into a man who was phenomenally successful with women. He had hundreds of flings with groupies and girls he met in bars, the kind of one-night affairs that were the domain of many a rock star.

However, Pete was different from the stereotypical bad man of rock in that he would also fall in love repeatedly with women who, despite his promiscuity, could not bear to let him go. The sincerity of his feelings and the charm with which he expressed them meant that he was forgiven for acts that, for most men, would guarantee rejection. He made no secret of his intention to live freely and have sex with anyone he pleased and would commit to nothing except his music, yet he loved to be in love, and women loved him.

Even the most open-minded girls on the music scene found Pete's contrary personality difficult to deal with. Tabitha Denholm, one-half of DJ duo Queens of Noize, had a predictably unpredictable relationship with Pete, who would treat her as the love of his life one minute and openly cheat on her the next. Their affair was based on an adventurous sex life, which included indulgence in sado-masochism. What Tabitha referred to as 'an enjoyable mutual torture relationship' soon grew into a close emotional partnership, although she admitted that her relationship with Pete was challenging. 'It was a total nightmare. A lot of people fell in love with him, and he fell in love with a lot of people, so I had no monopoly over him. I definitely had that feeling of wanting to kiss him and strangle him at the same time. It was like a rug pulling out from under me in every direction.'

While Pete slept with dozens of women to whom he didn't mutter more than a few words, before or after, many stuck around in the hope of becoming the one who would tame him and save him from himself. He was, however, unlikely to change; after all, it was his unpredictability that had attracted the string of beautiful women in the first place. Each girl became emotionally attached to him because of a combination of his fascinating intellectual complexity and unpredictability, reflected in the frequency of his flings.

Pete's habit was to romanticise and deeply analyse each relationship, just as he did every other aspect of his life, the feelings and ideas that conditioned it serving as fuel for his creativity. He borrowed some of his ideas about love from his favourite Romantic poets and philosophers of the eighteenth and nineteenth centuries, sharing their scorn for the convention of monogamy, which he saw as a social constraint that prevented the individual from fulfilling his true desires.

Pete read about the poet Percy Bysshe Shelley, who tried to overcome the pain of sexual jealousy by lending his young wife to friends, and admired the way in which Shelley's friend and fellow artist Lord Byron expressed scorn for sexual morality. Byron set himself the aim of having sex with an all-time record number of women in a year, having them delivered daily by gondola to his palace in Venice until he reached a total of more than 1,000. Like Byron, Pete believed that one could never be truly free while forming a partnership that would ultimately control him.

Pete's sexual adventures had also involved the beautiful French woman Carole Desbois, whom he'd dated in 2001 after the twenty-seven-year-old Carole had sent her mother to Filthy McNasty's to soak up the bohemian atmosphere. With his wide-ranging taste, Pete was in no time chatting up Mrs Desbois behind the bar. Mother told daughter, and

Carole went to have a look at Pete. The result was an affair that was enlivened by Pete's taste for women in uniform. Carole, it turned out, worked for the railways, and her uniform – a polka-dot blouse, knee-length flannelette skirt and pointed hat – drove Pete wild. She confessed that he loved to have a 'quickie' when she was in uniform, up against the kitchen table.

At that time, Pete hadn't started to use drugs intravenously, but even his extensive use of LSD and speed had begun to affect his sexual performance. Carole remembers how he couldn't keep going for more than a few minutes at a time and sometimes suddenly went limp. Nevertheless, in spite of his often shabby appearance, Pete made himself desirable through his charismatic, romantic behaviour. 'It was like standing next to a pile of manure,' Carole remembered of their first night together. 'The grimy odour would have put me off having sex with him. I did everything for him that night, from washing his hair to clipping his fingernails because they had so much dirt underneath.'

Pete was sometimes more interested in romantic rituals than in the act of sex itself. While this was charming to an extent, it didn't always provoke the same interest in his partner. Carole remembered one occasion when 'he put on my dressing gown and we walked hand in hand to the bedroom. He kissed me all over my body and stroked my hair, but he would often stop and read poetry and play his guitar to me. When we got down to sex, I could tell he was pretty inexperienced. We spent twelve hours in bed that night, but most of the time we slept or read poetry. We only made love twice.'

Pete couldn't have known how much his early days spent buried in books would later influence his sexual behaviour. He'd read the Marquis de Sade's tales of libertines and what later became known as sado-masochism, but he could never have believed he would one day be able to act out his every fantasy on a queue of willing females. He continued to draw on the inspiration of de Sade, who was addicted to freeing people from what he saw as unnecessary and damaging constraints on their sexual lives, and preached his sexual preferences with such fervour that his girlfriends believed that they were going on a poetic journey, not a depraved one.

Like de Sade, Pete was fascinated by the pleasures of pain. According to several girlfriends, Pete's activities included bondage, mutilation, sodomy and three-in-a-bed sex. Katie 'Bapples' Lewis, for example, who had first got together with Pete at a gig in London in April 2002 and for whom the song 'What Katie Did' was written, recalled that, at that time, Pete 'was becoming more violent and paranoid. Once, we were both high on crack and heroin and had a blazing row at my flat. He got a razor blade and started slashing at my arm. We both ended up going to hospital for stitches. I have huge scars for life.'

Like several of Pete's girlfriends, Katie put up with a lot to be near him, once spending a night in bed with him and Carl after a 'wild night out when they were high on drink and drugs'. Unlike many of his other lovers, however, she let rip when he left her, blaming him for encouraging her to try hard drugs and then leaving her to battle her addiction to crack and heroin on her own. She branded him 'poison' and was quick to speak out when news of his relationship with Kate Moss broke in early 2005. At that time, bitter after a year of fighting drug addiction on her own, Bapples condemned Pete: 'He's evil, twisted, and the only thing he loves is her money. He says he loves her and is trying to stop crack. Yes, he ruined my life. I would love nothing more than to see him crash and burn. He is pure evil. I hate him for what he did to me. She has had more men than I've had hot dinners. They are a match made in Hell. I have a beautiful soul and trusted him, and he killed me.'

Katie had been seduced by Pete's spell and developed a £1,000-a-day drug habit. She admitted that she soon became hooked and wanted to be in his private world with him, confessing, 'I loved him and would do anything he said.' She found Pete enormously desirable, and the fact that he'd previously loved and lost so many other women only served to enhance his attractiveness.

Pete was intelligent enough to understand what his girlfriends wanted, and he responded in kind, playing the minstrel and charming them with tunes made especially for them, after the manner of the troubadours of the early Middle Ages. He realised that exposure to such old-fashioned charm as being the object of song was fascinating for many women, such as The Queens of Noize's Tabitha Denholm, who remembered him climbing into her room and serenading her at the foot of her bed.

One characteristic of Pete's was to make typically unpredictable romantic gestures that grabbed at women's hearts just as they were preparing to let go, such as once taking a cab all the way back from a tour in Manchester to London to the woman who was at that point the love of his life. These impulsive moves left many of Pete's girlfriends with a lasting sense of devotion and forgiveness, even after things had turned sour. Tabitha, for instance, despite being made to suffer when he'd cheated on her, was very supportive and stood by him during some of his lowest moments, even dismissing his burgling of Carl's flat as a cry for help rather than a crime. In spite of the hurts he'd caused her, Tabitha had thought that Pete's jail sentence had been unnecessarily harsh, although she did hope that it might, almost by accident, prevent something 'really bad' from happening to him. She'd been delighted about his early release but disappointed that she hadn't got around to sending him a parcel she had been preparing, including an eyepatch, fake goatee beard and ideas of games to play when alone in a room.

Pete's spontaneity was part of his charm, yet it also inspired many an act of unfaithfulness. He didn't regard two-timing as sordid or shameful, believing even his one-night stands to be acts of sincere love. His approach wasn't a cynical one; he simply believed in following his true feelings, wherever they led him. For example, his diaries describe the occasion when he met a girl one Christmas Eve, attesting that, for that moment, he was 'completely in love', the tone of the entry indicating that he savoured the experience like an unexpected but delightful dish. In Pete's eyes, the experience of instantaneous love could be kept without being spoiled by his own or anyone else's expectations.

The consequences of spontaneity and freedom in love proved as serious for Pete as did those of his drug-taking. Pete took all the support he could get from Tabitha, but at the same time he betrayed her by sleeping with the singer of Kill City, Lisa Moorish, who he'd met on The Libertines' 2002 tour, on which her band had also performed.

His relationship with Lisa, of course, resulted in the birth of their son, Astile. At the time of the birth, Pete had wanted to call the boy Peter, because he was convinced that he was so low he was going to die and wanted his name to live on through his son. Lisa, however, wouldn't allow it, so they created a name out of letters from both of their first names. The baby would have parents with different surnames, but Pete's poetic way with words ensured that he would still take elements from both of his parents' names.

Lisa knew at the time that having a baby with the Libertine meant trouble, but she confessed that Pete 'got under my skin. I knew it was a bad idea. We were ultimately friends; we tried embarking on a relationship, but it wasn't meant to be. I was careless and it happened. I couldn't get rid of it. I didn't want to, even though there were a million reasons not to have it. I thought, I'm going to get it in the neck for this, but I don't care.'

Lisa had already had a daughter, Molly, by Liam Gallagher, former holder of Pete's rock 'n' roll rebel crown, conceived just a week after Gallagher married Patsy Kensit. Pete and Lisa managed to keep Astile's paternity a secret for almost two years, until Pete's fame and press interest in his life grew and the truth was revealed. Pete then struggled to deal with the demands of having a child and rarely saw his son. It wasn't that he ignored his responsibilities; he was just unable to take them on in full. Astile occupied his thoughts, but not much of his time. He carried a photo of the boy in his wallet, though, and was fond of showing it to people. As Pete saw it, 'I don't have a close relationship with his mother, but my family's been amazing. I need to buck up my ideas there, but, when I can claim to have any sort of control over my own life, I'm going to take some responsibility for Astile. I love the little fella.'

Lisa, who tried to avoid publicity because of the groupie label attached to her, admitted that she feared for her children, given the drug-taking reputations of their fathers. She wanted them to go to school and become teachers or doctors, but wasn't sure they would follow in their fathers' footsteps: 'They haven't picked up an instrument yet, but who knows? I accept it's funny for people to wonder if they'll argue about whose dad is more famous when they're older, but we just try to be a normal family.'

When questioned about his lack of contact with Astile, Pete would react badly, becoming emotional and defensive, even after having almost two years to get used to the idea of fatherhood. 'I do love him,' he once affirmed, before adding, 'I just need to take responsibility for myself before I take responsibility for him.'

While Pete was distant from Astile, his sisters, mother and grandmother welcomed the mother and baby and provided a loving family for the little boy. In spite of the well-publicised rows with Astile's father, Carl also visited the boy, almost in the manner of a godfather.

Lisa admitted that the distance between father and son was partly her choice, stating in early 2005, when Pete's problems were at their worst, '[Pete's] not well. He needs to get well and he needs to be there for my son – but not right now. Definitely not. He's seen him and been in his life, but, obviously, as things have got worse, it's been less and less. Now's the time to say we've got to cut this off until hopefully he sorts himself out.'

Despite admitting that their romance 'started on the tour bus', Lisa insisted that she hadn't been attracted to Liam or Pete because of their fame, because neither had been particularly famous when she'd met them. However, both had had the confidence and swagger of a star in the making. She admitted that she'd been attracted to them as leaders, but not as stars, and part of her wished that neither of their careers had taken off as they had. She also admitted to genuine concern as she watched Pete's rise and fall to the heights and depths of fame. 'He's a lovely guy, sensitive and gentle,' she said fondly, 'but unfortunately he suffers with a disease called addiction. It all smells of Princess Diana. Some people are pushing him into a corner he shouldn't be in.'

Many of Pete's women continued to show understanding and care for him long after he'd moved on as a lover. Not all of them, however, continued to say positive and respectful things about him, but many did. Primarily an artist, Pete might not have been a perfect father, but he paid his own very original style of maintenance when he wrote the brilliant and socially observant song 'Hooligans on E' for Lisa's band Kill City. It spoke volumes for his musical, if not fatherly, talents that a song he wrote in a couple of hours was better than any that Lisa's established band had been able to muster in years.

Pete's odyssey through the complications of love often

involved someone's desire to rescue him from himself. In the summer of 2004, he got together with Massive Attack's singer Dot Allison, a sensitive and pretty Scottish singer who Pete's friends hoped would be his soul mate, someone who would put his life back on track. The pair had already been friends for some time when they met, and they became inseparable for several months, with Dot touring with Pete on his first solo tour after departing The Libertines, and she was also by Pete's side when he appeared in court for sentencing that September for carrying a knife. Friends called it an old-fashioned romance and thought that she might capture Pete's heart for good. Here, at last, was someone who might easily be seen as his match.

A gifted songwriter, Dot posted her work regularly on the Babyshambles website, and she and Pete worked together at her east London music studio. Their mutual talent and obsession with music and poetry led to fans believing this was Pete's purest relationship to date, and many were upset when it came to a seemingly premature end. Like many of the women who had loved and lost Pete, however, Dot remained loyal and emotionally attached, continuing to make cameo appearances at Pete's gigs, despite their relationship coming to an end.

Other women caught in Pete's whirlwind were less sympathetic after he'd ended their romance, however. In spring 2004, student Lucy Evans publicly attacked Pete when their six-month relationship came to an end, after having witnessed first hand Pete's increased drug use after leaving prison. 'He's become a junkie, a different character,' she noted at the time. 'He used to be the most sensitive, laid-back guy, but now – I hate to say it – he has just become a junkie.'

Lucy still showed a good deal of concern for him, worrying about him idolising The Sex Pistols' Sid Vicious, who died from a drug overdose. 'It wouldn't come as a shock if Pete overdosed on heroin,' she mused. 'At the rate he's going, I think it would be a miracle if he sees Christmas.' An archaeology student, Lucy felt that Pete's drug intake had worsened since his release from prison, pointing out that he'd lost more than three stone after his incarceration.

The record of Pete's love life at this time shows a man addicted to being in love, sometimes with one woman and sometimes with many, but all of his relationships came to an end, sooner or later. Sometimes the affairs where he found himself more evenly matched in talent and creativity lasted the longest, but that wasn't always the case. Pete the minstrel danced with so many different personalities that the huge range of individuals involved makes any pattern of preferences impossible to see. The common factor was that *he* left *them*, drawn on in his romantic way to see what another experience, another woman, would be like, and what she would do for his music. He found it easy to move on without suffering the devastating effects of heartbreak, and so he left them all behind. All of them, that is, except Kate Moss.

CHAPTER 13

What Kate Did

'IT'S ALL IN MY HANDS. I WANT TO MAKE IT WORK. THE
DRUGS HAVE GOT TO STOP OR I'LL LOSE HER. I OWE IT TO HER.
WE ARE SOUL MATES. IT IS A BEAUTIFUL THING.'
– Pete Doherty

By the beginning of 2005, twenty-five-year-old Pete Doherty had had relationships with dozens of beautiful women and sex with hundreds more. The casual sex had come as an integral part of his hedonistic philosophy, while the relationships were the product of an emotional nature that had a tendency to develop close attachments very rapidly. Pete had derived a huge amount of enjoyment from both, but he'd never found what he truly wanted; the adulation of groupies was a welcome boost to his ego, but the idea of any long-term involvement with a girl who looked up to him because of his fame was distasteful. He liked being hero-worshipped, but only in small doses. If he was going to share his life properly with someone, he needed a woman on his own level, one who didn't buy into the fame game, who was confident. He needed someone who had a life beyond him and wouldn't try to take him over, someone who understood his music. Someone who would last.

Pete had always been looking for someone to love. Until this time, the nearest he'd come to this ideal closeness, this meeting of sprits, was in his relationship with Carl, whose attention Pete still hankered after and probably always would, although he was forced to accept that his desire for a reunion was unlikely – for the time being, at least – to be met. Pete's life had to go on, however; he needed to find someone who could be his closest friend. This is what he would discover in Kate Moss.

For a man who didn't like to follow the herd, falling in love with Kate seemed to be an unusually conventional thing for Pete to do. A large proportion of the male population were already in love Kate, who had been the stunningly attractive face of the 1990s. For once in his life, Pete found himself running with the crowd, pinning pictures of Kate to his bedroom wall, like thousands of other teenage lads, including a large poster of her in a revealing catwalk pose. He'd spent hours of his youth fantasising about her, and when by a combination of chance she ended up within his grasp it seemed as if once again his dreams were becoming a reality. The appearance in his life of his teenage self's ideal woman gave him a sense that the relationship was somehow meant to be. 'I think it's in the stars that we should be together,' he mooned at the time.

Their burgeoning relationship raised a few eyebrows in Pete's circle, because he was normally disdainful of the showbusiness hierarchy of which Kate was a member.

Indeed, Pete was renowned for being prepared to mix freely with anyone, homeless crack addicts included. He was known for scorning the superficially glamorous face of the entertainment industry and hating the kind of social climbing within the rock world that he identified in Carl. He'd even poked fun at Carl for lavishing attention on Jude Law's ex-wife, Sadie Frost, accusing him of playing a game of showbusiness snobbery. Now he was going out with Sadie's best friend, a multi-millionaire who lived in St John's Wood – exactly the kind of leafy north London district he'd once claimed to detest.

Those who found it difficult to understand Pete's affair with Kate were guilty of looking at just the image of the relationship and not bothering to see beyond it. For all Pete's teenage lust over Kate's pictures, it was the real woman and not her two-dimensional alter ego with whom he eventually fell in love. Her appearance on make-up adverts, on the covers of magazines and all over the newspapers painted her as a superior waif of the fashion world, haughty, high class and inaccessible. Of course, she was paid to look proud and aloof because the wealthy women who bought the clothes and cosmetics that she advertised wanted to feel proud and aloof.

Privately, Kate's real personality was totally different. She was the down-to-earth daughter of travel agent Peter Moss and his wife, Linda, and had been born and bred in the thoroughly ordinary London satellite town of Croydon. She'd always been one of the girls, having been given the affectionate nickname 'Mosschops' by school friends who remained in touch with her long after she'd become famous. At secondary school, she'd always worn jeans and had been a nifty attacker in the netball team, and at the age of twelve she'd announced in the school cloakroom her ambition to become an air hostess or a model. She was more enamoured of cigarettes than boys.

Two years later, two events changed her life: her parents split up and she was discovered at New York's JFK Airport by Sarah Doukas, founder of the Storm modelling agency. Doukas recalled, 'I was on my way home from New York with my brother Simon after a scouting mission for models when I spotted her at the airport with her father. She looked like a child, but she had exceptional bone structure. As soon as the seat-belt sign had been switched off, we rushed over.' Luckily, Kate's father had seen Doukas on the BBC programme *The Clothes Show* and, knowing her to be reputable, allowed the agent to sign up his daughter.

Success was slow to arrive for Kate, however, and there were many rejections. She later admitted, 'It's not easy for a girl to go to casting every day and get rejected by eight different groups of people who say, "You're too small," or whatever.' Indeed, at 5ft 7in she was one of the shortest women ever to make it to supermodel status.

Then, in 1990, Kate created a stir when grunge photographer Corinne Day shot the gawky schoolgirl for the cover of *The Face* magazine. The slow burn suddenly flared. Moss was adopted as the magazine's house model, she appeared on four consecutive covers of US *Harper's Bazaar* magazine, and Calvin Klein put her into his jeans. It was all a bit of a shock to the young girl. 'I didn't have a dream where I wanted to be a star,' she protested. 'It just kind of rolled along and suddenly I was in the papers.'

Kate led a new breed of slimline, wide-eyed child-women

with 1960s haircuts and unmuscled limbs who seemed to threaten the more womanly all-American models such as Linda Evangelista and Cindy Crawford. By 1995, she was earning £1m a year and going out with Hollywood film star Johnny Depp, although their four-year affair came to a painful end when he left her for French actress Vanessa Paradis. In interviews, Depp claimed that he'd cried for a week after they split up, reproaching himself for being 'so stupid' that he let work get in the way of the relationship. It emerged that Paradis was pregnant with Depp's baby, and the couple ended up living in France with their children, Lily Rose and Jack.

Kate was devastated. Her friends said that the split nearly drove her to a nervous breakdown and claimed that her continuing obsession with Depp derailed her relationship with Spacehog guitarist Antony Langdon, who proposed marriage while they were sharing a tent in Cornwall during an eclipse.

Then, three years before Pete turned up in her life, Kate thought she'd found the man who would finally replace Depp in her affections: publisher Jefferson Hack, co-founder of *Dazed & Confused* magazine, who set up home with her in Belsize Park. She and Jefferson went on to have a daughter, Lila Grace, but Kate's feelings for Hack faded and she separated from him a few months before meeting Pete.

Behind Kate's public persona of a fashion icon, of the woman with whom Pete first fell in love, was the very human face of a single mother with a history of heartbreak who was fast approaching her thirty-first birthday. From their very first encounter, Pete found Kate completely different from the way everyone expected her to be. Leaving her supermodel stardom behind her, she'd turned up incognito at a Babyshambles gig in a back-street pub. Dressed in jeans and out for a night on the town with a group of female friends, she didn't stand out from the crowd, which had been made up of like-minded people.

Pete, who at first didn't realise who she was, was bowled over when he found out that the woman he'd fantasised about for years was mingling with his bohemian audience. For her part, Kate was in raptures over Pete's performance before a small crowd of around a hundred people, describing the intimate occasion as being the most exciting, charismatic gig she'd ever been to. She declared to her pals that night she was 'after his arse'.

As Pete had developed into a star, the woman of his dreams had evolved into a real being who admired him and loved his music, someone on the same wavelength as he was. She was now an ideal combination of supermodel and Babyshambles fan. Along with that, she had added appeal in that Carl had once been infatuated with her, too, and used to discuss her beauty with Pete in the mid-1990s, back when she'd been the female face of those Cool Britannia times. But, when the pair had found fame themselves, and pulling Kate had become a possibility, it had been Carl who'd grown closer to her.

Now Pete's fame had eclipsed Carl's and he stood a chance of landing Kate. He knew that Carl, always fiercely competitive, would be bitter with envy if he opened a newspaper to read that his once less-desired partner had won Kate's affections. Since the break-up of The Libertines, Pete had already become the more musically successful of the pair and was now the centre of the media's attention, and becoming more successful than him with women would be further revenge for the hurt that Pete felt.

Kate was determined to recruit Pete for her thirty-first birthday party at her country home in the Cotswolds and let her interest be known to her friends, who were organising the event for her, and they approached Pete, who of course accepted. One of his friends at that time was Primal Scream frontman Bobbie Gillespie, who was also friends with Kate, and their mutual friendship helped Pete and Kate to grow closer over the weeks running up to her birthday. By the time of the party, romance seemed inevitable to everyone around them.

His head full of thoughts of seduction, Pete's ardour was fuelled further by the certainty that the event was going to be wild. He'd heard stories of the drunken goings-on the previous year at Kate's legendary thirtieth and was delighted to be asked along to the follow-up. The prospect was made still more attractive by the fact that his favourite producer and friend Mick Jones was going to accompany him on stage on guitar.

Pete was so enamoured of the idea of this decadent farmhouse gig in front of a girl he was desperate to impress that for once in his life he actually turned up early, having driven down to Little Faringdon in Oxfordshire on Friday, 14 January, a day ahead of the party. He was determined to turn that Saturday night into something special and so he wanted to check out the stage in advance, get his equipment set up and have a rehearsal. Anything for the woman who wanted his music.

The rock 'n' roll party in the seventeenth-century house built of Cotswold stone was given the added incongruous twist of a circus theme, with guests turning up in the guise of lion tamers and trapeze artists. It wasn't Pete's usual scene, but the gig went down a storm with Pete, Mick and Bobbie entertaining the party-goers with Libertines tracks mixed with classics like the Rolling Stones hit 'Gimme Shelter'. The guests loved the music, lapping it up along with the party's eccentric fare of pink champagne and lollipops.

Pete thought that Kate looked sensational that night in her yellow hotpants and jewelled bra top, her hazel eyes framed by high cheekbones and her delicate, lithe figure incredibly attractive. Soon the pair ended up together in a corner. Within minutes of opening the conversation, Pete had put his arm around Kate and was kissing her passionately. They were so lost in each other's company that they didn't care about their intimacy developing in full view of most of the guests. Kate was oblivious to the quizzical glances from her closest friends, Sadie Frost and Samantha Morton, and spent the rest of the night sitting on Pete's lap, before taking the stage with her friend Pearl Lowe – a former singer with Britpop band Powder – for a duet on 'Leader of the Pack'.

As the event wound up, Pete presented Kate with a framed envelope on which he'd written the lyrics to 'What Katie Did'. He penned the song before he'd met the model, and it was actually about a different Katie, but Moss still found the gesture romantic and charming. A little later, Pete and Kate could be seen disappearing upstairs together.

The following morning, Kate's garrulous 'friends' were

briefing the press about her falling for Pete, saying that she found him dangerous and exciting. This analysis might have contained some elements of truth, but the suggestion that this was a heady, fleeting fling was well wide of the mark. In fact, Kate felt so comfortable in Pete's company that she kept him by her side all through the next day, giving him a lift back to London in her chauffeur-driven car and even introducing him to her parents over Sunday lunch in a Belsize Park pub.

Pete found the instant progression to meeting the family a little daunting, yet he did his best to get along with Peter and Linda Moss, although he felt that they were less eager to get along with him. Unfortunately, they'd heard of Pete through reading the newspapers and, like so many people who didn't know his music, knew his name only because of his association with hard drugs and bad behaviour. Kate had had her own problems, and had been through a period in the Priory herself during a period of 'exhaustion'. Having seen their daughter in a perilous state once before, her parents were keen to protect her from any potentially dangerous influences.

'Kate got a lot of pressure from her family,' Pete noted. 'I went out for Sunday lunch with them and they nicknamed me "the Crackhead". They think I'm bad news. But I'm not after Kate's money, and I'm not interested in her fame. I just love being with her. She's an amazing woman.'

Despite the uneasy meeting with her parents, Pete's relationship with Kate continued to blossom at an exceptionally rapid pace. He felt completely smitten, and in the throes of his feelings he made little effort to smarten himself up for Kate's benefit. Calling her the next day, he invited her for their first proper date, to what turned out to be a run-down pool hall in Whitechapel. It wasn't a venue that would have impressed the average millionaire, but such was the chemistry between Kate and Pete that she had an enjoyable time there, chatting to the regulars and being taught to play pool. Despite being famous himself, Pete still offered Kate a sense of normality that she found invigorating. During that first week of their relationship, the couple spent most of their time together, with Pete staying at her flat in St John's Wood almost every night. She met his friends and he met hers.

For the first time, Pete felt a love that didn't appear to have any inbuilt problems. He'd been in love before, but each relationship had had aspects that gave him reservations, building up into a feeling that he should be cautious and hang back. The biggest long-term commitment he'd ever made was with Carl, but even in that intense situation there'd been a friction from the beginning.

With Kate, there was no such tension or reservations. He could see nothing about her that didn't fit with his image of the ideal woman. Being with her was the pure fulfilment of a fantasy for Pete, and the feeling only grew better as he learned more about her. So certain was he of his feelings, in fact, that he completed a tattoo on his arm that had been there for years: the red outline of a heart, an empty shape that he'd been waiting to fill with the name of the right girl. Although he'd known Kate for less than a week, he went down to the tattoo parlour with her and got a big letter K tattooed in the middle of the heart. Moved by Pete's gesture, she had a much smaller letter P etched on to her. (Kate told

Pete that the size of the initial didn't mean that she was less keen on him than he was on her; it was just the biggest tattoo she could get without risking being turned down for modelling work.) She bought Pete a chain as another token of her love.

Pete felt that his first week with Kate had changed his life. Just days after meeting her, he made a characteristically frank announcement on national television in an interview on ITV's *Orange Playlist*, saying, 'It's been the best week in a long time, because I've really found love. I think it will last. She's good for me because she's got a beautiful soul, and I think I can trust her. I think I can be trusted and she can trust me. I believe her when she says she loves me, and I know I mean it when I say I love her.'

Pete's statement of love for Kate was greeted with scepticism by many in the world of showbusiness. It seemed a bit much for Pete to be telling a woman he loved her after only a week, let alone announcing the move in front of millions of TV viewers. Whatever people thought, however, his comments were totally genuine. Pete didn't have any doubts about Kate. The relationship was going to work.

The full barrage of emotions that Pete turned on his new girlfriend understandably gave her cause for unease. She knew that she was in love with him, but she was taken aback and slightly scared by his level of commitment, coming as it did so soon after they'd met, particularly after she'd had so many disasters with men in the past.

The situation wasn't helped by Pete's reputation as the new bad man of rock. Kate could cope with her family's disapproval when it came to a low-key affair, but, with Pete upping the ante to such a degree, their reservations were bound to weigh more heavily on her mind. And the longer the relationship went on, the more difficult it would be if there were any problems.

Ten days into the affair, all these issues came to a head. Kate had been given an ear-bending by her family and some of her friends, who had agreed that Pete was a bad choice for her. They told her that she should end the relationship now, while she was still able to consider it as only a fling, rather than let it snowball further out of control under the impetus of Pete's enthusiasm. Kate was confused and didn't know which way to turn, so she decided to go on a night out and forget about the whole thing for a few hours.

On the night of 25 January, she went to the trendy Home House Club with a group of female friends and tried to put Pete out of her mind. Sensing that he was being excluded, Pete rang her mobile. She ignored him. In a panic, he called her again and again. The clinging behaviour infuriated Kate. In the early hours of the morning, it moved her to do what everyone said was best but what she hadn't been able to do when she was calm and sober. She sent Pete a text message telling him it was over.

Pete was shocked by the apparent callousness of the dismissal. It was as if he'd meant so little to her that she couldn't even do him the courtesy of dumping him in person, or even over the telephone. As the hours ticked by, however, he began to see the fact that Kate had dumped him by text as a sign that she was unsure of herself.

By the evening of 26 January, Pete had reached the

conclusion that she wouldn't meet him or call him because, if she did, she'd know that she wouldn't be able to go through with the separation. Armed with that hope, he turned up at Kate's flat in St John's Wood at 9pm that evening, carrying his guitar and some gaffer tape. He then proceeded to tape down the intercom button, get out his guitar and sing to her. He'd already wooed her with 'What Katie Did', of course, a track that he'd written about a previous lover with the same name, but that night he sang her 'What Katie Did Next', which he'd written for her. Pete later spoke publicly about penning the track for his new love, and it became much talked about before it had even been played live or appeared on the internet, becoming a romantic symbol of their love story. After several renditions of this song during a two-hour doorstep set, Kate finally let Pete in.

Pete found Kate's attempt to throw him out of her life painful, but it did nothing to dampen his desire for her. Since becoming famous, he'd grown used to girls flinging themselves at him and doing anything to stay with him, most of them a lot younger than Kate and much less sure of who they were and what they wanted. In many cases, Pete found that he could bend them to his will, making them do anything he pleased. Kate's appearance of being uncertain about him and possibly willing to leave him only made him pursue her all the more eagerly.

After winning her back, Pete spent the following weeks talking about her obsessively, telling everyone he met how he needed her in his life and how much he wanted to secure her for himself forever. Just a week after their brief split, Pete was sitting in The George Tavern and telling his friends, 'It's all in my hands. I want to make it work. The drugs have got to stop or I'll lose her. I owe it to her. We're soul mates. It's a beautiful thing. I'm a different person after meeting Kate.' He also mentioned that Kate had told him they could get married as long as he quit heroin. Their affair perfectly balanced the rock 'n' roll with the romantic.

Over the coming months, Pete's relationship with Kate faced many obstacles. He said that thoughts of Kate waiting outside kept him sane during his short spell in prison, although at the time it was unclear whether she felt the same devotion, and rumours surfaced that Pete's bad-boy antics had gone too far and Kate had dumped him again. The rumours were untrue, however, and the couple remained very much an item during this testing time. Kate was just frustrated that Pete kept talking publicly about their relationship, and rumours of a break-up were circulated just to keep her sweet.

If anything, the relationship was swinging further in Pete's favour. The more Kate got to know him, the more she fell in love with him – in contrast to the early days, when his commitment scared her. She was becoming more and more attached to him. Wolfman observed, 'Kate is besotted. She adores Pete. We all do. When Kate is with him, she is natural, childlike. It's as if she's under his spell.' Pete had worked his magic again, and now Kate wanted the world to know they were in love.

On St Patrick's Day, the pair made one of their first public appearances, at north London's Boogaloo bar, where Pete performed on stage with Shane McGowan, Allan Wass and

Dot Allison. Kate watched in awe from behind the bar, telling her friends how much she loved him and singing along to his Libertines songs. She giggled and danced along to the performance and said that Pete made her feel 'young and alive'.

Such public outings became more regular over the coming months. As Pete publicly fought his addictions in the rehab arena, Kate felt vindicated in her decision that Pete could be a boyfriend, a husband and even a stepdad to her daughter, Lila, who he was finally allowed to meet, even accompanying mother and daughter on a trip to Cannes. Kate had stuck to her promise: Pete could spend time with her daughter if he gave up heroin. She'd also said that they could get married if he kicked the smack. Pete was keeping to his side of the bargain – publicly, at least. Time would tell if she kept hers.

CHAPTER 14

A Night at the Circus

'IT'S MOVED ON ANOTHER LEVEL NOW. I CAN'T GO
ANYWHERE ANY MORE WITHOUT MY FACE STARING
BACK AT ME. THE WHOLE WORLD'S A CIRCUS,
AND I'M THE RINGMASTER.'
– *Pete Doherty*

I waited in The George Tavern pub in Stepney, east London, for Pete to arrive for another impromptu Babyshambles gig, organised via the internet just hours earlier. A couple of hundred fans did the same. Like me, they hoped (but did not expect) that Pete would eventually clatter through the pub's doors. Nobody knew for sure whether he would turn up or, if he did, what time he would arrive. That was part of the way he'd maintained the interest of his fans, continuing to intrigue them while many other musicians who had once caught their hearts, minds and ears had died early artistic deaths.

This gig was not unusual. Pete has been playing at pubs, clubs, bedrooms and street corners to crowds like these for years. In fact, Pete had already played at the venue twice in the last week. But that didn't stop an excited buzz from rising behind the fans' shaggy indie haircuts.

About an hour late – pretty good by his standards – Pete burst through the doors and into the dimly lit pub, wearing a long black coat over a suit and netted vest, with a large spliff tucked into the rim of his now-trademark trilby hat. (The following morning, that joint became the first to be pictured on the front page of a national newspaper in several years.) He gasped for breath and puffed out his chest as he fought through the photographers and emerged from the brilliant white light of camera flashes outside. The crowd parted as he staggered through in a way that only a rock star could. Pete had made wide-eyed stumbling look poetic, having done for the stumble what Liam Gallagher had done for the swagger. This time, however, the look in Pete's eye was even more frantic than usual.

I said there was nothing unusual about this gig, and there wasn't. Held in a small East End boozer, it was publicised only via an internet forum, with Pete turning up high and late. But the public interest in the event was something very new. Pete was now dating supermodel Kate Moss, one of the most famous and desired women of the previous decade. That made him a superstar to more than just die-hard Libertines fans, and he knew it. This was rumoured to be the first time the pair stepped out publicly together, and the Babyshambles devotees had been joined by dozens of journalists, photographers and various other thirty-somethings, all looking out of place.

But Pete arrived alone, guitar case in hand but no supermodel, and the fans filed through to the pub's back room for the evening's entertainment. The venue – a disused nightclub called Stepney's, attached to the pub –

was the perfect setting for the shambolic yet lovable Babyshambles and was one of Pete's favourites. Fans sat on the floor, in front of the makeshift stage, or danced on the lit-up dance floor that had rarely been illuminated since the 1980s. The dressing room was cordoned off by a tatty black sheet. The sound system was poor and the kit consisted of a single drum.

Pete took to the stage with his guitar and announced the night's special guest, then broke the news that his new millionaire girlfriend wouldn't be making an appearance. 'I'm on my own tonight,' he confessed. 'We've had a bit of a row. You'll have to make do with me.' He then broke into song, and the gig had begun. Kate wasn't there but his devotees didn't mind. Maybe now the *faux* fans and the press would fuck off and everyone could get on with listening to some music.

The beginning of the performance was strangely subdued. First, Pete staggered around alone on stage, his bandmates nowhere in sight. He strummed his antique guitar and slurred at the microphone. I considered the possibility that we wouldn't be seeing Babyshambles tonight, and that Pete would perform on his own. Such a scenario wasn't unusual; he'd captured my attention several times in the past while sitting alone on stage with just an acoustic guitar. Tonight, however, the focus of the audience and Pete himself were both wandering.

Soon the band joined Pete on stage. It turned out that he'd just got impatient and meandered on alone. Earlier, he'd seemed restless on arriving at the venue, barely acknowledging greetings from friends as he walked aimlessly around the hall, clearly uncomfortable despite the familiar surroundings and the fact that he was the proud new rock-star boyfriend of a supermodel. Even when he was joined by his bandmates on stage, the night failed to take off. It was one of new drummer Adam Ficek's first gigs, after Gemma Clarke had walked out over her issues with Pete and their management, although even the best drummer in the world would have struggled to hold such a chaotic ensemble together with the equipment available that night.

The band launched into their first song, but the audience didn't quite get it, prompting Pete to let out a derisory 'You can do better than that' after the first faint ripple of appreciation spread through the crowd. It wasn't until the band blasted out 'Killamangiro', the single that had been played well-nigh constantly on Radio 1 during the previous few weeks, that the crowd stopped chatting amongst themselves. It appeared that the intimacy of these small gigs was becoming lost under the Pete Doherty car crash being played out very publicly in the press. Many of the crowd weren't fans but rubber-neckers coming along to stare at the wreckage. They weren't libertines. Pete knew it and didn't like what he saw.

Just three songs in, Pete lost his rag with some photographers in the front row who were ignoring his request not to take pictures. His already waning patience shattered, he made a snatch for the cameras, grabbed bandmate Drew McConnell and burst for the back door. For the dedicated fans who had waited for hours to see their hero, the show was all over in less than fifteen minutes. They were used to that, of course – it was all part of the fun – while those who had come in the hope of seeing Pete fall on his face had their 'Pete lashes out and abandons gig' tale and could go home satisfied.

The mood that night was completely different from that at a gig at the same venue just two days earlier. On that evening, Pete told me how he felt 'fantastic' and, although he didn't exactly look it at the time, he was clearly more comfortable than he appeared forty-eight hours later. At the earlier gig, he'd shaken the hand of every fan, desperate to touch their friend and hero. Babyshambles had played a brilliant hour-long set, one of the tightest I'd seen from them and for the first time looking like a band who might rival The Libertines. Later that night, Pete had returned to the stage to sing songs and recite poems with his pal Wolfman until the early hours. The musicians and their fans were united in their love of music. Pete had sat on the floor, surrounded by dozens of youngsters, showing teenage girls how to play basic Libertines riffs on an acoustic guitar and handing out his phone number.

At one point that night, Pete had spotted a young lad, who couldn't have been much older than sixteen, looking enviously at the group gathered around his favourite rock star. Pete called over, 'Hello. I recognise you from that gig last week. How you doing, mate?' He then beckoned the star-struck teenager over and gave him a wink and a glass of champagne. It was exactly this kind of gesture that was what these impromptu knees-ups were all about. Pete could play big brother and get the acceptance and admiration he craved while in return giving his fans unrivalled access to their idol.

That night, Pete had jumped into a mate's car at 2am,

excited about continuing the festivities, then partied 'til dawn before grabbing a few hours' sleep in preparation for another gig – a concert at the Garage, Islington, staged to raise money for victims of the recent tsunami wave in the Far East.

At the Garage, Pete's pallid complexion and sunken dark eyes were even more pronounced than usual, and after the gig he wandered the streets outside the venue, charging at photographers gathered there to take his picture. A photograph taken that night, depicting him with his eyes rolled back in his head, became an iconic image of the man the press now called 'Kate Moss's junkie boyfriend' and was splashed over the front pages of several newspapers under headlines like 'THE LIVING DEAD'. Later that day, Pete wrote on his Babyshambles website, 'Ah dear, just a sigh to say that photo is all out of context.' He then invited fans to The George Tavern with the words, 'See you at 9 for a quick half before the set.'

However, by the time Pete had arrived at The George for his third gig in three nights – the second at that venue – it was more than dedicated Babyshambles fans who wanted to share a drink. The interest in him among people who had never owned a Libertines or Babyshambles record had moved to new heights. Pete had confirmed his rumoured relationship with Kate Moss in newspapers, and that revelation – coupled with the shocking pictures – had propelled him from newspaper gossip columns on to the front page.

The crowd that attended the gig was very different from the one that had appeared at the same place forty-eight hours earlier. Just two nights ago, he'd talked to them like old friends; now he eyed them with suspicion and caution, fleeing after just three songs. And, as Pete and Drew burst on to the street, a couple of paparazzi were waiting in a car. Pete went for one of them and swung a punch to back up the expletives flying from his lips. Despite Pete's fragile frame, the stocky young photographer looked terrified as the star danced around, throwing punches. The snappers then jumped – cameras and faces intact – into a car and followed Pete, as he skipped up the road in pursuit of some hard drugs.

Despite all the talk of music for music's sake, Pete loved and craved the fame. As he floated through the streets of east London that night, he seemed disappointed to have lost the photographers he'd threatened to 'fuck up' just minutes earlier. He then turned a corner and was greeted by the waiting car. 'Give us something good, Pete,' one of the photographers asked. Pete obliged and picked up a bag of rubbish from a doorstep, ready to hurl it at the car before he spotted some patrolling policemen and put it down. He seemed more like a naughty schoolboy than a wild man of rock, but that was Pete's appeal. He walked towards the camera, took one last deliberate drag of his cigarette and flicked it to the floor like a character in a Wild West movie. He then turned away and shouted, 'That's enough now. Show's over. Same time, same place, tomorrow.' It had become clear to me I was being taken on one of Pete's strange Dickensian journeys – with a very twenty-first-century twist – through east London.

A few more turns around run-down streets and darkened alleyways and Pete arrived at a black BMW parked on a street corner. The darkened window wound down to reveal four Asian men sitting inside. The car was shaking with loud drum 'n' bass music and Pete got in the back, shaking his head excitedly, to score a handful of drugs. It seemed strange to watch Pete appear so at home in this world so different from his habitual domain. The tracksuits and pimped-up cars clashed with Pete's old suits and antique guitars. The men in the car had drugs to sell, though, and that was all that mattered. Pete had been criticised by some of his oldest friends for deserting his people and places in pursuit of drugs, but maybe his world and the world of the dealers weren't that far apart after all.

We left the mobile drugstore behind and marched up some shabby stairs to Pete's friend's flat. At this point, Drew left in another direction, obviously having been taken on this journey before and unwilling to travel to the end of the line that night.

At the door to the flat, a beret-wearing figure in his fifties met us and ushered us inside. I'd thought that crack dens like the one in which I now found myself existed only in the movies, but apparently not. Poetry and doodles were scrawled all over the walls, while books and records spilled from every corner. Pete sat down on a flea-bitten armchair and picked up his guitar and crack, then plucked out the joint that had been perched in the rim of his trilby and lit it. The only part of the flat that wasn't covered in ash was the ashtray itself. As I flicked my cigarette ash into it, I was promptly told to use the floor. The ashtray was clean, I was told, because it was used for the mixing of hard drugs.

Suddenly, under the artificial, uncompromising light of the flat, Pete looked different, his face even paler than it had looked on stage and his fingers dirtier and browner. I noticed that the black suit I'd admired earlier was filthy and covered in holes while he recounted his journey to his pal in excited tones. 'You should have seen it,' he said. 'We've just been chased through the streets of London by some photographers. Every corner we turned, they were there.'

Pete's mate warned, 'I told you, Pete. Things are going to be different from now on. Now you're with Kate.' He handed Pete a copy of a newspaper bearing a front-page picture of his drug-addled performance at the Garage.

'I hate it,' Pete said, 'just like everyone hates seeing pictures of themselves, especially when they're fucked.' He kicked the newspaper across the room in rage, but he also seemed to be secretly basking in the attention he'd always craved. 'It's moved on to another level now,' he acknowledged. 'I can't go anywhere any more without my face staring back at me, without being photographed. The whole world's a circus, and I'm the ringmaster.' He then looked at the newspaper picture of his eyes rolling back into his head, held it next to his face and asked me sheepishly, 'I don't really look like that, do I?'

Pete emptied his pockets on to the table in front of him. Out fell a half-smoked ten-pack of Marlboros, a lighter, some weed, a rock of crack, some heroin, some cocaine and a crack pipe made from a miniature Martell bottle. He laughed as he delved deeper and deeper into his very own Pandora's box, then looked proudly at the contents lying on the tobacco-covered table. It was as if the vast array of drugs he was able to produce on request was a sign of how far he'd come. Others would say it symbolised how far he'd fallen.

Throughout the night, Pete and his friend reminisced about the birth of The Libertines. As they chased the dragon, smoking heroin off sheets of tin foil, they discussed how great writers and poets had used opium to aid the creative process. 'Writers have always taken opium,' Pete insisted. 'When I first took heroin, I just thought of it like that. I had a romantic image of it, that it would help me create.'

The conversation then moved on to the subject of Albion. Britain, Pete explained, is an island, and on an island you have to learn to fight. Here, Pete wasn't referring to a physical fight, or referencing the island mentality that's often blamed for England's problems with football hooliganism, but more the fight of minds and ideologies and the battle to get these thoughts across. As he talked about isolation, it became unclear whether he was still discussing life on an island and literal ostracism or his own self-induced exile of drug addiction; the two seemed deliberately blurred. Pete has contemplated these issues over many drug-filled nights, alone or in company, and his thoughts on the matter are best summed up in the poignant and brilliant autobiographical line 'Cornered, the boy kicked out at the world/The world kicked back a lot fucking harder' in 'Can't Stand Me Now'.

On three occasions during the night, the drug dealers we'd met earlier arrived with more provisions. Pete smoked weed, smoked crack, smoked smack, smoked more crack. It was clear that his drug-taking had reached a different level from where it had been in the early days of The Libertines. He proudly showed off his arm – battered by heroin abuse around his famous Libertine tattoo – like a trophy, then grinned as he told me he could no longer use that arm to inject the drug. Occasionally, he would disappear into the flat's only bedroom before returning to proclaim in a comedy northern accent, 'What a man sticks up his own arse is his own business.' For someone so obviously falling deeper and deeper into drug addiction, he didn't seem to be taking it very seriously, and despite his infectious boyish charm, I struggled to see the funny side of the situation. When I later grabbed a glimpse of the bedroom, the bed itself was covered with clothes and rubbish, looking like it hadn't been used for sleeping for a while.

Over the night, a strange mixture of men turned up, some looking like Pete clones with indie haircuts and distressed jeans while another looked more like Ali G, clad in rambunctious sportswear and shiny, tasteless jewellery. Pete had left behind many good friends who'd shared his incredible journey; now his friends appeared to be anyone who shared his drug habit. And, despite being the star of the show, Pete was often treated like someone's younger brother rather than their successful and gifted friend. Even though he'd been using the drug for five years, he claimed he still couldn't cook up crack and had to ask an old hand to do it for him.

Others hit him with money-making scams as they tried to grab a piece of his wealth, although as far as I could make out everything he'd owned had already been spent on drugs. He was ridiculed for his friendship with me, a middle-class lad who shared his love of music but not of crack and smack, although the comments were reminiscent of playground jealousy. They teased Pete about being a 'posh boy', too, and the army major's son defensively insisted that he was not.

One budding musician in the group even tried to make out he didn't know who Pete was, and asked him if he was in a band, although it soon became clear he was more in awe of Pete than anyone, listening attentively as Pete told him his face was too clean for his battered and paint-splattered jeans. Pete suggested that he should grow some stubble and not wash for a while to perfect his rock-star look: 'It just doesn't work. You've obviously climbed out of those jeans this morning to have a bath and a shave, then put them back on again.' Later, the now mesmerised lad, who had been staring at Pete as he'd chased the dragon, said that he'd never taken heroin before and asked what it was like. Although Pete didn't go as far as to condemn his drug of choice, he insisted to the enchanted musician that he shouldn't take it if he hadn't taken it before.

Another young guitarist cornered Pete and criticised him for 'selling out', now that he was a chart-topping artist. Pete turned to me for the assurances he often required, an indication of his endearing insecurity, and said, 'He's got a point, you know.' I convinced him that that wasn't the case, that he should be proud that his music and message had influenced more people than most musicians could dream of. Later, that same lad sat hypnotised and doe-eyed as Pete sang to us and played his guitar. His treatment of Pete was typical of what the ex-Libertine received from most of the group: with one hand they pushed him down, and with the other they begged for his approval.

Then Pete launched into a rendition of 'What Katie Did Next' – a song that he claimed he wrote for Kate Moss – on an acoustic guitar. I'd seen him in many intimate surroundings, but I still felt especially privileged to hear this song in a part of an audience of just two, especially as the song had been the focus of hundreds of newspaper column inches the previous week, after Pete had announced that he'd penned it for his new lover. The disordered chords and confused lyrics still sounded like work in progress, but the innocent honesty Pete exuded in small gigs was magnified in this, the most intimate of venues.

As the other lads arrived, the evening then turned into a sing-along around a rickety record player and Pete's guitar. But, as others tried to drown out the voice of the only talented singer in the room, I couldn't help but think that this was a long way away from the creative drug-fuelled sessions Pete had once enjoyed with Carl and his other musical partners. The atmosphere did more to squash talent than nurture it; as more drugs were consumed and more drug-takers arrived, less music was played.

Despite his obvious physical and mental scars, Pete still glamorised drugs to the watching disciples. 'Crack's gorgeous,' he enthused, 'and the brown's all right. It depends on the quality of it. But it's become more of a painkiller than a high.' And when someone suggested that Pete should let him make a Doherty doll to sell at Camden market, Pete replied, 'As long as it's holding a guitar and a crack pipe.' Although I couldn't stifle a chuckle, this was another gag that seemed somewhat tragic.

As the drugs and money ran out, Pete's mood soured. The jubilant singing and chatting descended into depressive deep thinking. Pete admitted that the circus he'd found himself at the centre of hadn't impressed his new girlfriend, and neither had the particularly telling pictures all over that day's newspapers. 'It's a difficult time at the moment,' he told me. 'We've had a bit of a row. The usual shit – she wasn't happy about all those pictures. I think I've fucked it up, as usual.'

Pete also struggled when asked about Astile, the son he'd had with singer Lisa Moorish and had seen only rarely since. After some criticism from his entourage, whose claims to be good fathers themselves amused me, he protested, 'I saw my baby last week. I do see him sometimes, but not that often. It is hard.'

Despite the cash rolling in from record-buyers and gig-goers all over Britain, Pete admitted that he was homeless, without a bed to call his own. 'I'm between places at the moment,' he confessed, then lamented, 'I always seem to be between places. I haven't had a real home for years. A mate is trying to get me into a flat in Primrose Hill. I don't really think that's for me.'

Pete began to sink into his thoughts, taking each criticism like a blow to the face. He then grabbed me and asked if we could leave alone and go to a pub and talk. I thought that maybe he'd seen through the jealous bullying of these so-called friends and the superficial nature of the drug-inspired friendships and wanted to speak to someone who genuinely admired his talent. Despite it being 3am, Pete insisted that he knew a pub that would let him in, whatever hour he banged on their door, but, as we retraced the steps we'd taken earlier that night, Pete suddenly halted. He wanted to return to the crack den, alone. He'd come down from what was left of his high and wanted more drugs.

As I wandered off, I thought to myself that something had to give. The drug-taking was overtaking the music as the most important thing in Pete's life, and it was going to take a huge event to change that.

Less than twenty-four hours later, I received a phone call from documentary-maker Max Carlish. He told me he'd been attacked by Pete, who was now locked up in a police-station cell.

CHAPTER 15

Chained Melody

'IT WAS HELL ON EARTH. AT NIGHT THE NOISE WAS
HORRIBLE, AND THERE'S NOTHING MORE TERRIFYING THAN
THE SOUND OF A PRISON WAKING UP.'
– Pete Doherty

Having overcome the first rocky patch of his relationship with Kate, Pete had believed that she was his. Her nervousness about the new affair had passed; the couple had outlasted the early stages and resisted negative input from Kate's family and friends.

As it turned out, the future would prove that he was right – for the medium term, at least – but what he didn't account for were the side-effects of his new status as Mr Moss. Pete was, of course, already a huge star in his own right, but his arena was the music world, with its relative tolerance of eccentricity and behaviour of all kinds. Kate, on the other hand, was part of the mainstream, famous in all fields, a household name. The moment that Pete had started seeing her, he'd entered another sphere, and it wasn't one in which he felt at home.

The first sign of the impending fallout over Pete's new affair came in the shape of film-maker Max Carlish, who over the past few months had been preparing a documentary about Pete. An Oxford-educated broadcaster who'd won a BAFTA during his time spent working for the BBC, Carlish was a man who had fallen on hard times. Brilliantly talented but emotionally unstable, he was a thirty-eight-year-old self-confessed crack-cocaine user with a history of manic depression. He'd been allowed access to film gigs and backstage scenes by James Mullord, Pete's new manager with Babyshambles, who had believed he had found someone who would produce a good film. Mullord had also thought the venture could provide the band with some helpful publicity, telling Pete that letting Carlish film the band could make them 'a million quid'.

The arrangement had been made the previous summer, but the situation had soured amid Carlish's increasingly odd behaviour around the band and Pete's diminishing patience with the project. All Carlish had managed was a few chaotic sequences that showed Pete backstage at gigs or at the recording studio, saying very little and repeatedly smoking heroin. The Pete Doherty documentary, it turned out, was the freelance broadcaster's own idea, and didn't have the backing of a TV company. With no funds and no more access, it appeared by the beginning of 2005 that the whole idea would fizzle into nothing. Then Kate Moss came into the picture.

With Kate on the scene, the fragments that Carlish had stored at his Birmingham home acquired a new significance. They were no longer just scenes of Pete the well-known heroin addict smoking heroin but rather pictures that proved graphically the shocking headline 'KATE MOSS'S NEW LOVER IS A JUNKIE'.

'Suddenly, my stock had risen enormously,' Carlish explained. 'When I filmed Pete taking heroin, I didn't think it was a big deal. Everyone knew he was a heroin addict, so footage of him smoking it wasn't news. But, when Pete started seeing Kate Moss, everything changed overnight. The slightest bit of information about Pete, whether it was new or not, was from that moment a reflection on her. It was important and saleable.'

Despairing of ever being allowed to finish his film, Carlish called the *Sunday Mirror* and struck a deal for the sale of the heroin footage. Pictures of Pete chasing the dragon appeared on the front page of the newspaper.

Pete was furious. It didn't matter to him in the slightest whether people saw him taking drugs or not – he'd always been completely honest about his habits and would smoke heroin, crack and cannabis and snort cocaine in front of fans, band members, studio hands and journalists alike – but, now that he was with Kate, his drug-taking was being viewed as a reflection on her. She was a household name going out with a junkie, and the images of Pete doing what everyone knew he did were seriously damaging to her reputation. There was a strong possibility that she could even lose modelling work because of them.

Pete's addictions, instead of being the stuff of banter within the music trade, had become much more shocking when displayed in the mainstream media. They even earned him the honour of being lambasted by then Tory leader Michael Howard, who accused him of corrupting the nation's youth and called for him to be banned from the pages of the newspapers. Pete, already battling against a weight of adverse opinion from Kate's family and friends, found that his enemies suddenly had allies in all kinds of places, and he feared that Carlish's photographs might tip the balance in her mind away from him.

Pete embarked on an exercise in damage limitation. First of all, he let it be known that Kate had delivered him an ultimatum, ordering him to clean up his act. She had to distance herself from the drugs; she did not condone them; she was trying to force him to stop, telling him that she would walk out if he didn't. 'The drugs must stop or I'll lose her,' he said. 'I owe it to her.'

Pete's assessment that the drugs were in danger of driving Kate away might well have been correct in the long term, but at the time the statement was intended as much as a PR exercise as a pronouncement of the truth. As such, it marked a change in the man who never used to give a damn.

In the aftermath of the *Sunday Mirror*'s front-page piece, Pete became the target of an intense effort by the newspapers to follow up the piece and confirm his smacked-out status. He found this a rather strange situation, given the fact that he'd never tried to conceal his drug use, although he particularly hated some photographs that had been taken of him at this time during a performance at a Babyshambles gig that made him look like a patient in an asylum, his eyes rolling and face blank. These photographs were printed across the land as an illustration of Pete's advanced addiction, and he found the easy reduction of his life to a negative image highly disturbing.

The furore surrounding the Pete-as-junkie pictures left their subject with the sense that his relationship with Kate was hanging by a thread, and indeed he had several heated phone conversations with her on the subject. Kate had made it clear that she was very unhappy at being dragged through this storm of bad publicity, while he pressed her for a face-to-face talk in a quiet place.

On 5 February, Pete booked himself into the Rookery Hotel in Farringdon, central London, for precisely that purpose. He knew the four-star establishment well, situated as it is near his old haunts, such as Filthy McNasty's and the Wolfman's former flat in Clerkenwell. Inside, the atmosphere is tranquil. Pete believed that Kate would like the Victorian fittings of the £400-a-night luxury bedroom, and he called her to tell her he'd get the Jacuzzi ready for her arrival that evening, before taking the opportunity to prepare himself a heroin fix. It was then that he got a call from the staff at the front desk, who told him that he had a visitor.

There are two radically different versions of what happened next. According to Max Carlish, he came to the hotel to talk to Pete about the pictures he'd sold and to discuss what he was going to do with the rest of his footage. He said that, when he arrived in the room, Pete flew into a rage about him selling the images to the newspaper, that Pete accused him of trying to blackmail Kate and then punched him repeatedly in the face, leaving him with two black eyes and a broken nose. Carlish went on to attest that Pete had been assisted in this by his friend Alan Wass of Left Hand, who had popped by for a visit.

Pete, meanwhile, argued that Carlish had been stalking him, that, while he'd been innocently waiting for Kate to arrive to share the Jacuzzi, Carlish had arrived at his hotel room brandishing a samurai sword and babbling incoherently. Pete said that Carlish attacked him with the weapon, and that he'd struck back only to protect himself.

One certainty about this incident was that it passed in a blur for both men. Pete had just taken a large dose of heroin and was drugged to the point at which he couldn't be sure what was going on, while Carlish had appeared to have been drinking heavily and was talking constantly.

Soon after the incident at the Rookery, Carlish had called me to report his side of the story. His garbled conversation had lasted for more than three hours before I felt duty-bound to meet him in Islington, just to make sure he was all right.

Meanwhile, Pete's encounter with Carlish had been followed by the arrival of the police. Disturbed by the afternoon's events, Pete had taken yet more heroin in a bid to calm himself down, and by the time the law turned up he was out of his mind, hardly able to speak, and found himself being pushed into the back of a patrol car and driven to Islington Police Station. The officers told him that he was under arrest on suspicion of robbery and blackmail, but Pete found it hard to figure out what they were saying. A doctor who examined him said that he was too high to respond to questioning, pointing out the track marks all over his hands.

Carlish, it appeared, had called the police and told them that Pete had stolen his phone and some money, showing them the damage Pete had allegedly done to his face, which was very badly bruised. His left eye, in particular, was so swollen that he could barely see out of it, while his nose was flattened and bloody. He was taken to University College Hospital for some treatment on his face.

The situation was a serious one for Pete. Earlier that day, he'd been plotting a way to wriggle free from the row over the heroin pictures, hoping to smooth things over with Kate. Now, when he should have been frolicking with her in the bubbles of the Jacuzzi in his hotel suite, he was locked up in a police station, facing another crisis of crushing proportions. He was already on a suspended jail sentence, following his conviction for possession of a flick-knife at Thames Magistrates' Court in September 2004, and, if he was convicted again, he'd definitely be going back to jail – and, given the gravity of Carlish's accusations, he could be in for a long stretch.

The following day, when Pete had finally come down sufficiently to understand what was being said to him, the police told him he was being charged with robbery and blackmail. He was told that, if convicted, he could go to jail for up to four years.

For Pete, it was the stuff of nightmares. As the drugs wore off and his mind began to register the detail of his surroundings, he noticed that he was locked in a bare, $6m^2$ cell furnished only with a metal bed. He knew that within a matter of hours he would experience the first symptoms of withdrawal, the first trembling that would become the shakes, the first nausea that would develop into vomiting.

Pete later remembered this experience as waking to find his world had fallen apart. 'One minute I'm waiting for Kate to arrive to join me in the Jacuzzi for a romantic evening,' he remembered. 'The next thing I can remember is doing cold turkey in a vomit-filled cell. It was supposed to have been a great night.'

Pete's priority was to get himself out of there as quickly as possible, but he found it difficult to get help in securing his release, with his friends, his management and even Kate all displaying a reluctance to come to his aid. They all believed that Pete had somehow brought this on himself, and that they'd be doing him no favours if they made it easy for him. He was going to have to learn a lesson some time, and it might as well be now.

In an appearance at Highbury Magistrates' Court, where he was formally charged, Pete was offered bail in return for a surety of £150,000. Having run up huge debts while feeding his drug habit, Pete didn't have that kind of money, and Kate – having retreated from this disastrous situation to stay in her house in the Cotswolds – wasn't going to stump up the cash. Rough Trade, meanwhile, was having trouble raising the necessary sum.

Pete ended up being stuck behind bars for six nights. For the first two, he was kept at Islington Police Station, and then for the remaining four he became a resident of HMP Pentonville, five minutes' drive to the north. Everyone who came across Pete at that time was struck by how unwell he looked. The policemen who escorted him noticed that he stank of decay and had thick black grime wedged beneath his fingernails. One of the other inmates at Pentonville, twenty-five-year-old Stephen Gascoigne, told his fiancée, Stacey Luck, how shocked he was when he saw Pete. 'Stephen saw Pete arrive and was gobsmacked,' recalled Stacey. 'He couldn't believe how scruffy he looked, and he was amazed that Kate Moss would fancy him because of the state he was in. Stephen said Pete was very quiet and his head was bowed as he was led along by a prison officer. He looked nervous and scared.'

When he'd been convicted of burgling Carl's flat in 2003, Pete had served a month in jail – more than four times the number of nights he was incarcerated on this occasion – but this second time round was a real low point, lower than the first had been. So many things had seemed to be going well – Babyshambles, his love life – and then he was back on his own, facing this, a place worse than Thamkrabok Monastery.

Pete was locked up in the A wing of Pentonville, a grim Victorian prison, with murderers and paedophiles for neighbours. He was given methadone to ease his withdrawal from heroin, but he was so depressed about drugs that he swapped it with other prisoners for some cigarettes. 'It was Hell on Earth,' Pete recalled. 'At night the noise was horrible, and there's nothing more terrifying than the sound of a prison waking up. My cell stank of vomit and I felt the walls closing in. I thought I was going to die.'

Pete felt too disgusted with himself to call Kate or his mother from inside the walls of a prison, so he exchanged his phone credits for more cigarettes instead. As when he'd served time at Wandsworth and Standford Hill jails, he felt afraid of both the officers and the inmates, experiencing surges of terror when forced to rub shoulders with them in the exercise yard or at mealtimes in the canteen. His fear was rational enough because, now that everyone knew who he was, his situation was potentially more perilous than the last time he'd been in jail. As thirty-eight-year-old armed robber Will Brown – coincidentally, one of Pete's 'brown people' – pointed out, there was reason for concern over Pete's safety: 'There's no way Pete will be able to do any serious time. He thinks he's a hard man, but he's just a pretty little rich boy. There'll be a lot of seriously hard bastards who will want to make mincemeat out of him inside. And, with his money, he'll have every skag dealer inside throwing drugs at him until he's bled dry and out of it. It's easier to get heroin inside than out, and at £80 a gram he can afford it. I'm seriously worried about what could happen to him. I'm worried he might swing.'

In this context, it was no wonder that Pete felt a sense of relief when he found that some of the other prisoners warmed to the idea of having a celebrity in their midst. His cellmate, nicknamed 'Bilko', took a protective attitude to him and nipped antagonism from other quarters in the bud. When Pete came out, he issued a public thank you to Bilko, who had also helped him to write a song.

Another of Pete's protectors was an individual known as 'the General', who had promised Pete that he would be OK. His prediction held good; no one laid a finger on Pete during his four days in the prison. The worst he'd to put up with during that time were the repeated strip searches carried out by the officers, who were determined that such a high-profile prisoner wouldn't walk out of Pentonville and proceed to show the world how easy it was to get hold of drugs in prison and conceal them without being caught.

After remaining in Pentonville over the weekend, Pete was relieved to find that Rough Trade and EMI had finally managed to raise his £150,000 bail money. At 4.30pm on the day of his release, he slipped out of a side entrance and was whisked away in a black Mercedes.

Pete's first act on his release was to call Kate and apologise for ruining the romantic evening they'd planned to share six days earlier. He found that she was surprisingly understanding, having calmed down from the state of fury she'd been in on first hearing that he'd been arrested. Pete then pacified her further by telling her that he he'd not touched heroin or crack during his time inside, assuring her that the worst of the withdrawal was over and that he was heading straight to a rehab clinic to make sure he wasn't tempted to start on drugs again. 'I want to clean my act up and look good before we reschedule that romantic evening in the hotel,' he said with frank determination. 'I felt like crying, but the thought of Kate on the outside kept me going. I'm determined to kick the habit for good for the sake of my relationship with her.'

Kate's understanding response to his call had given Pete a huge boost. Combined with the elation he felt at getting out of prison, it put him in such an upbeat mood that even the prospect of weeks of rehab wasn't daunting. He was determined to turn the Carlish débâcle into something positive. As long as he didn't end up with a conviction and a jail sentence, he could look on six days of misery as the short, sharp lesson he'd needed to inspire him to sort himself out. 'I'm going to stay clean,' he affirmed. 'I'm determined to do it for Kate and my mum, the two women I love. Everyone has been telling me for months, but I wouldn't listen. This is the shock I needed. Six days without heroin hasn't been as bad as I expected. I've been through the worst of the detox, and I want to prove to my mum above anybody else that I can do this. I also need to stay clean for the sake of my bandmates and all my fans.'

The conditions of Pete's bail meant that he had to stay in the detox clinic until 19 February, after which he could live a reasonably normal life, apart from having to observe a curfew that meant he couldn't leave his home between 10pm and 7am. Pete's legal team were optimistic about his chances of escaping prosecution, especially since Carlish appeared to be having second thoughts about giving evidence against Pete. Outside Highbury Corner Magistrates' Court, Pete's solicitor, Sean Curran, said, '[Pete] and Alan Wass ferociously deny the allegations against them. They look forward to a satisfactory conclusion at the Crown Court, where "not guilty" verdicts will be returned on both counts against them.'

Mr Curran's confidence was not misplaced. In fact, the case never made it as far as the Crown Court; the CPS decided to drop it. Pete had escaped the Carlish affair without the terrible consequences that could have ensued. This time, his tendency to live life on the edge had taken him right to that edge, and he'd been horribly close to losing everything: his band, his relationship with Kate, the freedom that he valued so much. But, now, instead of being locked away in jail, Pete was planning to marry Kate and honeymoon in his dream city of St Petersburg.

For all Pete's schemes of glory, however, he knew he'd ventured into territory so dangerous that it gave him a feeling of vertigo. Whereas surviving previous scrapes had added to his sense of invulnerability and served only to encourage his risk-taking, this time he realised that he'd escaped only by a stroke of luck, and so he vowed to live less dangerously. The question was, how long could he keep that promise?

CHAPTER 16

Babyshambles

'PETE IS AN ADDICT WHO NEEDS A STRONG, STRAIGHT EYE ON
HIM TO KEEP CONTROL, BUT NOBODY IS LOOKING AFTER HIM. THERE
WERE HUNDREDS OF HANGERS-ON. ALMOST EVERYONE WAS ON
DRUGS, EXCEPT ME AND THE ROAD CREW.'
– *Gemma Clarke, former Babyshambles drummer*

'I DON'T THINK I'VE EVER FELT THIS WAY ABOUT BEING IN A BAND
BEFORE. YOU STILL GET THE HEEBIE-JEEBIES BEFORE GOING ON STAGE,
BUT IT SEEMS LIKE THERE'S NO POLITICAL QUAGMIRE ANY MORE.'
– *Pete Doherty*

Pete had found his exclusion from The Libertines to be a painful and demoralising business. It wasn't just the matter of losing a band he'd co-founded; The Libertines had been a way of life for him, part of the identity he'd strived so hard to create for himself. Everything about the group bore the imprint of his character and his philosophy. It was as if he'd made a success of his band only for others to hijack it and rob him of it. And the manner of the theft was perhaps the worst aspect of all, for it was aided and abetted by his best friend, Carl. The betrayal was hard to take.

Pete was determined not to lie down and let himself be sidelined, believing that *he* had been the one who'd got The Libertines where they were. He *was* the band, and by cutting him out the other members were signing their own death warrants. Whatever people said about his drug habits, he was still a star in his own right. He could still write and perform songs and play the guitar. The group that had supported him was gone, but he could replace them more easily than they could replace him. That defiant intention was the shaping force behind Babyshambles.

Pete's formation of the breakaway band was a clear signal that he was out to rebuild his empire, and the fact that the origins of the project went back as far as the beginning of 2003 illustrates how early he came to feel marginalised within The Libertines. The very first Babyshambles recording took place in the Albion Rooms that January, after Pete had bought himself a portable digital recording kit, enabling him to use the Teesdale Street flat as a makeshift studio.

The use of this technology was significant; the financial basis of the Babyshambles project was formed by advances in recording and distributing equipment, meaning that Pete could bypass the formalities of professional studios and mainstream record labels. He would create music in his own living room, use cheap devices to record it, and then distribute it himself via the internet. Instead of relying on a team of professional managers and publicists, he would organise gigs in informal locations. Pete's intention was to free himself of the apparatus of the music business and use new technology to bring the process of making music back to being a communication between the artist and the audience.

Owing to the free material they'd made available on the internet, Babyshambles had a dedicated fan base before they'd had released a single. 'Those first Babyshambles sessions back in the Albion Rooms happened mainly because I'd got this digital recorder and wanted to try it out,' Pete recalled. 'It was me and the Wolfman – just a couple of mates messing about, really – but the stuff turned out to be good, much better than I thought you could get without loads of equipment. That was the beginning of the whole Babyshambles thing.'

Over the next few months, Pete developed this homespun approach to recording music into something radical and groundbreaking. At the time, Carl was spending less and less time in the Albion Rooms, in pursuit of a less dissolute circle, although he wouldn't officially move out until April. His departure had already left a gulf in Pete's life, particularly when it came to making music. In the early days of their residency at Teesdale Street, Pete and Carl had spent many a night writing songs together, and now that Carl had vanished Pete looked to his new friend, Wolfman, to step into that role of co-writer and companion. It was with Wolfman that Pete had one of his biggest and most surprising chart successes, the beautifully lyrical single 'For Lovers', released in April 2004 and later nominated for a prestigious Ivor Novello award.

For all the accusations from fans claiming that Wolfman was cashing in on his friend's fame, Pete hijacked what was essentially Wolfe's creation. Amid their crack highs and heroin lows, the new songwriting duo recorded a series of tracks, including 'Black Boy Lane' and 'I Love You But You're Green'. The sound they produced was surprisingly good in quality but unmistakably intimate; it was the sound of a gig being played in a living room. Pete loved it, christening the musical hotchpotch *The Babyshambles Sessions*, though others would later claim authorship of the name. Indeed, The Queens of Noize and even

Wolfman's mother have both been credited with coining the term 'Babyshambles' as an apt nickname for Pete, although it's certainly in keeping with Pete's poet-like appreciation of the meanings of words.

The tracks that Pete and Wolfman produced had that sound of shambolic chaos that had informed much of The Libertines' music, largely because the arrangement of individuals that the pair had used to create their music wasn't an organised group but a decadent bohemian shambles, a collection of misfits with no leader or structure. The association with the drink Babycham sent up the snarling, macho orthodoxy of rock music, while the prefix 'baby' contained suggestions that the band wasn't grown up, wasn't tough and streetwise and wasn't experienced, smacking of innocence and idealism. On top of all that, of course, it was Pete's own baby, his creation and nobody else's. It was his pride and joy. The close affinity he felt with Babyshambles was reflected in a tattoo he'd had done, featuring the name of his new band inscribed in a semi-circle around his right nipple.

Carl hated the name. Indeed, for him and many of Pete's other acquaintances, Babyshambles would be one of the worst-named rock bands in history. The idea of a group making fun of themselves in their title seemed a poor strategy in an environment where every musician was fighting to be taken seriously and to access the mantle of cool.

Pete, of course, was beyond such worries. He believed that self-deprecation *was* cool and that, with his identification with the moniker, he could carry it off. 'Carl didn't like the name at all,' he confirmed. 'He told me he thought it was shit, that the whole idea was a shambles as far as he could see. I wanted a name that was a bit different, and that's what I came up with, and it stuck. I liked it then and I still do.'

Initially, Pete saw Babyshambles not as a group but as a collection of performing artists and performances. He wanted them to be an outlet for the creativity he could no longer express through the increasingly controlled environment of The Libertines. The new material wasn't intended to rival The Libertines' music, he said, but to act as a supplement for those fans who wanted more, who were keen enough to accept less polished material. He spoke to Carl and confessed a need to write and perform more songs. For Pete, the record-label approach, whereby a small number of tracks would be relentlessly promoted in tours and other stunts, was too restrictive. It was stopping him from producing the new material he had inside him.

Pete wanted Carl to get involved with the new project, to be a key member of the shifting collection of musicians behind the sessions, and during The Libertines' first US tour in May 2003 Pete and Carl had been booked in for a recording session in studios in New York for just such a purpose. On that occasion, Pete brought along a collection of new friends, who were mainly fellow crack and heroin addicts, and tried to turn the recording into a spontaneous sing-along in which new tracks would be created. Carl, however, found himself repelled by the people with whom Pete had chosen to associate, while he also thought that the standard of the music was poor. He walked out of the studio and got a plane home.

Back in London, Pete made renewed overtures to his old friend about getting involved with Babyshambles, trying to pique Carl's interest by describing the project as an expansion of the guerrilla gigs they'd staged in the Albion Rooms and elsewhere. However, while Pete wanted to return to the underground and make it his domain, Carl didn't share that objective, and he failed to show at a gig organised on his birthday on a rooftop in Whitechapel.

Pete's reaction to Carl's lack of interest in all aspects of Babyshambles, from the name to their fans, was one of acute disappointment, but he was determined to push on regardless. He released the fragments they'd recorded in New York as *The Babyshambles Sessions* and began to stage guerrilla gigs on a more regular basis. 'I really tried to make Carl part of what I was doing,' he remembered. 'I was full of it at that stage. I'd just lost interest in promoting, promoting, promoting all the time, going on tour and doing so much other shit that we never got to make any music. I wanted to write songs. I needed that. That's why I started doing more Babyshambles stuff.'

As Pete's alternative project began to gather impetus, his situation with The Libertines was becoming more and more perilous. Throughout 2003, a series of incidents occurred that drove a wedge between Pete and the rest of the band: his failure to go on two tours of Europe and a tour of Japan, the experience of Carl telling him he wasn't wanted on stage in Paris, Carl's departure from the Albion Rooms in April and refusal to show for Pete's Whitechapel rooftop gig in May, and Pete's inability to turn up regularly for the recording of 'Don't Look Back into the Sun' in June. To cap it all, there was Pete's burglary of Carl's flat in Baker Street in July. The turbulence – described in more detail in Chapter 10, 'Can't Stand Me

Now', culminated in Pete being unofficially pushed out of The Libertines by the summer.

Despite his own role in contributing to the chaos, Pete felt utterly rejected by his exclusion. Indeed, he was determined that he wouldn't stand for it. For the first time, he began to see Babyshambles not just as an alternative outlet to The Libertines but also as a possible replacement for his old group. The effort to reclaim his band was reflected in his attempt to stabilise the underground version of the band into a permanent line-up, recruiting Scarborough Steve and Neil Thunders as his support acts.

Furious at the spectacle of The Libertines touring the world without him, Pete even tried to reclaim the name, calling his new group t'Libertines, because all of the members bar him were from Yorkshire. The joke was lost on London audiences, however, and one promoter refused to use the name, advertising the band as 'Babyshambles', the name of the first song in the set. The transition of Babyshambles as a sub-Libertines session to Babyshambles as a new band to replace the old was complete.

That summer, Pete's new outfit played gigs in pubs and squats all over London. The events were loud, energetic and packed with enthusiastic fans. Following Pete's month-long stint in jail, however, this first established Babyshambles line-up dissolved. There was also a thawing of relations with Carl, while Alan McGee was brought into the fold as the new Libertines manager. Pete experienced an upsurge of hope that he would get his old band back, and the Babyshambles project was put on hold – but not for long.

In December 2003, Pete's decision to relaunch his breakaway group as a more professional outfit was a sure sign that matters were still not perfect for him in The Libertines. Despite the change of management, he was still finding that the commercial business of music was cramping his style. He just wasn't getting to write or perform enough new songs, he complained; he just wanted to make music, not make music in order to make money.

In pondering these problems, Pete had identified the moment when it had all started to go wrong for him with The Libertines. Looking back, he pinpointed the period in which the band were being made commercially viable by Banny as the beginning of the compromises and the origin of his exclusion. It was then that he'd ceased to be in control of the project. 'We were so keen to get signed,' he noted of those times, 'and a lot of the things Banny did were things that needed doing. She deserves a lot of credit for the way she came in and got us a deal like that. But, after that, it wasn't just *our* music any more; there was a lot of other people's input, and a lot of that was just about making money out of it. There was a price to pay for getting signed, and that was losing some of what we were about.'

From that point on, the decisions concerning The Libertines were being made not according to what Pete the artist wanted but in line with what Banny and Rough Trade wanted. He came to feel that he'd sown the seeds of his own undoing in craving fame, that in a Faustian impulse he'd sold his soul to the devil of the music industry, allowing Pete the people's minstrel to be transformed into a mass-selling rock 'n' roll stereotype.

Pete's assessment of Carl, Banny, Rough Trade and

McGee was, of course, coloured by bitterness. He couldn't see that, along with their commercial interests, all of those parties had a genuine love of his music. In the context of a time when bands were being manufactured totally from scratch from members who had little talent, often in front of a live TV audience, Rough Trade certainly weren't the evil men of the industry.

Nevertheless, Pete felt that the compromises he'd gone along with in order to break into the big time had been the origin of his eventual disassociation with the band. That determination of Banny's to get The Libertines signed to Rough Trade had been about business, after all, not music. The band could have signed with the small independent label High Society, whose representative James Mullord had approached The Libertines before Rough Trade had showed an interest. At the time, Mullord had obviously liked the music and wanted to distribute it on a small scale to a dedicated fan base who would also enjoy it. Part of Banny's obsession with getting them signed to Rough Trade was in fact musical, inspired by the fact that it was a label steeped in an impressive tradition of modern music, but Pete regretted the direction his band had taken after signing to them. He wanted to turn the clock back. And so he recruited Mullord to manage Babyshambles.

The move perhaps ought to have caused more alarm at Rough Trade, where the intention remained to develop Pete's talents through the winning Libertines formula. To this end, Pete attended a meeting with company man Geoff Travis and The Libertines' current manager, Alan McGee, in which he managed to convince the other men that he was setting up his own side project as a supplement to his main interest. He told them that recording Babyshambles tracks with Mullord was 'a matter of honour' from which he couldn't back down. 'I wasn't bullshitting them,' Pete recalled. 'I didn't think at that time that I'd ever be out of The Libertines. I wasn't trying to escape from the band; I just wanted to do more stuff, the sort of stuff me and Carl used to do, only more of it.'

Having smoothed the situation over with his management, Pete proceeded to put much of his musical effort into the new, revitalised Babyshambles, first of all settling on a concrete line-up, comprising Patrick Walden on guitar, Drew McConnell on bass and Gemma Clarke on drums. The new band recorded their first single, 'Babyshambles', in a series of chaotic sessions over New Year 2004. Still a hard user at that time, Pete's indulgence in crack and heroin was at its maximum across the festive period and he spent much of the time out of his mind, but the group still managed to get the job done and 'Babyshambles' was released in May. Only 4,000 copies of the single were released, but they could have sold five times that. A year later, copies would be changing hands on the internet for up to £100.

During the first few months of 2004, Pete managed to juggle Babyshambles business with his commitments for The Libertines, which included the recording of his original band's self-titled second album. It proved to be a very busy period for Pete, as during this time he was also attending rehab centres in Roehampton, Paris and Thailand.

That June, Pete's new band were given a boost that Pete neither wanted nor expected. Following his failure to come off drugs, news that The Libertines would no longer be needing his services was the biggest shock of his life and, when Carl and the others made the announcement, he was distraught. Although he was hit hard, however, his response was to use Babyshambles to fight back. He invested all of his energies into the new outfit, determined to make it much more than a side interest that complemented the main band. From now on, Babyshambles would be the primary outlet for his talents.

'OK, I hadn't managed to get clean,' Pete confessed, 'but the thing was, I was still out there playing in a band, doing gigs with Babyshambles. If I'm doing that, how come I'm suddenly not up to doing the same thing in The Libertines? Carl made a mistake. I think he knows that, but he hasn't got the courage to own up to it. Being chucked out of the band was the last thing I wanted, but I wasn't going to lie down and let it stop me writing songs. So yes, it did make me concentrate harder on Babyshambles, and I guess that's the only good thing that came out of it.'

Pete embarked on a sell-out Babyshambles tour that received a rapturous reception wherever the group went. That summer, they travelled to venues in Sheffield and York in a green transit van, a makeshift tour bus that was often full of fans they'd met and picked up on the way. The van made irregular progress, frequently stopping so that its hungover passengers could vomit on the hard shoulder of the motorway. In many senses, Babyshambles offered the best of both worlds for Pete, as his notoriety meant that cash was flowing in from ticket sales, but he was in charge and there was nobody to complain about his late night drug-taking and sex with teenage fans.

The tour was an incredible journey that raised

interesting points about talent and fame. Never before had a band, who'd released one single that had barely made into the Top Forty, filled so many venues with such delirious fans. Indeed, the unrestrained hedonism of the gigs led some critics to claim they were too shambolic, that on occasions Pete's performance was the worse for his drug-taking, but to most of the band's fans, that was their appeal. The Libertines were equally disorganised when they'd first formed, and it was years before they tightened up their act.

Despite his extravagant behaviour, however, Pete was totally serious about Babyshambles and his music. 'Believe me, I'm not the sort of person who'll take a substandard alternative,' he affirmed. 'I've chosen this path because it's me. And this is the first time in three or four years that I've listened to my heart, as opposed to listening to my wallet, my gullet or my vanity.'

Babyshambles weren't about money and they weren't about puffing up Pete's ego. It was a project dedicated to making music and performing it while enjoying the process. Pete developed his aim of communicating directly with the fans to a new level, and he was able to keep them up to date with his every move, using his laptop computer to post diary entries and bulletins on the Babyshambles website on a daily basis.

Pete also staged guerrilla gigs at every opportunity. The loyalty he'd received from Libertines fans was, if anything, enhanced under the new outfit. Indeed, Babyshambles developed a very close following, a more extreme version of the bohemian crowds that had comprised the audiences of early Libertines gigs. The intensity of their interest in Pete's activities was reflected in regular coverage by the *NME*. On occasions when Pete failed to show for gigs, fans would bombard the magazine with phone calls, asking the magazine's journalists if their idol was OK.

Pete's no-shows were far from rare, although, considering the number of commitments he'd made, this was perhaps less surprising than it might seem. His sometimes erratic attendances were well illustrated in December 2004, a month in which he turned up late for a gig in aid of the charity Shelter and was ejected by security, was thrown out of the *Top of the Pops* studio for fighting with a member of the audience, was dragged off stage in a state of collapse by his management at a gig in Blackpool, and cancelled a concert in Aberdeen because he'd overdosed. And when he failed to turn up for Babyshambles' end-of-year gig at the London Astoria, the crowd, who waited for him until 2am, rioted and stole stage equipment. This incident particularly upset drummer Gemma Clarke, who was targeted by the drunken mob as they fought over her equipment. Gemma was the latest of Pete's musical partners whose patience was wearing thin, and this incident would later contribute to her leaving the band.

The progress of Pete's new band took the form of a chaotic careering across the country. It was a compelling spectacle and, although some fans were disappointed not to see Pete, those who did see him felt that they'd witnessed something special.

In total contrast to the no-shows, Pete saw in 2005 with four gigs in four separate venues. In what he called his 'apology' after the Astoria débâcle, Pete played at

Birmingham, Stoke, Oldham and Manchester in a single night, starting at 9pm and ending at 3.30am. The later gigs were riotous affairs, with fans invading the stage and bar, emptying bottles of hard liquor down their throats and all over the floor. A string of fights broke out in Manchester, with fans storming the venue. When he finally left the stage in the early hours, Pete was one of soberest men in the city.

The debauched behaviour eventually proved too much for Gemma and she quit the band in January 2005, no longer feeling able to cope with Pete either failing to appear at all or turning up so drugged that he'd be falling asleep on stage. It upset her to watch Pete, now in one of the most self-destructive stages of his life, separated from those who once offered a stabilising influence. She told him in an open letter, 'I will not continue to work under the management you have chosen for the band. I could no longer be part of the machine that I feel is destroying you... The Pete I know is sweet and caring, but when he is high he doesn't make any sense. Pete is an addict who needs a strong, straight eye on him to keep control, but nobody is looking after him. There were hundreds of hangers-on. Almost everyone was on drugs, except me and the road crew.'

Gemma was replaced by White Sport's Adam Ficek, but her concern was shared by many of Pete's old friends. Babyshambles' manager, James Mullord, was aware of every aspect of Pete's journey, drugs binges included. The contrast between his approach and the watchful eye of Banny could not have been greater.

The recording of Babyshambles' first album was hit with many delays, with Pete now unsupervised at the helm. At one of their many George Tavern gigs in early 2005, I asked Drew when the new album was coming out, and he nodded at Pete – deep in conversation with a group of beautiful blonde women – and said, 'We've got to get him into a studio for long enough to record an album first.'

Drew then spoke of his frustration at trying to organise things with Pete as the band's leader, but his words were all muttered endearingly. Without Pete, he knew, Babyshambles were nothing. Without Pete, The Libertines were nothing, although they hadn't realised that until he'd gone.

As it turned out, plans to record Babyshambles' debut in Bath were scuppered by the Max Carlish affair, with Pete under arrest and in a police cell the day they were set to travel to the studio. However, the band later worked around Pete's bail conditions to complete two of their biggest achievements to date: a sell-out gig at the Brixton Academy and a trip to Wales finally to begin recording an album.

The Babyshambles gig in Brixton in February 2005 was an incredible if bizarre night. From the moment Mick Jones stood up in front of the crowd of 5,000 paying customers (including myself) and introduced the fledgling group, hinting that 'they might have a decent album in them', the magnitude of Pete's achievements was clear: the fans had crammed in to watch a band who hadn't even released an album, and the anticipation was unrivalled. At earlier Babyshambles gigs, fans had chanted for The Libertines, but now thousands of fans all screamed, 'Babyshambles! Babyshambles!' Pete had been given a special exception from his 10pm curfew, a judge allowing him to stay out until midnight for one night only so he could perform at the venue.

That night, the atmosphere felt more like that of a

demonstration than of a gig, with many in the crowd wearing T-shirts emblazoned with the proclamation 'PETE DOHERTY IS INNOCENT (AND SO IS ALAN WASS)'. His co-accused friend Wass was there, too, playing an acoustic set as fans waited for the main attraction. A month earlier, he'd been the guitarist of virtually unknown group Left Hand, a former Libertines support act, but now he was thrust before thousands of fans, all singing his name, and he loved every minute of it.

With Pete still facing prison over the blackmail and robbery charges, the opening line of 'Killamangiro', in which Pete asks why people would pay to see him in a cage, couldn't have been a more pertinent way to open the set. Pete strutted around the stage, standing on speakers and puffing out his chest, his iconic status confirmed. Then, as he basked in the familiar cries of 'We love you, Pete!' and launched into 'Stix and Stones', Pete spotted some young fans being crushed at the front of the gig and stopped the show. 'Stop! Stop!' he shouted. 'Push back. Oi! Push back!' And, as security guards waded into the mass to pull out twenty or so crushed fans, some of whom had passed out under the weight of the crowd, Pete pleaded, 'You have to move back.'

It wasn't the last time the gig was suddenly halted that night, but, if that standstill was prompted by Pete's caring nature, the next was caused by more violent aspects of his character. As he stormed through 'Gang of Gin', Pete gave a playful push to Walden, who responded with a boisterous kick to Pete's backside. Pete then turned and landed a full-blown punch on Walden's face, and within seconds the pair were rolling around on the floor as stage crew bundled in to split them up. The crowd were divided over whether the punch was serious or a piece of showmanship, but the tension between the fighting pair once they'd returned from being dragged off stage suggested that, if it was part of the show, it was certainly not planned anywhere other than in Pete's head. And, considering that he was currently on bail, accused of violent theft, Pete's behaviour that night was a dramatic statement in front of the watching fans and press.

On the way home from the concert, I ran into a music promoter and member of The Libertines' original entourage. He called the chaotic performance 'a disgrace' and told me that Pete was wasting his talents and that he should have been on stage with The Libertines, not a second-rate substitute like Babyshambles.

I disagreed. Although the band were still inferior to The Libertines at their peak, they were in fact tighter than Pete's original band had been at a similar stage of their development and a worthy new outlet for Pete's song-writing ability.

After the Brixton gig, and with Pete still on bail, Babyshambles travelled to Wales in March to start recording their album at the picturesque Twin Peaks Studio, near Brecon. The album would be produced by Mick Jones, known for his raw style and lack of edits, and it promised to stay closer to Pete's preferred style than anything The Libertines had released.

Before setting off to record the album, Pete told me that he was looking forward to the session, that it was going to be 'like a live recording, just a band playing in a living room'. His new creative freedom meant that he could produce something more akin to the beloved sessions he'd released on the internet. He felt that The Libertines had been pushed into their albeit successful punky sound and image, while the forthcoming Babyshambles debut promised a brand of music that owed less to punk rock and more to decadent bohemia. It would, said Pete, be a deep and sincere record.

CHAPTER 17

The Legacy

'THERE'S ONLY ONE BRITISH HERO RIGHT NOW:
PETE DOHERTY.'
– Liam Gallagher

In 1996, when Pete and Carl had made a pact to 'sail the good ship *Albion* to Arcadia', British music hadn't needed a saviour; Oasis, Blur, Supergrass and others were keeping the public more than occupied and Britpop was at is peak. Perhaps it was only right, therefore, that the ship took several years to find its correct course. If The Libertines had found their feet in the mid-1990s, they would have been in danger of drowning under the devastating flood of homegrown talent, and their potential doomed never realised.

By late 1997, Britpop had disappeared under the weight of its own success. Opportunists including Tony Blair, Robbie Williams and The Spice Girls had since supped their fill, taking elements of the movement and manufacturing it for their own populist and commercial gains in their own unique ways. By the turn of the twenty-first century, dance music and MDMA were once again the escapism of choice for most youths, as they had been a decade earlier. The public were pretty satisfied with their lot, no longer needing Oasis to tell them how cigarettes and alcohol were the only things worth living for. They no longer believed them.

However, by the time the censor-battering 'What a Waster' became The Libertines' first Top Forty hit in 2002, as a double A-side with 'I Get Along', the nation was crying out for a new leader to drive a new rebellion. And any band who could mention 'fucking divs, spivs and two-bob cunts' in their debut single and still get to number twenty-seven were worthy of the crown.

The advent of The Libertines bore similarities to the rise of Britpop almost a decade earlier, not least the integral part supermodel Kate Moss would end up playing in both. More pertinently, the country's youth had again become frustrated with the establishment, and The Libertines' material was based around a strong sense of national identity, just as the thriving UK scene in the '1990s had been. The band were also partly influenced by movements across the Atlantic, just as Britpop had been largely informed by Nirvana and grunge.

With the release of The Strokes' debut album, *Is This It*, in October 2001, rock-music lovers had something to get genuinely excited about for the first time in several years. The problem for British youth was that, despite The Strokes being a genuinely exciting new band with a brilliant debut album, it was hard to relate to an American garage-rock band when you were living in a London council estate or playing football in suburbia.

Indeed, the mere word 'garage' left a nasty taste in many mouths in 2001. When Pete and Carl had first seen The Strokes playing in Liverpool that summer, they'd realised that the British public wanted their own heroes. It was time for The Libertines.

So there were similarities, but Pete and Carl's revolution was very different to Liam and Noel's. While the Gallagher brothers sang about using cigarettes and alcohol to escape the grim terraced streets of the North, Pete told tales of escaping benign suburbia with skag and bone. As Pete sang on the track 'Albion', the power stations Oasis sang about avoiding were now disused, anyway. The way in which Pete looked at Britain was more intellectual; lad culture, hooligans on E and Reebok Classics were one element of Pete's Albion, but so were gin in teacups and leaves on lawns. Liam had certainly never discussed 'the realm of the infinite' on national television.

The meteoric demise of The Libertines, who eventually imploded in a ball of punch-ups, burglaries, drugs and creative squabbling, meant that they could never suffer the same fate as the former holders of their 'Best Band in Britain' crown. If Oasis had split up after their second album in a blaze of brotherly hatred, they would have remained heroes and regularly topped 'Best Band Ever' polls, but instead they were criticised for slowly morphing into Status Quo, releasing album after album of inferior material as they milked their cash cow.

Pete vowed that he would never let that happen to his dream – and fortunately the rest of The Libertines also realised (although, unfortunately, not until they misguidedly tried to continue without him) that there was no Libertines without the libertine.

The band lived fast and died young, its development as perfect as it was tragic. Comparisons with Oasis are more cultural than musical. Both bands were popular, very British and made an explosive impact on the music scene, but, in fact, The Libertines were closer to more articulate British bands like The Kinks and The Smiths, coupled with the anti-establishment mentality of The Clash and a bit of Chas 'n' Dave's cheekiness chucked in for good measure.

Where The Libertines went, other bands soon followed. The success of Pete's first band opened the door for new acts, as well as for those who had been knocking around in the same circles as Pete and Carl had without having quite the strength or charisma to step into the light. One of the most enjoyable and best-selling albums of 2004, for instance, was *Up All Night* by Razorlight, whose frontman, Johnny Borrell, had been a one-time member of The Libertines, while acts such as Selfish Cunt, The Paddingtons, Wolfman and the Side Effects and Special Needs all forged careers out of sharing venues such as Whitechapel's Rhythm Factory with The Libertines and Babyshambles. Even bands from other parts of Britain with less in common with The Libertines, such as the hugely successful Franz Ferdinand, have the boys to thank for getting people talking about British guitar-based music again.

But it was a band named The Others who benefited most obviously and ruthlessly from The Libertines, and in particular from Pete. As Others singer Dominic Masters noted, 'Pete was very good in his selection of the support bands and how he carved up the support and divided it between the local bands.' Although from Somerset, Masters tried to follow Pete's formula and fly his flag around the East End of London, an approach that saw The Others play gigs in tube carriages, on buses and in Radio 1's front lobby. The numbers of their mobile phones were included on their website, while Masters shamelessly namedropped Pete in every interview and wrote a song called 'Stan Bowles' about him.

While The Others should be congratulated for doing something genuinely exciting for their fans, it was Pete who pioneered these techniques so that his art could receive a wider audience. This is the legacy he will leave behind: recording sessions and demos placed on the internet for fans to download for free; deeply introspective lyrics; the constant interaction with fans in internet forums; and mingling with his followers at gigs, in pubs and even in his own living room. All have a ticket to join him on his journey, to come aboard the good ship *Albion*. It is the ultimate access-all-areas pass. Listening to a download of Pete singing in his living room, pausing to take a drag of a cigarette, is almost voyeuristic.

As The Libertines tried to move away from this direction towards more commercially driven promotion, Pete chose his fans over his band. 'The kids on the internet, they're like my extended family,' he once noted. 'They've supported me through so much. I love them all.'

After he'd walked The Libertines plank, many predicted that Pete would drown. However, his talents were only confirmed by the projects that followed. The London of cocaine and riots he painted in *Up the Bracket* made way for deeper thoughts, a deeper contemplation of the thoughts that had inspired him to set sail on this incredible journey in the first place. A softer, more intimate sound resonated from Babyshambles and his later solo sessions, and he was able to release songs which would never have conformed to the more commercially driven needs of a Libertines album. His dream of Arcadia appeared as close as it had ever been, and the Babyshambles track 'Arcady' spells out this dream, which Pete claimed had been misunderstood and twisted by others in a way that The Libertines would have never allowed. Drawing on the lyrics of the now little-known 1909 musical play *The Arcadians*, Pete sings of a life in Arcady where life is 'pure and simple' and seraphic pipes play.

Pete felt that The Libertines had been pushed in directions he didn't want to go, and it wasn't the route to Arcadia he'd had in mind. But, even if this pied piper has to complete the journey on his own, his contingent of loyal fans won't be far behind.